WE BELONG DEAD

CONTENTS

2. Keeping Count – Alistair Hughes
3. Editorial
4. Dracula in Derby – Darrell Buxton
6. Dracula at the BBC – Stephen Hatcher
11. Ramsey Campbell interview – Simon J. Ballard
15. *The Return of the Vampire* – Matthew E. Banks
18. Marvel Comics' Dracula – Andy Allard
21. XXX/adult Dracula movies – Neil Pike
24. The Black Laboratory of John Llewellyn Probert
26. *Dracula: Pages from a Virgin's Diary* – Karen Joan Kohoutek
28. Emma Dark's Dark Corner
32. *Purple Playhouse* – Terry Sherwood
34. Robert Cremer interview – Matthew E. Banks
38. Dracula on Stage – David M. Nevarrez
42. David Skal interview – Alistair Hughes
46. ...*Hanno Cambiato Faccia* – Darrell Buxton
48. Cinemacabre – Steven West
51. Am-Dram-ula: My Night at the Village Hall – Darrell Buxton
52. Hammer Dracula LPs – Simon J. Ballard
54. Orson Welles' Mercury Theatre – David M. Nevarrez
56. Asylum for the Psychotronic – Ansel H. Faraj
60. *The Dracula Saga* – David Dent
62. Kim Newman's Daily Dracula – Ken Shinn
64. *Shadow of the Vampire* – Sarah Butler
68. Julia Kruk interview – Darrell Buxton
72. *The Last Voyage of the Demeter* – Paul PD Donaldson
74. *The Unquenchable Thirst of Dracula* – Parker Stewart
76. Son of Dracula – Mark Iveson
79. Dacre Stoker interview – Ian Talbot Taylor
84. Dario Argento's *Dracula 3D* – Dawn Dabell
86. Animated Draculas – Jason D. Brawn
88. Hammer Draculas in Leigh – Ian Talbot Taylor
90. *Mystery and Imagination* – Kevin Nickelson
92. Dracula comedy sketches – Steven West
96. *Dracula 2000* – David Gelmini
98. Crossing Running Water: Dracula overseas – Karen Joan Kohoutek

---

Artwork and articles always welcome on horror films of all eras. Contact us at wbdmagazine@yahoo.co.uk or darrellpbuxton@gmail.com

Publisher: Eric McNaughton
Editor: Darrell Buxton
Editorial Team: Dawn Dabell, Ian Taylor, Jonathon Dabell & Simon J Ballard

Design & Layout: Steve Kirkham – Tree Frog Communication
www.treefrogcommunication.co.uk
Printed worldwide by Amazon

We Belong Dead
www.webelongdead.co.uk
wbdmagazine@yahoo.co.uk

We are the stuff that dreams are made of.

Contributors this issue:
Andy Allard • Simon J. Ballard, Matthew E. Banks
Jason D. Brawn • Sarah Butler, Darrell Buxton, Dawn Dabell
Emma Dark • David Dent
Paul PD Donaldson
Ansel H. Faraj • David Gelmini
Stephen Hatcher
Alistair Hughes • Mark Iveson, Karen Joan Kohoutek
David M. Nevarrez
Kevin Nickelson • Neil Pike
John Llewellyn Probert
Terry Sherwood • Ken Shinn
Parker Stewart, Ian Talbot Taylor
Steven West
With thanks to: Julia Kruk
Ramsey Campbell • Kim Newman
Dacre Stoker • Robert Cremer
and Derek M. Koch
This issue is dedicated to David J. Skal

A BUZZY KROTIK BK PRODUCTION

We Belong Dead

KEEPING COUNT

* **Lugosi:** Reprised Dracula 'in all but name' for *Return of the Vampire* (1943).
* **Carradine:** Also starred in an NBC television adaptation of *Dracula* (1956).
* **Lederer:** Also played Dracula in an episode of *Night Gallery* (1971).
* **Lee:** Seven films for Hammer, French comedy *Dracula and Son* (1976), Jess Franco's *Count Dracula* (1970) and a cameo in *One More Time* (1969). Not included are Dracula-esque appearances in *Uncle was a Vampire* (1959), and *The Magic Christian* (1969).
* **Count Von Count:** Although clearly not Dracula, no other character inspired by him has appeared continuously for over 40 years.
* **Palance** was inspiration for the physiognomy of the Count in Marvel Comics' **'Tomb of Dracula'‡**, (a year before his television casting).
* **Kinski:** Appeared in the remake of *Nosferatu* as Count Dracula. The original character, Graf Orlok, was played by Max Schreck (A), then Willem Dafoe (B) in *Shadow of the Vampire (2000)*. Orlok will return at the end of this year in a new remake starring Bill Skarsgård.

Carlos Villarias 1931 (Dracula)

Bela Lugosi 1931-1948 2*

Lon Chaney Jnr 1943 (Son of Dracula)

John Carradine 1944-66 4*

Christopher Lee 1958-1973 10*

Atif Kaptan 1953 (Drakula Istanbul'da)

Francis Lederer 1958 2* (The Return of Dracula)

Denholm Elliot 1968 (Dracula)

*1972-

‡1972-1979

John Forbes-Robertson 1974

Narciso Ibáñez Menta 1970, 1973 2 (Otra vez Drácula, La saga de los Drácula)

Zandor Vorkov 1971 (Dracula vs. Frankenstein)

Charles Macaulay 1972 (Blacula)

***Jack Palance 1973** (Bram Stoker's Dracula)

David Niven 1974 (Vampira)

Udo Kier 1974 (Blood for Dracula)

Louis Jourdan 1977 (Count Dracula)

Frank Langella 1977 (Dracula)

A 1929

B 2000

***Klaus Kinski 1979** (Nosferatu the Vampyre)

George Hamilton 1979 (Love at First Bite)

Duncan Regehr 1987 (The Monster Squad)

Gary Oldman 1992 (Bram Stoker's Dracula)

Leslie Nielsen 1995 (Dracula: Dead and Loving It)

Gerard Butler 2000 (Dracula 2000)

Stephen Billington 2003 (Dracula II: Ascension)

Dominic Purcell 2004 (Blade III: Trinity)

Richard Roxburgh 2004 (Van Helsing)

Rutger Hauer 2005 (Dracula III: Legacy)

Marc Warren 2005 (Dracula)

Adam Sandler (voice) 2012-18 3 (Hotel Transylvania series)

Thomas Kretschmann 2012 (Dracula 3D)

Jonathan Rhys Meyers 2013 (Dracula)

Luke Evans 2014 (Dracula Untold)

Christian Carmago 2016 (Penny Dreadful)

Claes Bang 2020 (Dracula)

Nicolas Cage 2023 (Renfield)

Javier Botet 2023 (Last Voyage of the Demeter)

● Main players	○ Big budget adaptation
● Major production	○ Franchise
● Single appearance	○ Television
● Addenda	○ Film and television

We Belong Dead
Editorial Issue 40

We bid you… welcome! That's the only possible way to kick off our landmark 40th issue of 'WBD'. It can't have escaped the notice of keen vampire fans that we've featured renowned bloodsucking exponents William Marshall and Nicolas Cage on our last two covers, but those were mere tasters for what we are about to offer. If there were some way that I could make our front page sound like a creaking castle door as you turn it… yet I fear such a trick is beyond even the capabilities of our expert designer Steve Kirkham! However, that would be the perfect lead-in to this latest packed offering, since we are celebrating the centenary of Count Dracula's debut stage appearance, which took place in Derby (the city where your humble ed was born) way back in May 1924. Derby's Museum of Making, set within the historic Silk Mill, is marking the occasion with numerous planned events, and as a local boy myself, I wanted 'We Belong Dead' to be right at the staked heart of the proceedings. So, what better time to rise Dracula from the grave once again?

As you'll discover, our take on the Count honours his part-stately, part-savage screen past, but in true 'WBD' fashion we are delving deep, examining a few less familiar areas of Dracula's domain. Dracula has been represented or portrayed in the movies dozens, if not hundreds, of times, rivalling and almost certainly even surpassing fellow film 'frequent flyers' such as Tarzan or Sherlock Holmes (and he actually *can* fly, unlike the competition!) – so we've taken the opportunity to follow a less-travelled path through the Borgo Pass. Join us on our journey, where we'll cover unfamiliar fang films such as *Zinda Laash*, *…Hanno Cambiato Faccia*, *Dracula Sucks*, also taking a look at vampiric TV, comics, theatre, and other media besides. Plus, we speak with various experts in the field (including the late, great David J. Skal, to whom this issue is dedicated.) Surprises await!

Our new 'Euro Horror' book, with a foreword by the marvellous Lone Fleming, is currently out and getting a positive reception from readers – don't miss this one, a full-colour, expansively-illustrated, 350-page beast of a volume covering continental classics galore. Whether giallo, krimi, haunted castles, witchcraft, or eerie Blind Knights Templar are your thing, you'll find plenty within our covers to chill you to the bone. Naschy, Argento, Franco, Rollin, Bava, and many other key figures on the European scene are present, and the whole package comes wrapped in a spectacular new cover design from ace artist Graham Humphreys. The programme to unleash our out-of-print items into the world anew continues apace, too – you'll find many of our back issues available via Amazon, and our popular overview of 1970s British horror 'Chopped Meat' has also recently re-emerged (suitable for vegetarians, despite the title…)

Festival news! Our good friends Gill & Wendy from Sheffield's annual 'HorrorConUK' event have amassed a sensational guest list for their weekend bash on May 11-12, with Britt Ekland, William Katt, Griffin Dunne, Kane Hodder, Christina Lindberg, and not one but two major cast members from *Children of the Corn* in attendance! I'll be on interview and hosting duties at that one, alongside Tony Earnshaw and Bunny Galore. 'WBD' columnist Selene Paxton-Brooks continues to mark 'Fifty Years of British Horror', with her upcoming event on July 27th in Greaat Yarmouth featuring 1974 releases *Frankenstein and the Monster from Hell* and *Frightmare*. Manchester's Festival of Fantastic Films and Allan Bryce's DarkFest are in the planning stages and all set for October and November respectively; in between those two, Graeme Lloyd and Tom Lee Rutter from Treasured Films are inviting cult director Jeff Lieberman to Kidderminster for what is certain to be an unmissable occasion, screening as many of Jeff's movies as possible at the lovely little independent venue The Lume. Tickets for this one are extremely limited, so get in quick. And bring your own Blue Sunshine…

Congratulations to everyone who received a nomination and a place on the ballot for the 2024 Rondo Awards! I'm thrilled to say that 'WBD' picked up nods for 'Best Magazine', 'Best Column' (Emma Dark), 'Best Interview' (Emma again, via her thoroughly entertaining chat with Shaun Hutson in issue 35), 'Best Cover' (Selene's brilliant Lon Chaney/*London After Midnight* artwork adorning issue 36), 'Best Article' (for both Kevin Nickelson's issue 38 piece on *Blacula* and Steven West's career study of Willie Best and Mantan Moreland in the same mag), with 'Euro Horror' among the contenders as 'Best Book', with our columnist Ansel H. Faraj's *Todd Tarantula* in contention as 'Best Independent Film'. See rondoaward.com for full details.

But now it is time to enjoy Dracula's hospitality. Don't say we didn't warn you…

Darrell Buxton (editor)

RAM-PIRE!
DRACULA IN DERBY

Proud East Midlander and 'We Belong Dead' editor Darrell Buxton stakes a claim for his birthplace…

So, what's all this about a 'Dracula Centenary', then? You can't have failed to spot that the current issue of 'We Belong Dead' is marking 100 years of Dracula. But why? After all, Stoker's novel was published in 1897, Murnau's *Nosferatu* haunted cinema screens in 1922. Haven't we missed the rat-infested boat with this one?

Well yes. But then again, you probably aren't from Derby, and I am.

More than one local historian or journalist has put forward the notion that Dracula was born in Derby, and died there too. A suggestion that certainly carries some validity, especially if it is the stage that is under discussion. For Hamilton Deane's theatrical adaptation of Stoker's novel received its world premiere at Derby's Grand Theatre, still standing to this day on Babington Lane in the city centre (currently operating as an 'adult'-themed crazy golf centre named 'House of Holes'! Though at least with the gorgeous theatre frontage still largely intact.) And when Derby was host to the immortal Bela Lugosi during his notorious 1951 British tour of the play, it was here at our Hippodrome (close to the Grand) that producer John Mather delivered the news that additional dates were to be added to the run, in places such as Newcastle and Liverpool, only to be informed by a shattered Lugosi that "John, I can't go on. It's taking too much out of me. Please finish it quickly." Not the only haggard and sickly vampire to request a peace-granting termination, perhaps, but without a doubt the most significant.

Indeed, Bela was denied his wish in the immediacy, since dates were already booked and contracted for Portsmouth, but following that unwanted trek to the South Coast it really was all over for this particular caped bloodsucker (*Mother Riley meets the Vampire* and *Plan 9 from Outer Space* notwithstanding, of course…)

The 1924 production of Deane's play at the Grand Theatre is notable for many reasons, not least of which was the presence and apparent blessing of Florence Stoker! Bram's widow had, infamously, suppressed Murnau's illicit film version *Nosferatu: Eine Symphonie des Grauens*, but a mere couple of years on, seemed perfectly happy to avoid interfering in this theatrical take on her husband's material. Maybe Bram's own theatre interests (stage critic for the 'Dublin Evening Mail', business manager of Henry Irving's Lyceum off The Strand in Westminster) had eased Mrs Stoker's anxieties a little – actors treading the boards might have been judged as somehow classier than those performing before motion picture cameras, possibly? Whatever the reason, Florence endorsed the stage show and is reported to have attended the Derby world premiere. Author Deane had intended to take the title role himself, but ultimately decided that Van Helsing might be a more suitable character; thus it was that Edmund Blake became the first stage Dracula.

Cast oddities include Frieda Hearn as Quincey P. Morris – seemingly gender-altered by Deane out of expediency, due to the ratio of females to males

Grand Theatre, Derby

in the available troupe – and the presence of Jack Howarth some way near the foot of the bill as a warder, decades before radio success in *Mrs Dale's Diary* and TV superstardom of sorts in Granada's evergreen continuing drama *Coronation Street*. In one Dracula-linked occurrence that might well have fitted right into either of Howarth's popular soap-style hits, on July 25th 1929 Jack married his fianceé Betty in Hull, only for Deane to request that he perform in the play that evening in Sheffield! Florence Stoker might have approved of the script, but the Lord Chamberlain did not, entirely, with theatrical censors granting a licence only on their insistence that Dracula's demise could not be presented directly to the audience (an action, or inaction if you prefer, which of course found its way into Tod Browning's film for Universal seven years on.)

Following the short Derby run, the play made its way around the provinces for the next three years before eventually transferring to the West End, opening at the Little Theatre in the Adelphi on Valentine's Day 1927. By October of that year it was on Broadway, with Lugosi, Edward Van Sloan, and writer John Balderston on board – the latter streamlining and compressing Deane's plot considerably as well as combining or ditching major characters (no need for Quincey Morris here, male or female!) And the rest is history.

The early 1950s saw a number of fading American film talents crossing the Atlantic and treading the boards before live, and often disinterested, British crowds. Laurel & Hardy did so, as documented recently in the biopic *Stan & Ollie*; so too did Buster Keaton, who had a disastrous run at Derby's Hippodrome Theatre, resulting in one of the venue's worst box-office takes of 1951. Lugosi revived as the Count was a different matter, however – pretty successful around the country, though not without criticism from many regional audiences and local news hacks who often reported that the play was laughable, unscary, and cheap-looking. Yet in Derby Dracula seemed to strike a chord – there are numerous first-hand reports of Bela's kindness, accessibility, eagerness to meet and speak with fans, and even venturing out to the town shops on occasion to purchase stationery and other sundry items. The show itself is said to have been greeted in a hushed awe, and if this was to be Lugosi's swansong in his signature role (those final few shows in Portsmouth aside, and one senses he would have been going through the motions there), then for all his troubles he may have at least ended on a minor high, with the Derby public – far from the easiest audience in the world! – truly taking to him and loving the production.

Coinciding with the publication of this issue of 'We Belong Dead', Derby is marking 100 years of Dracula via various events in the city, and we are thrilled (if not 'shocked' or 'horrified' as per Edward Van Sloan in *Frankenstein*!) to be a small part of the festivities. I haven't sufficient space within this cursory overview to go into full detail concerning Derby's history with the Count, but highly recommend that you seek out 'The Bela Lugosi Blog' on Wordpress, an incredibly detailed resource crammed with info, contemporary reports, and more photos, programme reproductions, ticket stubs, and other ephemera than you could possibly imagine. One of those websites that you'll need to bookmark as it will likely become a regular haunt once you've delved in initially.

So yes, step aside, Whitby! Derby is staking (npi) its claim as the true home of Count Dracula…

We Belong Dead   Page 5

AUNTIE'S VAMPIRE
DRACULA AT THE BBC

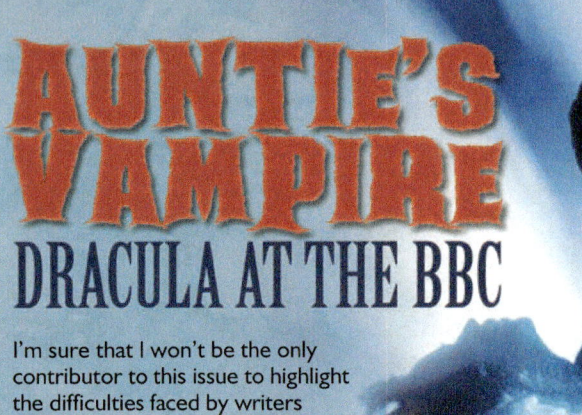

by Stephen Hatcher

I'm sure that I won't be the only contributor to this issue to highlight the difficulties faced by writers and producers in adapting Bram Stoker's 1897 novel 'Dracula' for film, television, or stage – not least the epistolary nature of the book, the variety of settings, and the many characters who appear in either main or supporting roles, several of whom have overlapping functions within the narrative. Writers have had to make decisions about which characters to focus on, and which to cut altogether or combine; whether to focus primarily on Harker's experiences at Castle Dracula or to take up the story from Dracula's arrival in Whitby – and then whether or not to move the action to London, and then back to Transylvania. Then there is the broader question of how faithful to the novel one wants to remain, or to what extent to be influenced by later adaptations – particularly the 1924 stage version, the 1931 Universal Pictures film, or that produced by Hammer in 1958, all of which added significantly to the mythos and have coloured public expectations of every new production of *Dracula*.

In looking at the three adaptations of *Dracula* produced for broadcast on the BBC between 1977 and 2020, we can see how different writers or teams of writers have approached the story and the differing creative decisions they took in facing these and other problems.

Count Dracula, written by Gerald Savory, produced by Morris Barry, and directed by Philip Saville – a very 'old-school' BBC team – was considered to be among the highlights of the BBC's winter 1977 drama schedule and was broadcast on 22nd December of that year, running to 155 minutes. It is considered to be one of the most faithful screen versions of the story and was produced in the traditional BBC way, using a mixture of multi-camera in-studio video for interiors and film for exteriors, although the occasional use of infra-red night-vision shots and black and white stock-footage add a welcome touch of variety.

Despite all the limitations of studio drama, *Count Dracula* is a lavish production, which all these years later still looks rather spectacular, and despite its length manages to hold the attention very well. Subsequent broadcasts have seen it divided into two or three parts.

Although Barry, Savory and Saville went for a traditional adaptation of the story, this did not prevent them from making changes as they saw necessary, including making Mina and Lucy sisters, thus establishing a more direct connection between the Westenras and Harker, and through him to Dracula. Lucy's three suitors in the book are reduced to just two, combining Arthur Holmwood and Quincey Morris into Quincey Holmwood, so allowing more focus on the husband and the rejected suitor (Seward).

Suave French actor Louis Jourdan was an interesting choice to play Dracula. At the time he was probably best known in the UK for his lead role in the frequently broadcast 1958 musical comedy *Gigi*. Jourdan has often received praise for his performance in *Count Dracula*, but I wasn't entirely convinced, finding him to be rather caught between two stools – without either the demonic, animalistic fury of Lee or the romance of Langhella. It's by no means a bad performance, but it doesn't rank among the very best.

There are very strong performances by Frank Finlay as Van Helsing and especially from Jack Shepherd as Renfield. Susan Penhaligon as Lucy and Judy Bowker as Mina are both excellent, succeeding in ensuring that neither are the weak creatures they sometimes appear. In contrast however, the younger male characters are somewhat anonymous, with neither Mark Burns as Seward, Bosco Hogan as Harker nor Richard Barnes as Holmwood being particularly memorable.

I'll highlight one scene which has tended to stick in the memory of viewers, when Harker leans out of his window in Castle Dracula, to find the Count crawling bat-like down the outside wall. It's very well-realised, although it is never really explained what Dracula is up to here – is there some reason why he cannot use the stairs?

Exterior filming at Alnwick Castle in Northumberland, and particularly in Whitby, is very welcome. This is one of the very few productions of Dracula to actually film in the North Yorkshire fishing port that is such an important location in the book, rather than use stand-in locations in Cornwall, the South of England or elsewhere.

By the time of our next BBC adaptation of *Dracula*, the landscape of British TV drama had changed considerably. Multi-camera studio productions had all but given way to the single-camera model, made all on film or filmized video. Following the success of the revived *Doctor Who* (2005), BBC Wales had become the centre for in-house produced drama, with most TV films being either co-productions with outside providers or made entirely by independent production companies. *Dracula* (2006) was written by Stewart Harcourt, directed by Bill Eagles and produced by Trevor Hopkins for Granada Television, for WGBH Boston and BBC Wales as a 90-minute TV movie, and was broadcast on 28th December 2006.

In contrast to *Count Dracula*, Hopkins and Harcourt chose to take a very different approach, producing a much-changed version of the story.

Lord Arthur Holmwood is our main character and is engaged to Lucy Westenra. He contacts Singleton, the sinister leader of 'The Brotherhood', a cult with links to a mysterious Transylvanian Count, who promises that his master can cure Arthur of his hereditary syphilis if he helps him come to England. Jonathan Harker (Rafe Spall) is sent off to Transylvania and killed by Dracula,

We Belong Dead

Page 7

who comes to England and fixes his attention on first Lucy and then her friend Mina (Stephanie Leonidas). Dr. John Seward, Van Helsing and a remorseful Arthur confront and apparently destroy Dracula at the cost of Holmwood's life, although we later discover that the Count has survived.

Clearly this is a very free adaptation of Stoker's novel. The role of Lord Holmwood is given much more prominence than in other adaptations, making him, for most of the film, the lead character, even though he is a deeply unlikeable antihero. Jonathan Harker's sojourn in Castle Dracula does not take up much of our time and he is very much dead as a result of it. This leaves John Seward, who, aided by Van Helsing, becomes the hero, confronting and apparently killing Dracula, and in a change from other versions, ending up with the girl (Mina). The 'final' confrontation with Dracula is transposed from Transylvania to London. There is no asylum or Renfield, whose role is filled by Singleton and the Brotherhood – new creations. Neither is there any sign of *Quincey P.* Morris, with just the wicked Holmwood and the heroic Seward left to woo poor Lucy.

The casting of Marc Warren as Dracula drew much criticism from some viewers. It was suggested that the attractive, young (39 at the time), blonde actor was far too pretty for the role. But for me, Warren's casting works very well. Cast against type, Warren's Count is very much a bestial, dark and brooding, animalistic vampire, which contrasts perfectly with his good looks. At the same time, he is just as believable as the seductive Dracula.

Sophia Myles is a more sexually voracious Lucy than is often seen. Frustrated and disappointed by her husband's apparent rejection of her physically, she is easy prey for Dracula.

David Suchet makes for an interesting Van Helsing, although his is hardly more than a cameo appearance with the vampire hunter reduced to a much less prominent role than is usual.

Dan Stevens is terrific as the despicable Holmwood, who comes good in the end, and Donald Sumpter is wonderfully hissable as Singleton, who more than makes up for the absence of Renfield as Dracula's UK ally. Although he has fewer interesting things to do than the others, Tom Burke, as Seward, is a solid heroic, if slightly bland leading man.

From what I remembered of it from 2006, I hadn't expected to enjoy this version of *Dracula*, however to my surprise, I found it to be great fun, well written, with strong performances and some terrific visuals. Great care has been taken with the design and lighting, using a dominant green and blue palette with occasional flash of deep red, which is, at times, a little reminiscent of Hammer's *Dracula*. Mention should be made too of the music by Dominik Scherrer, in which I detected occasional echoes of James Bernard's score for the 1958 film. Very effective.

The biggest criticism is that this *Dracula* feels all rather rushed, which it has no excuse for being, given how much of the story has been left out or altered. 2006's version of *Dracula* won't be to everyone's taste. It's certainly not *Dracula* for the purist, but it is an enjoyable riff on the theme, and for me, a thoroughly entertaining 90 minutes.

When it was announced that Mark Gatiss and Steven Moffat would be following their popular modern-day *Sherlock* (2010-17), with a three-part adaptation of *Dracula,* it was generally expected that the pair would do something similar with the Count. In fact, Gatiss and Moffat managed both to have their nineteenth century gothic cake and eat a slice of rich 21st century gateau, by setting the first two episodes in the 1890s, before pulling off an unexpected time-shift to 2020 for the third instalment. Produced by Sue Vertue for Hartswood with the three 90-minute instalments directed by Jonny Campbell, Damon Thomas and Paul McGuigan, *Dracula* was filmed in Slovakia and Bray Studios, the home of Hammer, and broadcast on 1st, 2nd and 3rd January 2020.

The serial is remarkable in that the three episodes, although telling a single story, could easily be watched and enjoyed separately, each having its own narrative and a different cast, with only Claes Bang as Dracula and Dolly Wells as Agatha and Zoe Van Helsing appearing in all three. Dracula is right at the centre of the story – very much the leading man, appearing in the majority of scenes and allowing us to observe his evil at close quarters.

The Danish actor Claes Bang is terrific as the Count, managing to combine the animal ferocity of the fanged vampire with the suave sophistication of the European aristocrat to perfection. He is dangerous to the core at every moment. Perhaps the biggest surprise, however, comes from Dolly Wells, who is just wonderful – especially as Agatha, the atheist nun, the strongest character in the show. She is just magnetic, stealing every scene she is in, even from the excellent Bang, and demanding the viewer's attention every time she is on screen.

Episode One 'The Rules of the Beast' is in many ways, the most traditional of the three and is a very well-told version of the story of Harker in Castle Dracula. Where it scores particularly highly is in managing to reflect the epistolary nature of the novel, by telling the tale via a series of interviews (accompanied by flashback scenes) between the undead Harker and Sister Agatha, in the convent in Budapest. John Heffernan shines as the tragic Harker, as does Joanna Scanlan as the Mother Superior.

The second episode 'Blood Vessel' is very unusual, focussing on the voyage of the Demeter, an aspect of the Dracula story to which very few adaptations have given much attention. It's almost a twisted version of Agatha Christie's 'Death on the Nile', as a disparate group of passengers and crew – including Sacha Dhawan as an Indian doctor, and Catherine Schell as an aristocratic lady – are picked off one-by-one. Could the killer be the enigmatic Count, or maybe the mysterious passenger Inside (cabin) Number 9? (Gatiss paying a little tribute to his League of Gentlemen confederates' hit comedy horror show there). Dracula demonstrates a new power here, acquiring the knowledge, memories, and experiences of his victims when he drinks their blood.

Some critics, having loved the first two episodes, were badly disappointed by the third 'The Dark Compass', especially by the time-jump to the 21st Century, but this felt absolutely right to me. As Gatiss and Moffat point out during the accompanying interview on the Blu-ray release, it's precisely what Stoker did in the novel, starting his story in the medieval society of Transylvania, then transporting the vampire to (then) present-day Britain, where he was able to avail himself of all the accoutrements of modern life, to prey on an unprepared and unbelieving population.

Dracula's submerged body is found and revived by scientists from the Jonathan Harker Institute. He is imprisoned in a glass cell but manages to acquire a mobile phone and calls in a lawyer, Frank Renfield (Mark Gatiss), who secures his release. Once free, Dracula pursues his interest in a young woman, Lucy Westenra (Lydia West) who quickly falls for his charms.

Gatiss and Moffat pull off the same trick with this episode that they did with Sherlock, updating a popular icon of Victorian literature, and examining how that character would operate in the modern world. This final episode could easily have served as the pilot for an on-going Dracula series, in the mould of Sherlock, which I have no doubt would have been every much a success as the detective show.

The ending has also proved controversial, as Zoe Van Helsing, dying of cancer, explains to Dracula that he has allowed himself to believe in all the legends of vampire weaknesses, as a way of avoiding his terrifying shame at what he is. Zoe dies and Dracula tenderly takes her body and drinks her blood, which he knows will kill him. The two come together in death almost as lovers in the sunlight.

It's a conclusion like that of no other Dracula adaptation, for which Moffat and Gatiss should be commended. It's breathtakingly daring and original, and looks just beautiful. However, it might be best not to think too deeply about it, as I'm not entirely sure it works. It doesn't detract though, from what is a terrific take on Dracula.

So, three BBC adaptations of Dracula that tell essentially the same story, each of them excellent in its own way, and each entirely different to the others. But which is the best of them? I honestly don't think there is an answer to that. The purists will undoubtedly go for the 1977 Louis Jourdan version, quoting its accuracy and faithfulness to the text. Those who prefer an updated Dracula will probably choose the Gatiss/Moffat/Bang version – especially if they enjoy their vampires with a good dose of black humour. The Marc Warren version will probably not be anyone's favourite but will have elements that appeal to both sides of the traditional/modernist debate. I have absolutely enjoyed revisiting all three versions and will, no doubt return, at some point, to each of them. It's a testament to the strength of the source material – both Stoker's novel and subsequent influential adaptations – that three so very different versions can be made, each producing such pleasing results.

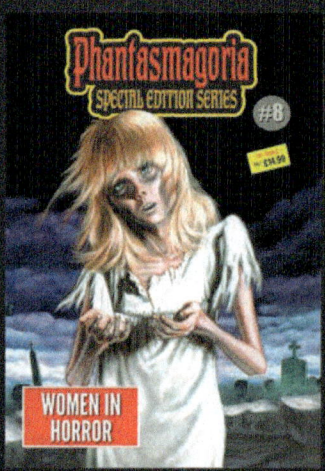

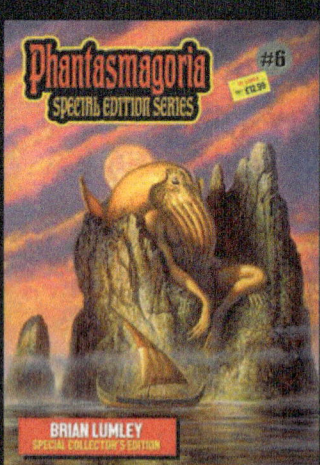

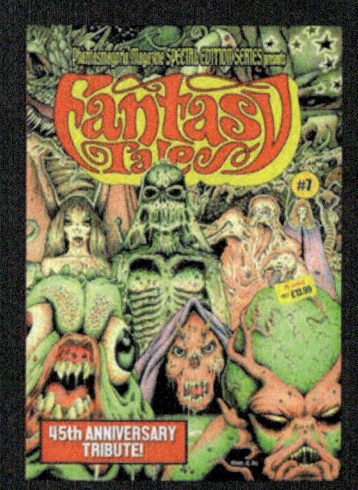

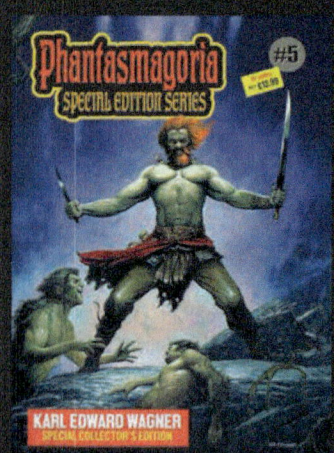

THE COUNT AND ALL HIS WORKS
A Chat with Ramsey Campbell on the many facets of Dracula
By Simon J. Ballard

When Darrell asked for an interview with legendary horror writer Ramsey Campbell, I jumped at the chance. Not only is he an incredibly nice man, but he is also highly knowledgeable on the horror genre – a geek if you like, just like you and me – so I knew it would be a fascinating chat. Having made the trip from Oxford to his house just outside Liverpool, we sat down in his living room, and I had all my questions concerning Dracula in front of me in chronological order. But something about the geniality of the man caused me to largely abandon this list and just chat to him informally. What follows concerns aspects of Dracula in no order at all, but I did start by asking Ramsey about Bram Stoker's novel.

"Well, I first encountered 'Dracula' when I was maybe ten or eleven. This was the old Arrow paperback. I'd been forbidden before because my mother thought it wasn't quite nice, you know, along with Dennis Wheatley. Ghost stories were all right, though. I found the first few chapters grippingly intense, frightening even, and then I was surprised that Dracula drifts to the periphery of the narrative, glimpsed in an adumbrative fashion although crucial to the story. It was an unconventional approach to the classic horror story – you get this gradual accumulation of detail with M.R. James and Lovecraft, but with 'Dracula' you get the revelation at the start and accumulated details after.

"The only other novel I know that does this is Richard Marsh's 'The Beetle' which was a kind of competitor to 'Dracula.' Marsh, as a point of interest, was Robert Aickman's grandfather. You have in the opening chapter this Beetle, a shape-shifting entity, and again he hovers on the edge of the narrative and makes himself felt only by implication for quite a time.

"I'd already read 'Dracula's Guest', which was originally meant to be one of Jonathan Harker's chapters at the beginning of the book, which as a young creature was why I sought out the

We Belong Dead

Page 11

novel. That again greatly impressed me with the atmosphere. 'Dracula' is still a seminal work today- Steve King calls it the wall he bounced "Salem's Lot' off."

I said to Ramsey, "I've always thought it a shame Christopher Lee was disdainful about his portrayal being kept to the shadows for most of the running time of his Hammer Dracula films, given the novel's approach."

"Well," Ramsey replied, "look at *Dracula Prince of Darkness*, which benefits greatly from that gradual build-up, with old Klove as a sort of Saint John the Baptist to the vampire, announcing his coming before Dracula eventually shows up."

Indeed, the resurrection of Dracula with the help of Klove and the liberal spilling of Alan Kent's blood takes place three quarters of an hour into the movie. "Which gives us lots of Barbara Shelley," Ramsey nodded with understandable enthusiasm.

I then asked Ramsey his thoughts on *Nosferatu*. "I'm not sure which version is my favourite Dracula, but that is certainly one of them, and overall, for me one of the most frightening. Partly because you get a sense of belief in the material and also those curious occult references the estate agent employs, for some reason. It echoes the runic parchment from 'Casting the Runes'. Max Schreck is by far the most inhuman Dracula, until *The Last Voyage of the Demeter*, which gives it a run for its money but obviously to some extent derived from Murnau's film. As is Reggie Nalder as Mr. Barlow in *Salem's Lot*. I gather those warehouses still exist!"

I told Ramsey about Andy Ellis – famous on Facebook horror groups for his 'then and now' location shots – and friend Adrian Charlton's trip to those self-same warehouses, with the latter in full Count Orlok costume, which caused Ramsey great merriment.

"Well, that reminds me of *The Tomb of Nosferatu*, the remarkable 2023 silent short film by Arthur Dark and Nathan D. Lee, in which a young couple tour Murnau's locations and encounter more and worse than they bargained for."

Mention was then made of Francis Ford Coppola's *Bram Stoker's Dracula*. "It's flawed," Ramsey commented, "but I do have a lot of time for it. There is a love of the material, and the first half hour feels like a love-letter to almost every vampire film you've ever seen."

I ventured that, given its fast and loose use of the source novel, using the author's name in the title was misleading and worked against the movie. "It is Coppola's Dracula, and he should have said so," Ramsey replied.

This led me to onto the BBC's 1977 adaptation, *Count Dracula*, which, with its 155-minute run time, is perhaps the most faithful adaptation of Stoker's book. "That's true, yeah. I do think Louis Jourdan's is one of the best Dracula interpretations by any means. He's good at the suavity."

"So, who would you rare highest in the role of Dracula?" I asked.

"Overall, probably Christopher Lee," Ramsey replied in an instant, "I mean certainly after *Dracula Prince of Darkness* he gets visibly tired, but the power of his Dracula in Terence Fisher's *Dracula* – the most aristocratic Dracula but also the most physically terrifying!"

What of *Dracula A.D. 1972* and *The Satanic Rites of Dracula*, I ventured? "I'm less interested in those, but Hammer had to do it to keep the series going, to find new things to do with the character. You could certainly argue the quasi-immortal Dracula should pop up in modern London, but they don't have the same power as the original, or indeed *The Brides of Dracula*, even though he isn't in it."

"That film," I enthused, "is the ultimate gothic fairy tale, even with allusions to Rapunzel in the blonde-haired Baron Meinster trapped in his tower, a malevolent twist on 'Romeo and Juliet', and even echoes of M.R. James' 'Count

Magnus' thrown in with the magical dropping of the padlocks from Gina's coffin. "And the great Martita Hunt, and Freda Jackson," Ramsey smiled, "Quite a line-up! Jackson amounts to a mid-wife at the grave of the girl in that extraordinary scene." One of the most disturbing scenes in any Hammer film, I reckon.

I next asked Ramsey about Jack Palance as Dracula in Dan Curtis' 1974 TVM. "He's not bad, he has the menace and an uncanny quality. I think he brings conviction to the role, a romantic quality that precedes Coppola." Without any need of prompting from me, Ramsey then brought up Jess Franco's attempt at a faithful version of the novel with his 1970 El Conde Dracula, "Sadly, I'm probably increasingly heretical these days in thinking Franco isn't terribly interesting, whereas people are now hailing him. I remain unpersuaded on the whole. I'm a fan of The Awful Dr Orlof for certain, however.

"Lee did at least get to play Dracula as authentically as possible, and you do have Klaus Kinski as Renfield for Heaven's sake, which cannot be a bad thing. But apart from that, I don't remember much about it that impressed me."

Famously, Bram Stoker took years to research the Carpathian regions around which the top and tail of his novel is set without setting a single footstep there. I wondered if this was something Ramsey had ever done in his writing. "Oh gosh yes, quite a number of times. Of course, these days with the internet, there is a temptation towards laziness – you can easily take a video tour of your intended location!

"The earliest example of this was for a pretty ramshackle book of mine called 'The Claw' from the early 80s. Quite a lot of it is set in Nigeria, with the leopard men as the source of the Talisman. To be honest I wouldn't do that now, it's a bit suspect. At a convention after publication, this chap came up to me and asked, 'So how many months did you spend in Lagos?' which I thought was quite the compliment! If you can relate the location through the character's eyes, that's how you make it work. We were talking in the car [Ramsey, bless him, picked me up from the Mersey Line station] about 'Ancient Images'. I did drive to the Redfield area quite a bit for that."

"Would you say Stoker was a pro-feminist writer?" I wondered.

"Well, it's an interesting question, and depends if you feel it's a matter of female sexuality being something that the book doesn't view as evil, that it's the society that needs to control it and put it down. You can read the book that way."

I postulated that Mina is strong and proactive, as though the essence of his lifeblood Dracula infused her with brought out hidden characteristics that Victorian society would rather stay suppressed.

"That's a very good possibility," Ramsey agreed, "like with Barbara Shelley [in Dracula Prince of Darkness] when she finally becomes liberated, it's very exciting and rather positive. You regret her being put to the stake!

"As you say, Mina does become the controlling element of the narrative as it nears its end, so to that extent you can argue there is a certain undercurrent of feminism."

So, what of Ramsey's thoughts on Bela Lugosi, I'm sure you're all wondering?

"Well, he remains one of the greatest Draculas, of the urbane kind. But one thing Jimmy Sangster brilliantly solves in Hammer's Dracula is that you never get the sense of the structure falling away, which you do get with Tod Browning. The first ten minutes, though, are wonderful and extremely atmospheric. When it gets to England it does become rather more staid and stage-bound, with people saying that they saw a wolf crossing the lawn. Well, we would have liked to have seen that wolf! Lugosi holds it together, as does Edward Van Sloan. And how can we forget Dwight Frye [as Renfield], one of his greatest hysterical performances? Browning certainly has his moments of inspiration for sure, but it does sadly rely too much on the stage play."

I've recently written an article on Dracula's Daughter for 'Scream' magazine, a film I adore, so I was keen on Ramsey's thoughts.

"I'm fond of that and wrote the novelisation (to use that horrible term) back in the 70s. My first paperback editor was Piers Dudgeon of Star Books, whom I'd been recommended to by Hugh Lamb of Star's parent company W.H. Allen. That's who published my anthology 'Demons by Daylight' and my first novel 'The Doll Who Ate His Mother.' 'Dracula's Daughter' was a separate deal with Universal to do six of their horror/ monster films. I also did 'Bride of Frankenstein' and 'The Wolf Man.'

"It is a very interesting film, and the BBFC turned down a rather gruesome prologue set centuries past. The restraint actually works rather well, and I think it's more consistent in tone than Browning's Dracula. It has these real moments of subtlety, with Nan Grey as the model Lili. There are obvious but subtle hints of lesbianism. I brought that out, again subtly, in the novel – I didn't want to overdo it because I wanted to match the tone of the film. I've always liked its dark atmosphere."

I then asked Ramsey on his thoughts on vampirism from a story-telling point of view.

"Well, for a long time I felt it had all been done, and that I had nothing to say about it. I'd done the occasional short story, but not a novel. But then Jenny and I stayed on the Greek island Zakynthos, and we got an off-road jeep trip. We were one of the first to be picked up and we drove through a Club 18-30 resort just after dawn, with the occasional person brushing broken glass outside a taverna, and the driver commented, 'They've all gone now, they only come out at night,' and I thought, 'Hang on!' and for the rest of that trip I was scribbling notes. By the end of it I had the basis for the novel 'Thirteen Days by Sunset Beach,' my vampire book – there is new blood to be found in tourism! I wanted to rediscover the monstrous."

After I extolled the virtues of *Buffy the Vampire Slayer*, which Ramsey is keen to give a go, I asked for his thoughts on the Steven Moffatt/Mark Gatiss *Dracula*. "I did like that a lot," he said, "I like the fact that they did their own thing with it. You know, if you want the original, read the novel, or watch Louis Jourdan. I thought it was a pretty witty thing, and the black jokes have their roots in Lugosi; 'I never drink… wine'! I also liked the jump to the present." So do I and was amazed at the backlash this plot development received.

As my chat with Ramsey was drawing to a close, it seemed only right to touch on another anniversary taking place this year – his 60th year as a horror writer. That deserves a mention, I know you will all agree. Ramsey's thoughts on his diamond date? "My god!" he exclaimed, "My first collection ['The Inhabitant of the Lake and Less Welcome Tenants'] came out in 1964 from Arkham House, under August Derleth. Not to sound like a boast because it's true, but I was the first of the new generation of Lovecraftian writers to come after those who had known him; Robert Bloch, Frank Belknap Long, Derleth himself.

"You may find this difficult to believe, and certainly some of the readers will, but in 1960 there hadn't been a single paperback collection of Lovecraft's stories in Britain. Maybe the odd tale in an anthology, and a hardback collection in the early '50s but that was your lot. So out came this book 'Cry Horror!', a complete collection of Lovecraft, which I found for half a crown in a general store-cum-bookshop over in Liverpool. I managed to scrape together all these farthings which I dumped on this poor guy's counter, took it home and read it from cover to cover. I even skived off school!

"I thought his was the greatest horror I had ever read, and wanted to do this myself, so I sent off this fan fiction to Derleth and he sent back a long letter saying that it needs a whole lot of work, that I need to expand on the stories, set them in England, write some more, and then said he might be prepared to publish them. I was fifteen years old! So, my first book came out when I was eighteen, very much imitation Lovecraft, and I spent the next five years basically doing myself, with stories rooted in Liverpool, based on my own experiences. This then became 'Demons by Daylight'. My American agent, Kirby McCauley – now sadly gone – then encouraged me to do a novel, which became 'The Doll Who Ate His Mother', and on we go!

"We're going to do a special limited edition of my new novel, 'The Incubations' this November, with a matching collection of M.R. James and another of Lovecraft, and I'm doing a story in each, so it will make a nice trilogy collection. More power to Flame Tree Publishers!"

And on that delightfully positive note, it was time to take my leave, thanking Ramsey for his time, and for such an entertaining time. "My pleasure!" he graciously replied, before driving me back to the station, and I can honestly say it was one of those afternoons I never wanted to end. If only there was some way to prolong life beyond the grave…

THE RETURN OF THE VAMPIRE

by Matthew E Banks

1943 should have been the year of the Vampire for Bela Lugosi and taken him out of the poverty row films that he had had to do, to make ends meet. Between January and February, Universal filmed *Son of Dracula*, with Lon Chaney Jr. in the title role. It was a snub to Lugosi, who had played the Count in their 1931 film and who to the American audiences was Count Dracula. Lugosi would be bitter about this for decades, and in his autobiography, Curt Siodmak states, "Lon was wrongly cast. Bela Lugosi should have played the part." (Siodmak, 277) A point that 'Film Bulletin' made in its review: "And Lon Chaney Jr. is unable to give his portrayal of Count Alucard (that's Dracula spelled backwards) the eerie quality that Bela Lugosi originally imparted to the vampire role." (Nov. 29th, 1943)

It wasn't the first time that Universal messed him around. Bela was due to appear in a prologue sequence in *Dracula's Daughter* (1936), but with continuing script changes and shooting schedule, the studio ended up having to pay to use his likeness. With *Son of Dracula*, Universal had a chance to give the audience what they wanted, Lugosi as the Count

On March 6th, Universal released *Frankenstein Meets the Wolf Man*. Instead of being a triumph for Lugosi, it would be a disaster. Universal decided to strip the soundtrack of Lugosi's voice, thus making the Frankenstein Monster mute, despite several scenes where its mouth is moving and making his performance possibly the worst out of the proceeding Frankenstein films. If Lugosi was aware of this or not is not known; what is clear is again Universal hung him out to dry.

Whether to prove to the studios that he was the definitive Dracula or to remind audiences of his greatest role, Lugosi went on the road with a stage revival of *Dracula* – something that he would continually do throughout his career. In April, he arrived in New York, and in May took the play to Boston. May also saw Kurt Neumann sell his story 'Vampires of London' to Columbia pictures, who also wanted him to direct. On June 1st, Lugosi landed in Washington, his play replacing *The Bat* with SaZu Pitts. 'Variety' also announced that "Bela Lugosi also being booked by Kantz and McCoy for a revival of *Dracula* in mid-June under a policy of rotating guest stars with a permanent repertory company" (June 3rd). In fact June was a good month for Bela; in Pittsburgh, *Dracula* for the second week at The Locust, took $7,500 and in Washington at the end of June, 'Variety' announced, "In the face of blistering heat and housed in a non-air-conditioned theatre, Bela Lugosi in *Dracula*, eight performances grossed $8,000 last week, considered exceptional in the face of atmospheric opposition" (June 30th). At the end of June, in Chicago, Lugosi was named president of the nationally organized Hungarian American Council for Democracy.

Over at Columbia, things were moving for their vampire film. On July 22nd it was announced in 'The Film Daily' under 'Title Switches': "*Return of the Vampire*, formerly *Vampires of London*, Columbia." So, their production now had a new name, and on August 20th it was announced that Nina Foch would star. She had been under contact to Warners via a very strong screen test, but when she went before the cameras, she had Strep-throat, and her face was swollen. On seeing this, Jack Warner terminated her contract with immediate effect. That was on a Friday, by Monday she was signed to Columbia (based on that screen test) and her first production for them would be *The Return of the Vampire*. Also on August 20th, it was announced that Lew Landers would be directing, with Sam White producing, and on August 24th, the main casting was announced: "Bela Lugosi,

Miles Mander, Matt Wills, Frieda Inescort: *Return of the Vampire.*" By the 31st, Sherlee Collier and Roland Varno were added to the cast list. Added to the cast by September 3rd were Gilbert Emery, Donald Dewar and Ottola Nesmith. Shooting had already begun on August 21st. This would be the last time that Lugosi would receive top billing in a major studio film, the second time that he would portray a vampire on screen, and would receive £3,500 for his performance (the same as he received for *Dracula*.) Universal, on hearing that Lugosi was going to portray a vampire on the screen again, threatened to sue Columbia (as they had done with M.G.M. for 1935's *Mark of the Vampire*), but as Lugosi's character was not Dracula per se, Universal could not stop Columbia going forward. As Gary D Rhodes speculates, "Whether or not Lugosi's involvement with *The Return of the Vampire* had any effect on Universal's subsequent avoidance of him in 1944 is difficult to substantiate. At any rate, the studio did not hire him again until 1948." (Rhodes & Kaffenberger, 'Bela Lugosi in Person', 350)

Columbia, to some degree to pacify Universal, did not release the film nationwide until January 1944, this being done so as not to compete with Universal's *Son of Dracula*, that was released on November 5th 1943. *The Return of the Vampire* had an initial release on November 11th. Advance synopses and information in both 'Motion Picture Herald' (October 23rd) and 'Showmen's Trade Review' (November 6th) both gave away the story. By the end of November, the National Legion of Decency gave the film a Class A-II rating, unobjectionable for adults.

On February 2nd, 1944, 'Variety' gave the film a glowing review, saying: "Lugosi's villainy remains standard for him and Frieda Inescort, as one who saves the life of a vampire victim and helps trap Lugosi, contributes the outstanding portrayal. Miles Mander makes a realistic Scotland Yard operative. Nina Foch shows promise as the gal saved from the vamp. Matt Willis is excellent as the servant turned wolfman. John Stumar and L.W. O'Connell have done topflight photography." ('Variety', 18)

The Return of the Vampire is unique in horror film history. It is the first film to feature a vampire and a werewolf in a master and servant role, the first to show a vampire attack a child (the Bloofer lady in *Dracula* is not shown) and to break the fourth wall rule [character speaks directly to the audience]. In the UK the final scene of Lugosi's face melting in the sun was edited as it was deemed to be too much for a British audience.

The opening scene of *Return* is reminiscent to one in *Dracula*, where Dracula attacks the flower girl; here Tesla attacks a young lady in the London fog. This leads into a comparison scene in *Dracula's Daughter* (USA, 1936) – where Dr. Jeffrey Garth (Otto Kruger) fails to save vampire victim Lili (Nan Grey) after Countess Marya Zaleska (Gloria Holden) has attacked her, here it is perfectly mirrored in the scene where Professor Walter Saunders (Gilbert Emery) and Lady Jane Ainsley (Frieda Inescort) try to talk to the girl (Jeanne Bates) that Tesla has attacked, and she dies of fright whilst recalling her encounter. The relationship between Andreas Obry (Matt Willis) and Tesla (Bela Lugosi) is very similar in nature to that of Dracula and Renfield (Dwight

Frye) in the earlier Universal film, with the exception that Obry is turned into a wolf man whenever he is summed to do the vampire's dirty work. This double bill of monsters may have been influenced by the success of *Frankenstein Meets the Wolf Man* that had been released on March 5th, 1943. Frieda Inescort as Lady Jane Ainsley is the personification of Professor Van Helsing in female form, and in the confrontation scene between her and Tesla this could be seen as a parallel to the earlier film, where Dracula, realising that Van Helsing is a threat, goes to kill him, only to be thwarted by his strong will and a crucifix. The final scene is a reversal of Lugosi's earlier vampire outing, in that instead of the servant being killed by the vampire, it is reversed, although the redemption for the servant is also death!

Here, Lugosi, is not playing the aristocratic and suave Count Dracula that he portrayed in film and on stage; here he is playing a depraved Romanian scientist, whose thirst for knowledge made him a vampire – and this is Lugosi's strength here – he is portraying a very different type of vampire altogether. Tesla has the power to kill by the power of his mind – as seen when his first screen victim is describing her attack, she screams out, "No, no I didn't tell them…" before dying. After being staked the first time, he placed a curse Professor Walter Saunders from beyond the grave – "It was my curse that caused Professor Saunders' recent death." Here it is interesting to note that Tesla claims that this 'staking' imprisoned him, rather than killing him: "Lady Jane Ainsley and Professor Walter Saunders imprisoned me – deprived me of life for the past 23 years." – which leads to the question, how does Tesla know the names of his attackers? – is there some fine telepathic link to Andreas or Nikki that he is able to access, during his 'imprisonment'? Also, during the attack on the six-year-old Nikki, he can enter the house uninvited, which goes against vampiric folklore!

Incidentally his shadow on the wall shows him wearing a top hat – not unlike Dracula when strolling through the streets of London! Another interesting fact is when Saunders and Ainsley are hunting the vampire during the opening sequence, they come across the werewolf's footprints in the mud and dust, but there are no footprints for the vampire! As the werewolf, Matt Willis sometimes over-emotes, but that can be overlooked. His utter look of fear when he is confronted by a reanimated Tesla shows versatility and more importantly, believability. As 'The Brooklyn Citizen' says in their review: "a horror film of the first order. It is certain to send thrills and chills up and down one's spine … Mr. Lugosi spends his days in his coffin and his nights seeking out girls, and to make things more terrible, there's a wolf man as an assistant… Lugosi, as usual, gives a suave and polished performance in the title role … As Andreas Obry, a servant turned wolf man, Matt Willis is all that one could ask for." (Bojarski, 201). Frieda Inescort and Nina Foch are good too, but the real let down is character actor Miles Mander as Sir Frederick Fleet, who is the foil to Inescort. His utter refusal, despite mounting evidence, to believe what Lady Ansley is telling him leads to them bickering, slowing the pace.

The film has a 'Universal' quality to it and that elevates it. Griffin Jay had written scripts for several Universal films: *The Mummy's Hand* (1940), *The Mummy's Tomb* (1942) and *Captive Wild Woman* (1943), Lugosi and Landers had both worked for that studio, and a further connection to Universal's horror films is Billy Bevan and Gilbert Emery, both of whom had had roles in *Dracula's Daughter* (1936). Willis' wolfman make-up is more like a dog man and makes him cuter rather than something to fear, yet the scenes where he is running through the bombed-out streets of London are very effective. The sets of the abandoned Priory cemetery conjure up a claustrophobic atmosphere, where you really can believe that a supernatural manifestation will occur. The sets were constructed and shot at Fine Arts Studios as Columbia's lot on Gower Street was fully booked on other projects.

The Return of the Vampire was scheduled to have a sequel, *Bride of the Vampire*, but that project fell through and evolved into the dire *Cry of the Werewolf* (USA, 1944), starring Nina Foch, with Lugosi nowhere to be seen. After this, Bela would only play a vampire on screen one more time. He would resurrect his portrayal of Count Dracula for the comedic farce *Abbott and Costello Meet Frankenstein* in 1948, but as Tesla he showed the world the darker side to his Count's personality.

DRACULA IN MARVEL COMICS

by Andy Allard

To a nine-year-old kid feasting on 'The Mighty World of Marvel', 'Spider-Man Comics Weekly', and 'The Avengers', British Marvel's weekly dose of black-and-white superhero reprint comics, Saturday 19th October 1974 stands out as a very special day. Suddenly, there were two extra weekly comic titles on the racks, and neither of them featured superheroes. The first, 'Planet of the Apes', capitalised on the huge popularity of the Apes TV show and cinematic re-releases of the original pentalogy. The second, 'Dracula Lives', featured the exploits of everyone's favourite movie monsters, reprinting 'Tomb of Dracula', 'The Monster of Frankenstein' and 'Werewolf by Night' in weekly instalments. At a time when the BBC and independent networks regularly screened classic Universal and Hammer horrors on Fridays and Saturday nights, this was guaranteed to be a massive hit. The inclusion of huge, full colour posters with both new comics only made their release that much more special.

Of course, 'Tomb of Dracula' first appeared as a full colour monthly comic in the United States cover dated April 1972, introducing the vampiric count to the legions of Marvelites with the relaxation of the restrictive Comics Code. The Comics Code had been introduced in the 1950s after a group of concerned citizens argued successfully that comics were corrupting the minds of the nation's children. Horror, violence, bondage, juvenile delinquency, immorality... how could any self-respecting publisher want to feature these in four colour publications aimed at children? Fortunately, at the back end of the 60s/early 70s, pioneering moves in the industry such as releasing a three-issue run of 'The Amazing Spider-Man' without the Comics Code seal of approval led to amendments in the rules and paved the way for Marvel's excellent run of horror comics in the 70s and beyond.

This wasn't exactly the bloodthirsty Count's first foray into Marvel Comics, having appeared in two shorts just prior to the implementation of the Comics Code at a time when Marvel was still known as Atlas – and a good few years before Christopher Lee first donned the cloak and fangs. A 6-page tale of terror in 'Suspense' #7 (March, 1951) foreshadowed the title of American Marvel's own black-and-white magazine 'Dracula Lives!', whilst 'Journey into Unknown Worlds' #29 (July, 1954) gave us the 4-page 'Of Royal Blood'. Both were unmemorable O. Henry type tales, although they do give us an inkling of how Dracula may have fared without the intervention of the Code.

Fast forward to 1972 then, and as the initial run of stories develop we meet Frank Drake, descendant of Dracula and all round good guy; Rachel Van Helsing, versatile blonde vampire slayer with a crossbow long before Buffy took the reins; her mute, powerful Indian assistant Taj; Quincy Harker, wheelchair bound descendant of Dracula's 19th century nemesis Jonathan Harker and, in issue #10, one of the most popular creations of the 70s, Blade, the hip black vampire slayer reflecting the hugely successful blaxploitation movement of the time.

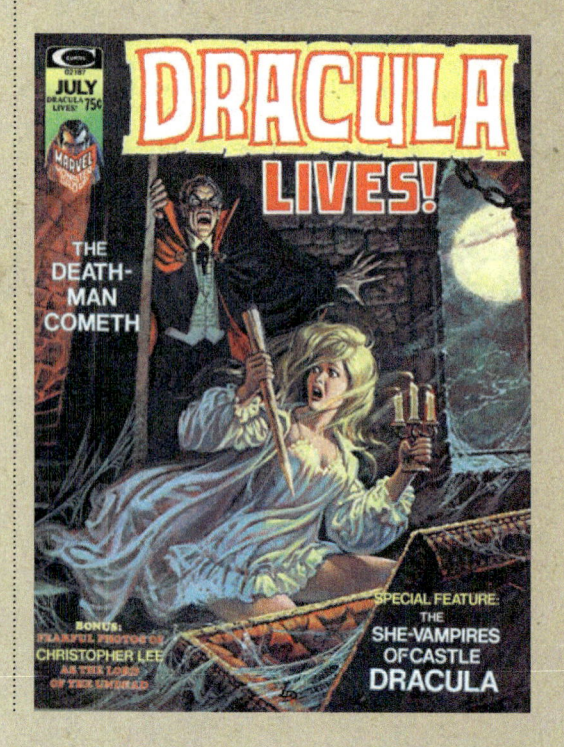

I remember reading 'Marvel Preview' #3, a 1975 black-and-white Marvel magazine and therefore subject to even less restrictions than the colour monthlies, which was a Blade special. Blade's introduction still resonates with me almost fifty years later: 'Born bastard to a prostitute...' How gripping were those five words? I was hooked!

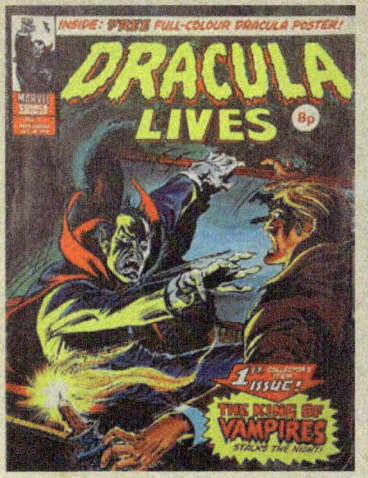

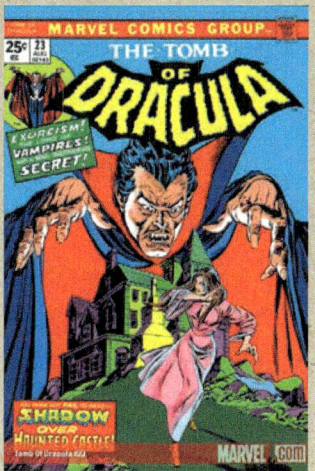

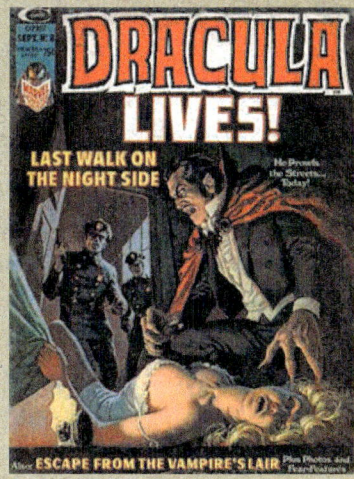

With Dracula's cast of characters firmly established, and the more adult-targeted black-and-white magazine 'Dracula Lives' running concurrently, it was time to integrate the Lord of the Vampires into the wider Marvel universe, beginning with the obvious crossovers featuring the Frankenstein Monster and Werewolf by Night. Following this, and a one panel appearance in the final chapter of the Avengers-Defenders war – 'Avengers' #118 (December 1973), the Lord of the Undead teamed up with everyone's favourite web-spinner in 'Giant Size Spider-Man' #1 (July 1974). The cover promised a whole lot more than the story actually delivered as our two superstars never meet, with Peter Parker brushing shoulders with Dracula in just three panels out of a thirty-page strip.

The 1975 'Mighty Marvel Calendar' featured a whole month devoted to Marvel monsters with a full colour page featuring Dracula, the Frankenstein Monster, Werewolf by Night, and relative newcomer Man-Thing. One thing was for sure; after a ropey start (the first few issues of 'Tomb' had been heavily criticised with several lengthy readers' letters calling for an early change), the now-established writer/artist team of Marv Wolfman (his real name!) and Gene Colan had breathed life into the cursed creature. Dracula was here to stay!

Soon, Marvel's latest sensation was pitting his wits against 'Doctor Strange' and appearing in all manner of colour monthly titles including 'The Invaders', 'Nova', and 'Ms Marvel'. August 1976 even saw an adaptation of Bram Stoker's original novel in 'Marvel Classics Comics' #9 (an earlier adaptation had started in 'Dracula Lives' but was not completed until decades later).

From the outset, Dracula had mirrored the fearsome demon of Hammer horror movies, with little in the way of back story, spending most issues seeking out victims to munch down on whilst at the same time avoiding his ever-growing band of stake-wielding enemies. In an incredibly creative move, Marvel began fleshing out their Vampire Lord, giving him a wife (his third genuine bride, completely different to his usual band of coffin-groping groupies he keeps hidden away in the castle basement) and even a son! In a complex, intricate and quite thrilling storyline spanning the final ten issues of the bi-monthly four colour 'Tomb of Dracula', we meet Janus, son of Dracula, see him transform from ugly baby into life size costumed supervillain, watch as Dracula is restored to humanity, see him face off against Mephisto, do the unthinkable and pray to God, become a vampire again, leading to a final explosive showdown with Quincy Harker in Castle Dracula, the place where it all began in 'Tomb of Dracula' #1. Toei Animation chose to adapt this storyline in their 1980 *Dracula Sovereign of the Damned* feature length animated movie, a production which featured stunning animation but didn't really capture the essence of Marvel's characters.

After seven years of publication, in #69 Marvel announced #72 would be the final issue of the comic. Months passed, and when the double-sized #70 appeared on the stands, cover dated August 1979, it was with the very sad announcement that this was to be the final issue. Marvel had replaced half a dozen titles in recent months and 'Tomb of Dracula' was the latest victim, although the exploits of the Lord of the Undead would continue in a new black and white magazine retaining the title 'Tomb of Dracula', recommencing from #1. Although this meant a release from the restrictions of the Comics Code, there wasn't a great deal to distinguish it from the earlier 'Dracula Lives' which only lasted thirteen issues. Without a strong cast of continuing characters, the new comic failed to generate much support and was itself cancelled after just six issues.

Was this the end of Dracula? It certainly defined

the end of the vampire's Golden Age as far as I was concerned, and 'X-Men Annual' #6 (November 1982) really drove the stake home! In one of the most bizarre X-Men stories, written by master scribe Chris Claremont with art by Bill Sienkiewicz, we discover what happened to Rachel Van Helsing. When we last saw Rachel, she and Frank Drake appeared to be embarking on a (hopefully) happy relationship, together in each other's arms, but oh no, that love affair ended badly, no reason given, and she is now a teaching professor at a college north of New York City. By the second page, Dracula has found her, and Rachel, our fearless vampire-slayer who survived endless battles with the Count, looks terrified (and so badly drawn)! Dracula then vampirises Ms Helsing, makes her his consort, and battles the X-Men. After he's defeated (was that ever in doubt?), Rachel demands to be put out of her misery and Mr Adamantium himself, Wolverine, does the honours, reducing the beautiful vampire slayer to a pile of ashes. Was I angry?! After years of investing in this character and having loved Claremont's earlier work on 'The Uncanny X-Men' ('The Dark Phoenix Saga' being one of only two comic sagas to have me in tears in my younger days), I was astonished to see this horrendous waste of such a centrally important character. Claremont definitely made a mistake with this one, and Sienkiewicz' rendition of Rachel is appalling.

So whither the Vampire Lord thereafter? Well, the great thing about old Dracula is you can kill him off, time and time again, and always find a reason to bring him back. You don't have to clone him (as with Gwen Stacy), create an inter-dimensional rift to bring in a Dracula variant from one of the many merry Marvel multiverses, or swing backwards through time to save him from certain doom. All Dracula demands is the swift removal of a stake, perhaps a few mystical words, maybe a pint or two of fresh Type AB negative, and he's back on his bloodcurdling feet ready to dance. And dance he did...

From 'The Fantastic Four' to 'Spider-Man', from 'S.H.I.E.L.D.' to 'Deadpool', Dracula became Marvel's undead slapper, occasionally headlining his own short-lived limited series, but more often than not featuring as villain of the month in more prestigious titles. He's pulled together his legions of the damned, developed a serum to enhance his followers' already formidable abilities, and tried to establish a whole new vampire kingdom. Sometimes, however, simple is best. Dracula's appearance changed too: gone were the long, flowing cloak, the high-necked collar, and the sleek, black hair – sometimes his hair turned grey, revealing pointy Vulcan ears; other times his locks flowed like an aged sixties hippy with only an eye-numbing supervillain costume to worsen the illusion. In these cases surely it was the artist who needed staking!

Just as the Hammer Dracula movies worked best when they remained simple and formulaic, and only really lost their way when they deviated from this structure, Marvel's Dracula worked best as the lone, powerful Lord of the Vampires facing a determined group of hunters who'd all lost loved ones at his hands. The seventy-issue run of 'Tomb of Dracula' is amongst Marvel's most creative and original works, and at the time of its demise was one of two of Marvel's most consistent sellers ('Conan the Barbarian' being the second). Keeping it basic was the key, yet Marv Wolfman infused each issue with excitement and wonder, and Gene Colan's intricate pencils inked by Tom Palmer gave each issue an artistic grandeur beyond its comic book limitations.

In hindsight it was a mistake to make Dracula a part of the wider Marvel universe. Pitching him against the Silver Surfer, Captain Britain, and (heaven forbid!) Howard the Duck, only diminished the gothic majesty of this once proud monarch of Transylvania. But then, there is a danger of repetition, and after seven years 'Tomb of Dracula' ended on a high note after an intoxicating story arc which gripped the reader for almost two years.

Recently, Marv Wolfman returned for a one shot: 'What If...? Dark: The Tomb of Dracula' #1 (2023) which answers the question... What if Dracula turned Blade the Vampire Slayer into a vampire? It's not a bad story, although the modern David Cutler artwork isn't a patch on Gene Colan. Basically, Dracula turns Blade, and then Blade still has enough strength of character to resist his 'master' and stake him. And we get to see Rachel Van Helsing, Frank Drake, and Quincy Harker again, like in the glory days.

Somewhere out there Dracula is resting. I'm sure it won't be long before some enterprising creative team decides to resurrect him once again. Maybe this time they'll get it right. And if not, they can always kill him off... and try again!

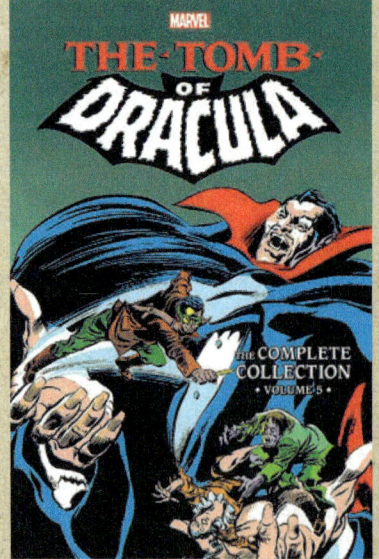

IS THAT A STAKE IN YOUR POCKET OR ARE YOU JUST PLEASED TO SEE ME?

by Neil Pike

DRACULA AND THE ADULT FILM INDUSTRY

One of the common traits across most film adaptations of Bram Stoker's most famous novel is that they tend to play up the sexual subtext that weaves its way through the narrative. There's a reason why, when casting directors were searching out actors to play the pointy-toothed aristocrat, they went for Christopher Lee, Frank Langella or Louis Jourdan and not Jack Elam (I'm still figuring out the thinking behind John Forbes-Robertson). It was inevitable then that once the adult industry became established enough to attract semi-reasonable budgets, Dracula capes would start rocking up on sets all across the San Fernando Valley.

The problem with documenting dirty mac Draculas isn't about finding enough movies to talk about; it's sifting the wheat from the chaff. To put it bluntly, there's a lot of erotic movies that promise vampiric action alongside the slap-and-tickle, but frankly lie about it. If there's a universal truth that applies to almost all adult movies, it's that plot is subservient to getting enough naked flesh on-screen and as a result, many of these movies (particularly the more modern examples) are reductive – in this case they tend to be the standard depressing gonzo output with an occasional set of plastic novelty-store fangs on display. I can't imagine anything more likely to induce misanthropy in me than sitting through hour-after-hour of modern porn or endless 8mm loops, so instead, let's consider the classic adult movies from the so-called golden age of the industry that involves our favourite Romanian. If you're genuinely interested in every hardcore incarnation of the noble bloodsucker, I'd direct you to Kim Newman's website, as the archive of his Daily Dracula social media posts (documented by Ken Shinn in these very pages) forms perhaps the most complete list of these appearances online and has proved enormously helpful when I started the research on this subject and no, 'research' isn't a euphemism.

Whilst Stoker's character makes numerous appearances in sixties nudies and softcore flicks (most notably in Modunk Phreezer's 1970 sexploitation movie *Sex and the Single Vampire*, starring John Holmes as 'Count Spatula'), the earliest hardcore example of the count on-screen came from cult Nevada-based film-maker Ray Dennis Steckler. *The Mad Love Life of a Hot Vampire* (1971) features a horror host Dracula operating as a pimp in modern day Las Vegas, who sends his girls out to collect blood from their clients. Played largely for laughs and saddled with a painfully low budget, Steckler's movie is a bit of a chore to sit through even though its running time barely stretches to 50 minutes. It does contain the occasional oddly compelling image (Drac sends his hookers out onto the streets of Vegas in full vampire garb) and Jim Parker as the Count is a paunchy, middle-aged take on the character but the perfunctory plot and unerotic sex scenes makes for an unappealing experience. Nevertheless, as the first American hardcore take on the subject, *The Mad Love Life of a Hot Vampire* does deserve at least some recognition. Steckler was busy in 1971, as he also directed *The Horny Vampire* aka *Count Al-Kum*, another comedic take that features Jerry Delony (here credited as Victor Alexander) as a Dracula lookalike with problems meeting women drifting through Las Vegas looking for hook-ups. With almost no plot and a budget sourced from behind sofa cushions, *The Horny Vampire* is even harder work to sit through than its stablemate.

With the mainstream acceptance and box office success of *Behind the Green Door* (1972), *Deep Throat* (1972) and *The Devil in Miss Jones* (1973), it's unsurprising that the seventies saw a mini-explosion of hardcore Dracula rip-offs. Early adopters include Anthony Spinelli's *Suckula* (1973), yet another comedic take on the subject about a reporter (George 'Buck' Flower) presenting a series of hardcore scenes as an expose of vampire activity in Los Angeles. Two sequences, shot like early silents (complete with title cards), include a character made up to look like Lugosi's Dracula. The actor playing the vampire may be Art Gill – however, as we'll find, credits on these movies aren't always easy to decipher. *Suckula* feels like a bunch of short loops linked together by a pretty thin concept, but the two Dracula-themed scenes at least generate a couple of minor laughs, so you could probably do worse. Also dating from 1973, Duncan Stewart's *Demon's Brew* features Marc Brock as The Count (in elaborate make-up that is oddly reminiscent of Richard Jay Silverthorn's

We Belong Dead

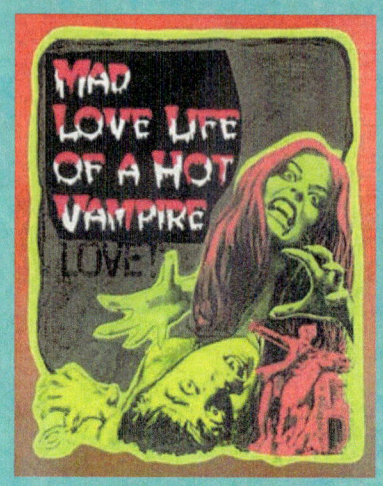

in Frank LaLoggia's *Fear No Evil* – 1981) who, in league with a witch, attempts to use magic to ensnare a young bride he takes a fancy to. Like Spinelli's flick, Stewart's movie is played for yucks but the painfully poor acting and some horrible editing makes it even more of a trial to endure. Completists who insist in subjecting themselves to it will appreciate the fact that the vampire gets plenty of screen time, and the black magic sub-plot represents a new wrinkle on the form.

Perhaps the first straight horror-hardcore take on the subject is Reginald Puhl's *Heisse Nächte auf Schloss Dracula* (1978) – released in edited form in English-speaking markets as *Hot Nights at Castle Dracula*. The plot involves a pair of young newlyweds being lured to Castle Dracula to take part in an orgiastic ritual aimed at ending his undead curse. There may be more to it than that, but the movie only seems to be available in its original language and my German isn't up to the potential subtleties. The second half of the movie is one big orgy that quickly gets very dull, but the flick demonstrates some gothic chops in its opening half hour, and has better production design and benefits from its middle European backdrops compared to the ultra low-budget American efforts produced to this point, so multi-linguists may get something from it. Dracula here is played by Mariano Perez and he doesn't partake in the muckier antics, happy to sit on his throne watching everyone else go at it like rabbits.

The best known of the hardcore Dracula movies is Phillip Marshak's *Dracula Sucks* (1979), in part no doubt thanks to its punworthy title. Clearly a pastiche of the Lugosi movie rather than a direct adaptation of Stoker's novel, Marshak delivers a very watchable, if distinctly odd, take on the subject matter. *Sucks* benefits from excellent production design and strong cinematography from lenser Hanania Baer, who'd go on to shoot mainstream flicks for Cannon and *Elvira: Mistress of the Dark* (1988) – not only is it better-looking than most hardcore flicks, it puts a number of contemporary mainstream horror films to shame. Performances vary as you'd expect from a work featuring largely adult performers; John Leslie, Kay Parker, Paul Thomas and Annette Haven acquit themselves reasonably well when not pawing each other, though, and Richard Bulik really climbs the walls as an impressively insane Renfield. The movie belongs to Jamie Gillis as Dracula, however, doing an entertaining Bela Lugosi impression and hitting all the right notes as he walks the fine line between parody and genuine magnetism with hardly a foot wrong. He's assisted by Reggie Nalder as Van Helsing, who gets most of the best lines. With hardcore scenes taking up a fairly small proportion of the running time, *Dracula Sucks* genuinely feels like a crossover work and belongs in a relatively small collection of porn movies – alongside *The Devil in Miss Jones*, *The Opening of Misty Beethoven* (1976), *Tropic of Desire* (1979) and *Roommates* (1981) – that could be shown at any mainstream film festival and not feel too out-of-place. If there's a criticism of *Dracula Sucks*, it's that its tone is uneven, mixing broad comedy (I could live without the *Airplane* style announcements over the sanatorium intercom) with reasonably effective Hammer-style gothic horror set pieces. This may explain why the movie was re-edited to play up the comic elements and to add a lot more sex before being re-released as *Lust at First Sight* in 1980, to cash in on the Richard Benjamin/George Hamilton mainstream comedy. Off-cuts from the film were edited together with new material shot by *Sucks* co-writer and actor William Margold to create *Dracula's Bride* (1980), often assumed to be another re-edit of *Sucks* but which was, in fact, a different work, though one I haven't been able to track down. As a final point to underline its horror movie chops, one of the assistant directors on *Dracula Sucks* was Norman Thaddeus Vane who'd go on to make several low-budget genre flicks in the early '80s including the vampire-themed *The Black Room* (1982).

Gillis would return to the cape and fangs a year later in *Dracula Exotica* (1980), directed by notorious hardcore helmer Shaun Costello under the *nom de guerre* Warren Evans. Rougher, more pornographic and cheaper than Marshak's effort, *Exotica* suffers in part because it has a distastefully misogynistic attitude and is saddled with an overly busy plot that mixes Gillis' Count with Cold War spy antics, a noirish murder mystery and most bizarrely a Broadway production, all of which drowns out the central story of the Count meeting the reincarnation of his dead love (Samantha Fox – no, not that one). Gillis and Fox are both good but they get less effective support here than the star was afforded in *Dracula Sucks*, and the screenplay is more interested in kink than playing witty riffs on the subject matter. One of the movie's high points is its finale that sees Fox and Gillis consummate their love after which both are transformed into doves, rather than bats. It's a surprisingly upbeat end for a Costello movie, a director better-known for his bleak world view. There are a few good ideas in Kenneth Schwartz's screenplay (Costello, who died last year claimed on his blog that Schwartz was heavily influenced by *Love at First Bite* (1979), something Schwartz denied) and it's played straighter than *Dracula Sucks* but like a lot of Costello's work it seems more informed by his own personal fetishes than any traditional cinematic convention; as a result it's nothing like as engaging or as pretty to look at as Marshak's picture.

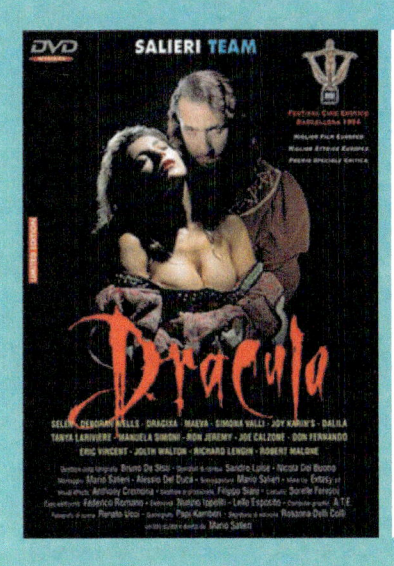

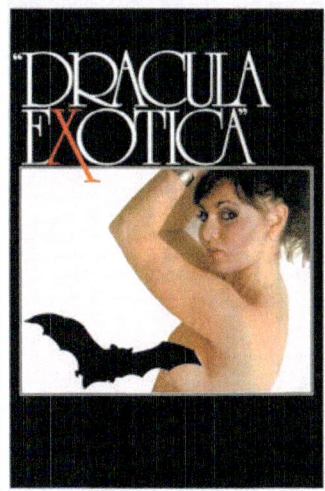

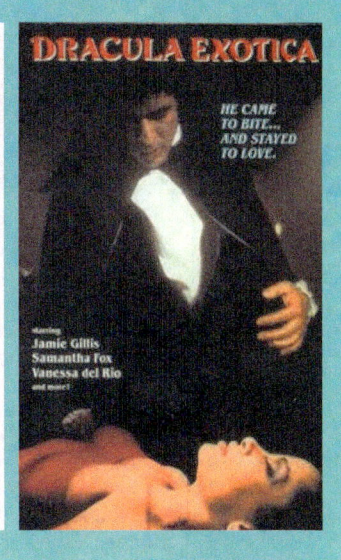

Dracula Sucks and *Dracula Exotica* represent the high points of the count's appearances in hardcore movies and, other than a few cameos in anthology-style movies (*Star Virgin* from 1979 includes a black and white scene reminiscent of the silent movie pastiche in *Suckula*), the last of note before the industry moved beyond its 'Golden Age' and into the videotape era of ultra-cheap plot-free productions. There are lots of flicks in this tedious realm that feature Dracula, but in the few that I've seen, the character is reduced to "I vaant to suck your…" schtick and there's not enough tequila on the planet to make me sit through them all. If you must, *Mario Salieri's Dracula* (1994) is better looking and has a bigger budget than most recent efforts (but is depressingly misogynistic) and Scotty Fox's *Leena Meets Frankenstein* (1993) is an occasionally witty and cine-literate take on the Universal monster mash-ups of the '40s, but these are the best of (from what I've seen) painfully slim pickings and very minor fare compared to the best of the Golden Age.

Despite the merits of *Dracula Sucks* and, to a lesser extent *Dracula Exotica*, we've probably missed the boat on the definitive erotic Dracula movie, given the current artistic wasteland that characterises the modern adult industry. Whether this represents a missed opportunity or a lucky escape will depend on your own tolerance for this most reductive of media. Initially I'd put myself in the latter category, but *Dracula Sucks* does at least hint at what might have been had someone like Radley Metzger taken a swing at it during the height of his powers – that's a movie I'd be interested to see. Now, if you'll excuse me, I'm off to take a shower. I'll see you in about 6 months.

We Belong Dead   Page 23

THE BLACK LABORATORY OF JOHN LLEWELLYN PROBERT

Jess Franco, Prisoner of Dracula?

"Welcome to my house. Enter freely. Go safely, and leave something of the happiness you bring. Oh, and watch out for that chap with the zoom lens because he's going absolutely mental in here today."

Oh yes, if we're going to talk about Dracula then we have to talk about Jess Franco, who provided his own unique variations on the theme of Bram Stoker's character in the early 1970s. This was after he had had what some might consider a proper try at adapting the novel in 1969. Toplining Christopher Lee and heralded as the first 'authentic' adaptation (at least according to producer and screenwriter Harry Alan Towers), *Count Dracula* aka *El Conde Dracula* really isn't that interesting, either as a traditional Hammer-type Dracula film or as a Franco film, because Bram Stoker's Dracula and Jess Franco's style just don't really suit each other. The traditional gothic elements that audiences had become used to were too constricting for Franco, and when he tried to include his own touches they grated against what was intended to be an entry in a well-established (and by then well-worn) genre. Jess's partnership with Towers yielded at least one classic (*Eugenie… the Story of Her Journey into Perversion*), some more run of the mill stuff (*The Bloody Judge*) and the perhaps a misjudged sequel or two (e.g. *Castle of Fu Manchu*). It was only after his partnership with Towers was dissolved that Franco was able to have some fun with the gothic, much to the delight (or exasperation) of those who got to see the results.

Titles open over a shot of a castle so wreathed in fog it quickly becomes invisible. In the first five minutes we see a series of repetitive crash zooms of a dog, a town square, a pub sign, a lady without her bra on, and a cat. Not a word of dialogue is spoken until we are fifteen minutes in, by which time we've already seen Dracula (Howard Vernon) sucking blood from the neck of Anne Libert, a crypt filled with coffins, thunder and lightning, a really poor bat on a string being wobbled behind a window, and a host of other Gothic trappings.

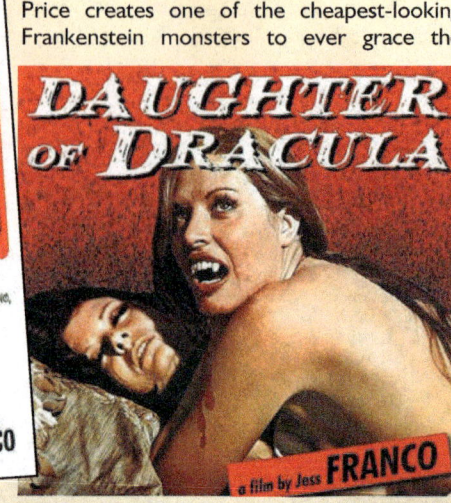

Thus begins *Dracula, Prisoner of Frankenstein* (1971), a film in which Dennis Price creates one of the cheapest-looking Frankenstein monsters to ever grace the screen. It grunts as if heavily constipated while it goes about its lady-abducting duties. Towards the end an even cheaper-looking werewolf turns up and does little to help resolve what has gone before. Coming across less as a traditional horror film and more like an avant-garde experiment in non-verbal communication, this is the kind of Jess Franco film his fans adore, playing with conventions, shaking up well-worn tropes in a big bag and then emptying them into the screen in an almost random, stream-of-consciousness manner. We're a million miles from Hammer here, and yet at the same time one can see the influence of the Universal monster mashes and American horror comics including, as some 'WBD' readers will recall, the Neal Adams and Dick Giordano's 'Frankenstein, The Werewolf, Dracula' strip from 'House of Hammer' issue 18.

In fact, so off the wall, lunatic and implausible is the film, that one might almost consider it Franco's reaction to his own previous Dracula outing and the critical drubbing it received. The film seems to be set in the nineteenth century with costumes and carriages appropriate for the period, but Dr Frankenstein gets driven around in a Mercedes Benz and what's that lurking in the bar at the start? Is it a juke box? And is that a cash register? Sitting beside an espresso machine? These, plus Howard Vernon's bizarre interpretation of the role of Count Dracula mean that here we have a film that will either drive you insane with its illogicalities, or give you 81 minutes of defiant eccentricity that will just fly by. I know which camp I'm in.

One of those illogicalities / eccentricities is the presence of Britt Nichols as a vampire sleeping in the same crypt but who is completely ignored by Alberto Dalbés' Dr Seward while he busily stakes Dracula with a little tap of his tiny hammer. Ms Nichols (real name Carmen Yazalde) is actually the best and most effective element here. After memorable performances in this, *The Demons* and *Virgin Among the Living Dead* she married a footballer who didn't want her to be in any more. While that's perhaps understandable, it's also a great shame because she's a genuinely magnetic presence in the few pictures she appears in.

The sequel to *Dracula, Prisoner of Frankenstein* is the delirious and superior *The Erotic Rites of Frankenstein*, in which Vernon returns not as Dracula but in a different role as Dr Cagliostro. Nichols got her own 'spin off' sequel to herself, and while it's not as crazy as its progenitor, if you had a good time with *Dracula, Prisoner of Frankenstein* then you may want to check out *Daughter of Dracula* (1972).

The third of what can be considered Franco's rag-tag Gothic trilogy, *Daughter of Dracula* features a number of Franco's obsessions for fans to spot, including his eye for architecture, which here is in part the same location used for *Erotic Rites*. The familiar staircase Britt Nichols descends to discover her birthright had featured previously in *Dracula,* *Prisoner of Frankenstein*, but also in *The Bloody Judge* and would pop up again in 1973's *Countess Perverse*. Also as in *Countess Perverse* (and its hardcore variant *Sexy Nature*), *Daughter of Dracula* features a body washed up on a beach, in this instance as the latest of a series of vampire killings. Howard Vernon is back as Dracula, even if his three scenes are strictly limited to him sitting up in his coffin and snarling. This seems to be enough, however, to give Britt a pair of fangs that allow her to bite Anne Libert (looking quite different and almost shockingly normal after her bizarre turns as the naked bird woman creation of Dr Cagliostro in *Erotic Rites of Frankenstein* and the strange blind girl in *Virgin Among the Living Dead*). There's also a Franco floor show shoehorned in (as there is in *Dracula, Prisoner of Frankenstein*), the performer in question becoming another vampire's victim. As in the first two films, Alberto Dalbés is the one investigating the case, although this time we're definitely in a contemporary setting. There are a couple of lengthy lesbian sex scenes that you can either fast forward through or play the regular Franco game of 'guess what body part his camera is too close to for it to be made out clearly'. It all ends rather insipidly, causing this one to fall into the category of 'films Franco got a bored with making halfway through'. Still, once you've acquired the taste, even half-good Franco is worth your time. *Daughter of Dracula* isn't as interesting or raving mad as *Dracula, Prisoner of Frankenstein*, and neither are as good as *Erotic Rites of Frankenstein*, but that doesn't feature Dracula so we'll have to wait for the 'We Belong Dead' Frankenstein special to talk about that one.

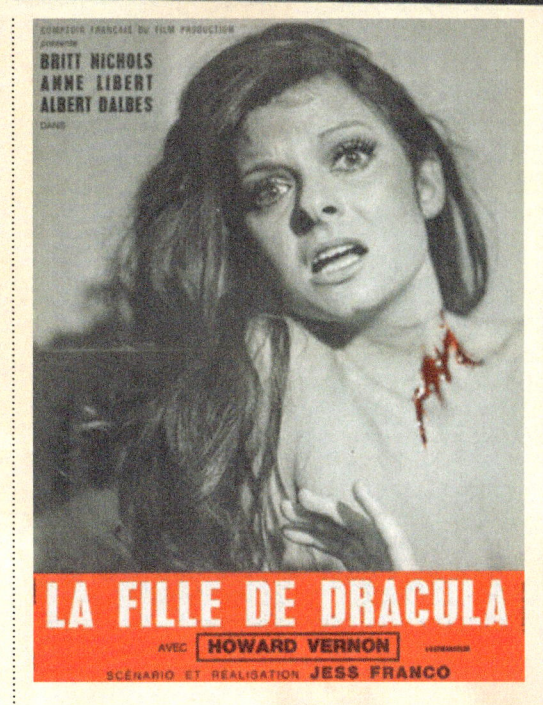

by Karen Joan Kohoutek

Dracula
PAGES FROM A VIRGIN'S DIARY

A pale, beautiful woman and a darker, handsome man dance in a field of fog, in a quietly falling snow. All the possible words are clichés: ethereal, luminous, a vision of elegance and grace. But this intimate, romantic scene is intercut with shots of a doctor, seemingly gleeful as he brutally restrains a patient; and in the background, a group of men are lurking, voyeurs, ready with wooden stakes to destroy the dancers, however transcendent their gracefulness.

The skill and lightness of Lucy Westenra (Tara Birtwhistle) and Dracula (Zhang Wei-Qiang) as they dance in the snow, their sheer beauty, makes them sympathetic. Even as vocabulary fails the essence of ballet, the visual language works in their favor. Of all the attempts to romanticize Dracula, this may be the most successful I've ever seen. The fact that he doesn't speak also helps, since expressing himself through dance makes him appear more sensitive, more unearthly. Similarly, the split between the vampiric "false Lucy" and the innocent "real Lucy" doesn't seem so clear, so that her eventual staking and decapitation just seems cruel.

Canadian auteur Guy Maddin, the director of *Dracula: Pages from a Virgin's Diary* (2002), has said that "when I began, I was pretty much resigned to the fact that it would be unwatchable." Instead, his adaptation of the Royal Winnipeg Ballet's production of *Dracula* has been called (by the 'AV Club' blog) "arguably the finest adaptation of Bram Stoker's novel ever filmed." That's a strong statement, especially in a whole publication bursting with fascinating versions of *Dracula*. I doubt there is a single best one, each take having different strengths, and weaknesses that come from never being able to fully capture the original, but Maddin's version is at least a contender.

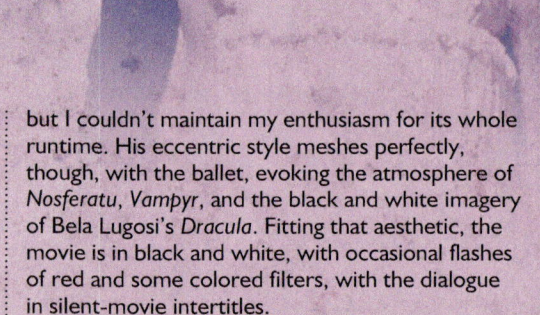

Over the years, his movies, full of silent movie stylings and non-linear stories, taught me the hard truth that, in some ways, I'm more conventional in my taste than I like to admit. While I can appreciate the beauties of surrealism, at some point I need the anchors of narrative or character development to keep my interest. Maddin's *Careful* (1992) opens with what might be, for me, the funniest five minutes in movie history, brilliantly satirizing Scandinavian stoicism, but I couldn't maintain my enthusiasm for its whole runtime. His eccentric style meshes perfectly, though, with the ballet, evoking the atmosphere of *Nosferatu*, *Vampyr*, and the black and white imagery of Bela Lugosi's *Dracula*. Fitting that aesthetic, the movie is in black and white, with occasional flashes of red and some colored filters, with the dialogue in silent-movie intertitles.

Rare for him, Maddin came into a pre-existing project. The ballet's choreographer, Mark Godden, is credited on the movie as the writer, so the script, and the music from Gustav Mahler's first two symphonies, were already in place, as was the cast, with most of the original dancers from the 1998 premier reprising their roles. Zhang was the company's male principal dancer, and since he's Chinese, that added an element that Maddin found in line with the novel's themes of xenophobia, the fear of "others from other lands!" as one of the intertitles shrieks.

Maddin has said that "to be honest, I don't know much about ballet," and multiple times that he doesn't like Bram Stoker's novel, even that "I couldn't care less about Dracula." Nonetheless, he "read the book pretty carefully," using as much of its actual dialog as possible. "Strangely enough, in spite of this being a danced version of 'Dracula', I aspired to make this the most faithful adaptation of the novel filmed yet." While compressing the events, it is surprisingly true to Stoker. Almost all versions change the names of some characters, or their relationships, and this one sticks to the book on these points.

No time is wasted getting to the center of the story. As Dracula scholar Elizabeth Miller says in her review of the ballet, "Unlike the initial readers of Stoker's novel, we know what a vampire does to his victim, so the suspense is not as essential an element." After a striking opening with some visual exposition (Dracula's voyage, the introduction of Renfield), Dracula enters a room and attacks/seduces Lucy. After that, the choreography begins as she dances, joyous and sprightly, with her maids, and then with her three suitors.

In this version, it's not even clear in the beginning how much Lucy has been injured. Her dancing is apparently effortless, her flowing gown dancing as much as she is. Some exhaustion starts to show, but she still seems full of life when Van Helsing enters as a threatening figure, with a dramatic clash of music, a reddish light filter, and an immediate dampening effect. It's with his entrance that her condition takes a turn, and his medical testing seems to only make it worse.

When Van Helsing diagnoses Lucy as "filled with polluted blood", the director's commentary reveals, "this is one of those Bram Stoker intertitles in which the men are continually blaming the women for their own libidinous thoughts." He adds that "the whole story of the novel is just men insisting on getting their way." The blood transfusion scene illustrates the sense of male dominance, staged from Lucy's point of view to almost like a gang rape.

The whole Jonathan Harker part of the novel, often the main focus of adaptations, occurs here during sped-up, orgiastic flashbacks, with intertitles like "Infants for supper?" and "Flesh-pots!" and "Vampyr harem!" When Dracula reaches out as if to nip Harker, they read "A manly temptation!"

About the intertitles, Maddin said he was told "you're bringing people out of the dance with these intertitles", but that the dancing's on the screen. "It's not real life. People don't bite each other and suck each other's blood, first of all, and second of all, they wouldn't dance if they did do it. It's art. You're not fooled by a painting in a museum."

As he recuperates, Jonathan (Johnny Wright) gives Mina (CindyMarie Small) his diary to read, and she responds with an acceptance toward his experience, becoming sexually forward in her dance. Her fiancé goes back and forth about this, dancing with her, then pushing her away. His conflicting feelings come to the forefront when she becomes Dracula's target. As the men nearly stake Mina, Maddin speaks for the characters in the commentary: "Wait, that's your fiancée, for crying out loud. Let's not make the same rash decision we perhaps made last time. No, as a matter of fact, let's make the same rash decision we made last time. She's got teeth marks on her neck!"

Despite his films often being so opaque, Maddin isn't mystifying about them in the way that, say, David Lynch is. In interviews and the commentary on the Zeitgeist Films DVD, he's very forthcoming about his ideas and intentions. A creator's statements can't always be taken at face value, but his thoughts on the Dracula story in general would be insightful from anyone. For me, his most striking comment is: "See, I don't even think Dracula exists. He's just kind of an embodiment of female lust and male jealousy."

With its gorgeous lighting and imagery, with Lucy buried in an enormous bed of garlic and Mina dancing with nuns, this version projects the familiar story into a dream of seduction. Can that really be defeated? After all, whatever his form, Dracula still endures.

We Belong Dead

EMMA DARK'S DARK CORNER

EMMA DARK is an award-winning filmmaker, and actress.

Hello readers! When I saw a few Facebook memories of past Women in Horror Month (WiHM) events (panels, screenings, etc.) it got me thinking. Women in Horror Month ran for about 13 years with a plethora of events supporting female filmmakers, actors and other women in horror annually each February. Sadly it finished a few years ago with the idea that we'd see more independent events supporting women in horror on a more general basis all year around. That hasn't really happened, I'm sure the pandemic didn't help things – it certainly killed off many smaller and independent film events. Facebook also reminded me that back in 2016 I graced the cover of issue 39 of the now defunct independent filmmaking mag 'Digital FilmMaker Magazine' with a feature article on female filmmakers called 'Women in Film – Emma Dark charts the rapid rise of female filmmakers'.

So, I had a chat with Darrell Buxton, We Belong Dead's editor, and asked if I could expand my column as a one-off for this issue and spotlight some lovely fellow ladies in horror. Darrell agreed so I asked a range of women in horror I know if they could answer the following question for me:

Q – In your opinion, what does horror mean to you as a woman working in horror, either in front or behind the camera, or simply a horror fan?

JUDY MATHESON

First up we have actress Judy Matheson, who probably won't need much introduction for you classic horror fans. Judy is well known for her iconic role as the innocent woodsman's daughter in Hammer Films' *Twins of Evil* (1971) who sadly gets burned at the stake as a witch by Peter Cushing.

> IN THE 70S, I APPEARED IN SEVERAL HORROR FILMS...[I] WAS, AND AM STILL, HONOURED TO BE DUBBED A 'SCREAM QUEEN'.
>
> **JUDY MATHESON**
> ACTRESS

Not to forget starring in other horrors such as *Lust for a Vampire* (1971), *Crucible of Terror* (1971) and *The Flesh and Blood Show* (1972). I worked with Judy on Misty Moon and Robo Films' short comedy-horror, *Frankula* (2017), where we both played vampires alongside Caroline Munro. What a fangtastic trio we made!

A "In the 70s, I appeared in several Horror films, alongside other work in television and theatre, and to be honest, it was simply the routine work of a jobbing actress, back then.

However, after many years, including a spell living in South Africa, and starting a family, I began very gradually to appreciate the appreciation my films were receiving. And this was entirely due to the internet. I began chatting to fans, and people who loved the films and amazingly knew so much about each one. That brought so many vivid memories flooding back.

I became much more interested in the whole extraordinary genre, and was, and am still, honoured to be dubbed a 'Scream Queen'."

Follow Judy on her Facebook fan page at: bit.ly/3IqLL2M

BARBIE WILDE

Next up we have actress and author Barbie Wilde. Best known for her role as the haunting female cenobite in Clive Barker (writer) and Tony Randel's (director) *Hellbound: Hellraiser II* (1988), also cited as "One of the finest purveyors of erotically-charged horror fiction around" by 'Fangoria' for her books 'Voices of the Damned' and 'The Venus Complex'. Amongst other things, Barbie also performed in many 1980s music videos as a dancer and once auditioned for the role of the heroine in Apple and Ridley Scott's iconic *1984* advert, which I'd love to have seen Barbie playing. I first met Barbie back in 2018 when we shared a dinner table in a nightclub around the corner from FrightFest in Leicester Square with Tim Dry (*Xtro*), Neal Jones ('Without Your Head' podcast) and more.

A "I've been fascinated by horror ever since I was a kid. Not only the supernatural elements but the real-life horror of human beings and what they can do to each other. Humans are truly the scariest monsters of them all.

As far as my career as an actor and author is concerned, horror is what I am best known for. For that, I have to thank Clive Barker and his vision.

Horror certainly has woven its siren song throughout my life. It's been a wonderful, cathartic journey where I can channel my darkest, most paranoid thoughts into something creative."

Find out more about Barbie at: barbiewilde.com

SARAH DALY

I wanted to get a quote from independent producer/writer Sarah Daly, co-founder of Hex Media/Studios and the new Amicus Productions who've been wonderful in championing British women in horror talent with a series of interviews recently (including an interview with me, thank you very much). Sarah's written/produced several films, including *Lord of Tears* (2013) and *The Black Gloves* (2017). Sarah's talents also extend into music as independent singer/songwriter Metaphorest, her work is well worth checking out. For example, Sarah describes her track 'In the Fire' as "An acoustic demo track inspired by tales of local witch hunts…" and it is rather beautiful and worthy of your listening time.

A "For me, creating in the horror genre is a way to confront the darkness in all of us, as individuals and as a society. This darkness is something we all possess, and have all experienced, but women face our own distinct horrors, and so we can bring a

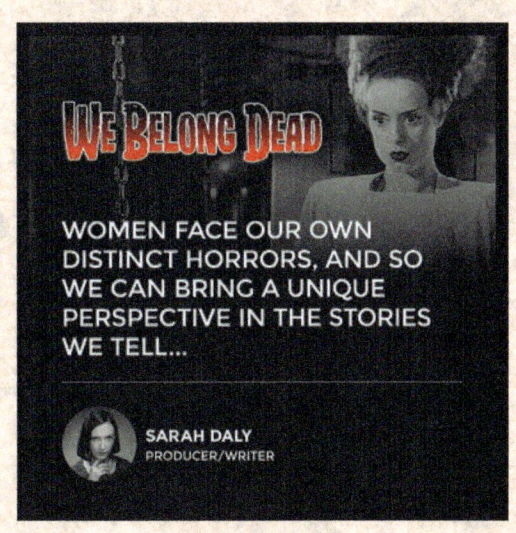

> AS FAR AS MY CAREER AS AN ACTOR AND AUTHOR IS CONCERNED, HORROR IS WHAT I AM BEST KNOWN FOR. FOR THAT, I HAVE TO THANK CLIVE BARKER AND HIS VISION.
>
> **BARBIE WILDE**
> ACTOR/AUTHOR

> WOMEN FACE OUR OWN DISTINCT HORRORS, AND SO WE CAN BRING A UNIQUE PERSPECTIVE IN THE STORIES WE TELL…
>
> **SARAH DALY**
> PRODUCER/WRITER

unique perspective in the stories we tell, and the way we tell them."

Follow Sarah on her Facebook fan page at: facebook.com/Metaphorest

SARAH APPLETON

A good friend of mine and our next woman in horror is Sarah Appleton, a filmmaker/director best known for the spine-tingling documentary features *The Found Footage Phenomenon* (2021), *Damaged* (2023) and *The J-Horror Virus* (2023). Sarah works through the film company she founded, CapriSar Productions Ltd, often having a hand in producing and filming a lot of the DVD/Blu-ray special features you'll find on your new releases from Arrow Video, Severin Films, 101 Films etc.

A "Being a horror fan is strange because most of the people you will ever meet in the world will make the same face at you when you say you like horror movies. When discussing *The Texas Chain Saw Massacre* with my mother-in-law she said, 'Why on earth would I want to watch that?' All horror fans know this feeling and it's an interesting one. This might not answer your question, but I don't personally believe there is much difference being a 'woman' in horror to being a man in horror. What I can say is horror fans are alike in one way, and that is that we love watching blood and guts over dinner."

Find out more about Sarah at: caprisarproductions.com

NINA ROMAIN

Now on to another woman in horror friend, Nina Romain, who's had her hand in so many different projects I lose track! A writer/producer (*Alice in Nightmareland* (2012), *Fright Corner* (2017)), journalist (Raindance etc.), script reviewer, PR maestro and many more creative talents I'm sure. Nina loves the dark side of Hollywood, often visiting LA – one day I'll join her and we'll visit the infamous Cecil Hotel and go searching for bloodsuckers in Santa Cruz. Until then a day trip to Brighton will probably have to do!

A "Horror genuinely has something for everyone, whichever genre you love. Maybe especially women with horror's many strong female characters, whether you're inspired by Laurie Strode, Ellen Ripley, Sarah Connor, Nancy Thompson (*A Nightmare on Elm Street*) or any other no-nonsense Final Girls. They could also be Sarah Carter (or indeed nearly anyone in *The Descent*), Angela of the *[*REC]* series, or Maggie (one of few survivors of Brit slasher *Severance*) – they're all here to take on the bad guys with a weapon and witty one-liner. So keep an eye out for future kickass horror heroines… especially those taking out the villain with a metal coat hanger. Not quite sure if I can quote: "You're terminated, f*cker…" but it's probably my favourite female one-liner. That and: "Get away from her, you b*tch", of course."

Find out more about Nina at: girlfright.com

> WHAT I CAN SAY IS HORROR FANS ARE ALIKE IN ONE WAY, AND THAT IS THAT WE LOVE WATCHING BLOOD AND GUTS OVER DINNER.
>
> **SARAH APPLETON**
> FILMMAKER/DIRECTOR

> BEING A HORROR FAN GOES BACK TO WHEN I WAS A YOUNGSTER, READING HORROR BOOKS SUCH AS FONTANA'S THE ARMADA GHOST BOOK...
>
> **DOLORES HARRINGTON**
> HORROR FAN

SARAH GIERCKSKY

There are quite a few Sarahs in this article, so either I know a lot of Sarahs, or perhaps women called Sarah are naturally drawn to horror. This Sarah is 'Sarah of Horror' herself, Sarah Giercksky – director, writer and actress best known for *Sargad* (2017) and *Bunny Man Slaughter* (in production). I first met Sarah several years ago when she flew over to London from Sweden for a WiHM event where I was moderating a panel talk, I believe – back when Sarah and her friend Jasmine had a film review site named 'Bitches of Horror'. I saw Sarah fairly recently at FrightFest 2023 and it was lovely to catch up, albeit briefly.

A "I mostly think about how the horror genre has changed me as a filmmaker by allowing me to get out of my comfort zone, which used to be focused on revenge horror, and today my main focus is creating horror comedies."

Find out more about Sarah at: sarahgiercksky.wixsite.com/sarahofhorrorfest

DOLORES HARRINGTON

I couldn't finish the article without getting a quote from a horror fan. It's not to say that people working in horror and film aren't fans, but I wanted to get an answer from someone who watches and reads horror, because at the end of the day that represents a good portion of people who are in horror or certainly into horror! So thank you very much to Dolores (Dee) Harrington for being willing to share her views.

A "Being a horror fan goes back to when I was a youngster, reading horror books such as Fontana's 'The Armada Ghost Book' and Herbert van Thal's 'Pan Book of Horror Stories', with covers that caught the eye – a knife in a wedding cake with blood dripping or a mouth with worms inside – they made want to read the book!

As a teenager, watching particular shows with memorable creepy visuals and soundtracks, like *The Tomorrow People*, *Armchair Thriller*, *Saturday Night Thriller*, *Tales of the Unexpected* and Hammer Horror films made an impression.

In adulthood, this continues through festivals, such as the Fantastic Films Weekend in Bradford and FrightFest in London. I also attend the Duke Mitchell Film Club and the West London Film Society. When I started going to FrightFest from its launch in 2000 it was mostly men, now it's half and half."

Dee also had another part to her quote we originally removed for space reasons, but I really wanted to add it back in as we've all had something like this before:

"When growing up, finding it not very easy to talk to boys/men about horror films; on one occasion a man said 'Why is a nice girl like you, enjoying horror films?' I said, 'Why is a nice bloke like you asking me a stupid question?' Unsurprisingly never saw him again!"

I don't think we'll get a comment like that in the company of 'We Belong Dead' readers, ladies, but remember guys, watch out for us nice girls as we may well be the horror hounds your mother warned you about!

Social links
Website: emmadark.com
FB | IG | Threads: @EmmaDarkOfficial
Twitter/X: @EmDarkOfficial

PURPLE PLAYHOUSE DRACULA

by Terry Sherwood

Who could have known back in 1973 that Dracula would invade Canada? Well, he did just that, despite Hammer Productions and others on the horizon. The vampire appeared in a hard-to-find adaption of the classic novel on Canadian television, as part of a limited-run series called *Purple Playhouse*.

The CBC (Canadian Broadcasting Corporation) has a long and distinguished history of producing drama. Today the company produces fine dramas, usually co-productions like the detective series *Murdoch Mysteries*, that are marketed worldwide on various platforms and languages. In 1968 Canadian television was involved in the wonderful adaption of *The Strange Case of Dr. Jekyll and Mr. Hyde* starring Jack Palance and Billie Whitelaw. This videotaped well-mounted show was directed by Charles Jarrott, produced by Dan Curtis, and was an American television co-production.

In February 1973, the CBC decided it was going to cancel a series that was not performing well on its schedule, so it was decided that the replacement program was to be *Purple Playhouse*. The eight shows were produced by George Jonas and Paddy Sampson. Video-recorded versions, with no live audience, of *Sweeney Todd* and the play *The Bells* (one of Henry Irving's greatest successes) are among the works that make up the brief replacement series.

Noted Canadian-based actors such as a young soon-to-be Hollywood-bound Leslie Nielsen, Norman Welsh, and Blair Brown appeared. One of the eight dramatizations was *Dracula*. This adaptation of the Bram Stoker book is the third of its kind for the small screen, after the UK's *Mystery and Imagination* (1968) and *Hrabe Dracula* (1971) from Czechoslovakia. The one-hour adaptation was scripted by Rod Coneybeare and the director was Jack Nixon-Browne. Nixon-Browne was a journeyman of sorts, as a story such as fantastic as *Dracula* and its themes did not seem to be his forte. He later went on to direct episodes of the long-running series *The Littlest Hobo*, featuring the adventures of a German shepherd.

The version of *Dracula* currently available is certainly edited badly: at least a quarter of an hour is missing from the 60 minutes announced. A journeyman director, plus a brief running time, and likely budget restraints with a story like *Dracula* meant that getting it right for all people was a tall order. The production has the look of a seventies in-studio produced show, which means with darkness, limited small room sets, and some film work in the great outdoors.

The Count was played by actor stage actor Norman Welsh, and Harker by nondescript Dan MacDonald. MacDonald, through no fault of his own, reminds one of some of the Hammer milquetoast romantic male players such as young Anthony Higgins as the 'pork chop' haired Paul Paxton in the stylish *Taste the Blood of Dracula*. Casting-wise wise, the most interesting element was character actor Nehemiah Persoff as Van Helsing. Persoff was a television veteran with many series behind him, ranging from comedies to straight dramatic roles. His speech patterns and slightly dark looks made for a different if not offbeat Van Helsing; considering that the venerable esoteric physician in the book is a Dutch professor. This has never stopped the story from being told in its way, as actors in any Dracula film are fitted to the specifications of the production. This wasn't the only aspect of the Dracula story that this production tried to alter and failed at.

The series opens with an introduction by noted author Robertson Davies, who expounds nicely when he tells us what we are about to see is the "true" Dracula. That statement could not be further from the truth. One hopes Mr. Davies was led to believe his introduction was for a proper version of the Stoker story. The opening scene in the castle with Harker and Dracula is nowhere near the novel in speech or intent, as the dialogue between them has the sound of a pulp paperback gone wrong.

The story begins with an exchange between Dracula and Harker, once the latter has arrived at Dracula's castle and is finishing his meal. The entire atmosphere represented by the young lawyer's journey is erased. His character faces a Dracula with shoulder-length white hair and pale skin. Physically, he is closer to the description of the novel than those who previously embodied the vampire. However, the actor overplays, and his forced makeup doesn't help matters.

Norman Welsh as Dracula has a pleasing appearance, much like Dracula in the novel, complete with that white hair and a slightly poor attempt at giving his skin a deathly pale look.

Camera resolution has since been upgraded, and today's transfers highlight the little cutbacks that escaped the lenses of the day. His speech pattern carries no hint of his supposed native country, instead, it is filled with well-pronounced stage thundering. The worst is when Harker cuts his finger on a wine bottle, and we see Dracula quivering and licking his lips. One drinks brandy in the Count's rather spare set designed castle: not wine. *Purple Playhouse's* Dracula has two brides, at least in the version I saw.

The Count's arrival via the Demeter, plus Lucy's death and rising as one of the undead are left out. So are the characters of Renfield and Quincey Morris. Mina is the one who is facing Dracula as the production skips to that. Other moments include bargain store jewelled crucifixes used to repel Mina and Dracula. I will spare you the tumultuous ending, except to say it is like the Dan Curtis/Jack Palance version. The other similarity between this production and the Dan Curtis one is that they use German Shepherd dogs in place of wolves.

Welsh's Dracula laughs like a villain in a cape and top hat who has just tied a helpless female to the railway tracks. Persoff does his best as Van Helsing with his well-modulated, accented voice spilling dialogue, often while chewing scenery.

The vampire conforms to the characteristics given to him by Stoker. He can hypnotize and maintain a strong bond with the vampires he breeds. He fears crucifixes, and cannot lie in a coffin that has been consecrated using a host. A stake to the heart will be the surest way to overcome him. It should also be noted that the vampire's attitude changes completely when he hears the rooster crowing, as a nod to Murnau's *Nosferatu*. In one of his final monologues, the character finally presents himself as a father betrayed by his children. This is how he considers Mina and Jonathan; the latter having been attacked by the Count in the first part of the story.

Of the three oldest TV adaptations of the novel, this is not the most successful. However, it would be interesting to be able to watch a complete version without a timecode and in full. If the cuts in the original plot are justified by the relatively short length of the episode, the tendency to overdo it undermines this adaptation.

And there we end – it's a competent but stagy version of the story. Locations were limited (and extras were minimal), as though we were watching a play, and that was the point of the series. Despite falling into melodrama on occasion, Norman Welsh is not the worst Dracula, and there are brief moments of genius – in the looks given, while I also enjoyed Nehemiah Persoff as Van Helsing. As the play is short there is little room to get all the strands of *Dracula* running. Still, some of the changes were interesting in themselves – transfusing Lucy with Mina's blood, Dracula and Lucy hunting together, and the effects of Mina's hypnosis all being prime examples. You get to see Dracula slithering down the castle wall in the best sequence; however, the camera cuts to a lower angle shattering the brief mystery of how it was accomplished.

The lasting image for me is Dracula laughing inanely as he whips his carriage containing his coffins and then unloads them in the night. It's one that struck me as being contrary to the image of the vampire. Mind you every viewer brings with them a preconceived conception of the story and the Count himself. I draw the line on that abomination I will not mention by title with Gary Oldman which some people revere; which is their personal choice. It is not fair to rate productions for budget or talent on screen or behind the camera, as often the money is what holds some together. Not to say that money and spectacular effects make the best film, yet even such as *The Last Voyage of the Demeter* (2023) have their moments.

This entry in the *Purple Playhouse* series is a small digest version of a very ambitious story, told with a budget and 'jobbing' actors. I would suggest this production is a curio in its slightly butchered version, or as viewed as a completist. The BBC *Count Dracula* (1977), dramatized by Gerald Savoy, with Louis Jourdan and Frank Finlay, is still the television production to beat. Mind you, is this a competition, as all as these examples keep the interest in Dracula and vampires in the public forum? The saga of the vampire simply sleeps in its grave, to rise again in a different form when that white spider-like hand reaches across time for the dominion of the night.

AN INTERVIEW WITH BELA LUGOSI'S BIOGRAPHER
ROBERT CREMER
AUTHOR OF 'BELA LUGOSI – THE MAN BEHIND THE CAPE'

by Matthew E. Banks

In 1976, Robert Cremer's seminal biography of Bela Lugosi to the world and now 48 years later, he's about to release the definitive version of his ground-breaking book, 'Bela Lugosi – The Man Behind the Cape,' through Clover Press and a Kickstarter campaign that saw its goal reached within hours. Such is the power and legacy of both Bela Lugosi and Bob's original biography. Mr Cremer kindly took time out for me to interview him about his book and Bela Lugosi.

Hi Bob, what was it about Bela Lugosi that got you interested in him as both an actor and as a man?

I first saw Bela when I was 10. Universal had released its horror package to TV. I was, of course, expecting a horrible monster to appear as the vampire, and it actually took me a short while to realize that this amazingly sophisticated man with a fascinating accent was the villain – the vampire! And yet, I was terrified of him as the movie continued. That aspect of his portrayal – combining the sensual with the sinister – is what made him my favorite horror actor. Later, of course, I saw every Lugosi film I could, and was taken with the intensity and variety of his performances in different roles such as Werdegast in *The Black Cat*, Dr. Vollin in *The Raven* and Ygor in *Son of Frankenstein*. I asked myself what was responsible for him standing out as an actor in this respect, and I began researching his life. I found tantalizing bits and pieces of information from his personal life that convinced me that I was on the right trail, and that these extraordinary experiences in his life were one key to his unique artistry. I chose the title 'Lugosi: The Man Behind the Cape', because I wanted to focus on the personal aspects of his life that paved the way for his immortality as Count Dracula.

Arthur Lennig's biography of Lugosi came out two years prior to your original biography. Was he able (or willing) to share any information with you?

No. As a film historian, Lennig chose to focus primarily on Bela's film career with extensive descriptions of the film plots, in-depth analysis of the films, and some general biographical information. Our paths never met, because my goal was to focus on Bela's personal life with only very general information on specific stage productions and films. To achieve my goal, I needed information that no other author had. I needed the unqualified support of Bela's son, Bela, Jr., Lillian, Bela's wife of 20 years, and his closest Hungarian relatives and confidants, especially those who knew him back in Hungary. These sources provided the main focus of the book. I spent months in exclusive interviews with his wife Lillian, a relative by marriage, Béla Loósz, and his closest personal friend Vili Szittja, I also conducted exclusive interviews with Dr. Nicholas Langer, his attending physician during his rehabilitation at Metropolitan State Hospital, and had access to his medical logs. Lillian and I also went on an extended research trip to Hungary and Romania together to uncover additional information about his childhood and early career.

Finally, I spent 4 days interviewing Ed Wood concerning his relationship with Bela between 1952 and his death in 1956. What emerged from all of these sources is an exclusive portrait of the man behind the cape that provides in-depth insights into Bela's personal life and their relevance to his stage and film career.

Your original biography came out in 1976 – which many consider to be the definitive work on Lugosi. In the intervening years there have been many books about Lugosi – what is it that made you want to revise your original tome?

First of all, the original publisher placed limitations on the book regarding its length and the number of illustrations that could be included. I was only able to use roughly half of the research I had at hand due to the limitation on the length of the manuscript. Further, the original edition contains a mere 42 photos for this same reason. This left me completely unsatisfied with the published edition. In subsequent discussions with the family, we decided to expand the book in every respect – both in terms of textual content and illustrations. In this new edition, entitled 'Bela Lugosi – the Man Behind the Cape', the text has been increased by well over 50%. Further, in the intervening years, Bela's granddaughter Lynne Lugosi Sparks, as the curator of the Lugosi Family Archive, has uncovered a variety of new documentation and photos on Bela's personal and professional life that have never been seen before. This resulted in expanding the original 42 photographs to over 700, which includes not only rare stage and film stills, but also unseen documents, correspondence, artwork and handwritten poems by Bela in Hungary and the U.S. Lynne was successful in finding a publisher, Clover Press in San Diego, that shared our enthusiasm for the greatly expanded edition of the biography. For these reasons, I would say that this new edition of the book is beyond a doubt the most comprehensive, if not definitive, book on Bela's life.

What 'new' material does it contain, and does it answer questions like why did Bela inflate his dependence on drugs? Did he and Karloff like each other or was there rivalry between the two actors?

The aforementioned exclusive interviews remain the unique basis for this biography but have been significantly expanded in this new edition. Through intensive collaboration with Hungarian and Romanian historians and film archivists, we have greatly expanded the information on Bela's childhood and his early career. We have also been able to correctly identify photos from stage performances and films in Hungary and Germany that were previously unidentified or incorrectly identified. In addition, I greatly expanded the information from my interviews with Ed Wood for the original edition. This interview material has been significantly expanded in this new edition to include more information on Wood's relationship with Bela between 1952 and 1956 and production details concerning the films *Glen or Glenda*, *Bride of the Monster*, and *Plan 9 from Outer Space*. Finally, several topics are dealt with in detail, such as the circumstances surrounding Robert Florey's plan to cast Bela in the role of Dr. Frankenstein in *Frankenstein*, and the true story behind the hiatus in horror film production in 1936 is presented, debunking popularly held beliefs about the subject.

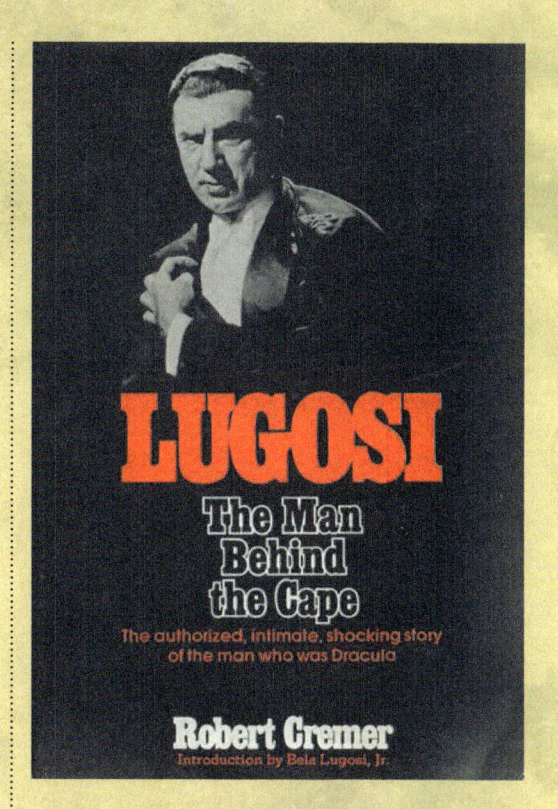

Bela exaggerated his dependency on drugs as painkillers deliberately and the reasons are not all obvious. Exclusive access to Dr. Nicholas Langer, his attending physician at Metropolitan State Hospital, and to the daily hospital logs, together with extensive comments by Lillian regarding Bela's use of painkillers, offer unique insights into the nature and extent of Bela's dependency on drugs. These interviews disclose Bela's true motivations for his exaggerations. The inaccuracies regarding his use of drugs depicted in Tim Burton's film *Ed Wood* are also corrected.

Interviews with Lillian and Sara Karloff, among others, place the relationship of Bela and Boris in a factual context that lays much misinformation to rest.

It's 93 years since Lugosi's portrayal of Dracula hit the screens, in the intervening years there have been many other actors that have portrayed the Count (Christopher Lee and Gary Oldman to name but two), but Lugosi's portrayal after all this time is still the definitive characterisation – why do you think that is?

I think Bela erased the boundary between actor and role, for openers. He never portrayed himself. As Lillian told me, "He communed with his character and submerged himself in the role." Furthermore, I think it is fair to say that the tragedies and horror he experienced in his life were the negatives from which his characterizations were developed. Finally, he had an instinct for creating unique characters drawn from his own imagination and soul. Count Dracula blends a sensual undertone with blood-curdling terror so seamlessly that it has never been matched in subsequent portrayals. Other actors have, of course, provided thoroughly professional accounts of Count Dracula, but they do not measure up to Bela's unique interpretation, in my estimation.

With so much material about Lugosi out there – where does the focus of your book now lie – Bela the actor or Bela the man?

The book remains true to its title – the *man* behind the cape. There is no need to reinvent the wheel, when there are already outstanding works on various aspects of Bela's career available to Lugosi fans. The works of Dr. Gary Rhodes, Bill Kaffenberger, Frank Dello Stritto and Andi Brooks have provided groundbreaking research on Bela's early Hungarian and German career, his *Dracula* tour in Great Britain, and his stage and film work in the U.S. My goal was to provide a personal perspective on Bela that only my close collaboration with the Lugosi family could provide.

In your opinion, do you think Universal sabotaged Lugosi's career? By all accounts, Laemmle Jr. certainly did not support Lugosi when it came to *Frankenstein*. What I mean by this is that Lugosi could have played Doctor Frankenstein rather than the monster – What are your thoughts on this?

With regard to the casting of *Frankenstein*, Lillian put the miscasting into perspective in very succinct terms. She said to me, "Bob, the Frankenstein monster was Karloff's monster, but Universal was Bela's monster." The plan to follow Florey's plan to cast Bela as Dr. Frankenstein instead of the monster had been agreed to by Laemmle in a number of conversations with Florey. Suddenly, without Florey's knowledge, Laemmle replaced him as director, and both he and Bela were shunted off to *Murders in the Rue Morgue*. Universal remained a thorn in Bela's side throughout his association with the studio. Universal negotiated his salary down to a pittance in every production he appeared in, including *Son of Frankenstein*, when Universal took advantage of his grave financial situation resulting on the ban on horror films. Although Bela saved Universal financially twice in his career, Universal showed its appreciation by making him a junior partner in all salary negotiations, never accorded him the respect and recognition he deserved. Later in his life, when he was financially strapped, Universal did not buy one ticket to the *Bride of the Monster* Benefit for Bela while he was in the hospital, nor did they send a representative to his New Year's Eve appearance at the California Theater in San Bernardino. Finally, they did not appear at Bela's funeral to pay their respects. Universal was, in the truest sense of the word, Bela's "monster".

How did the new project come to be? Did the Lugosi family come to you with the idea of fully revising the book, or did you go to them?

When I began working in Los Angeles as a syndicated columnist covering prime-time television for 'The Hollywood Reporter', I was eager to use the Margaret Herrick Library to research Bela's life and career. My fascination with Bels Lugosi grew as I grew older. When I discovered in my research that Bela Lugosi, Jr. was a practicing attorney in Los Angeles, I contacted him with the proposal to write his father's biography. Bela, Jr. and I met for lunch and I described my approach and goals for the biography. He explained that, since his mother, Lillian, would play a major role in the project, he would arrange for me to meet her and discuss my proposal with her. I met with her at her home in Culver City shortly afterwards, and there was an immediate rapport between us, because she wanted nothing more than to set the record straight on a variety of issues, most notably the exaggerations concerning his drug dependency. After months and months of interviews with her and others close to Bela, Lillian accompanied me on a trip to Hungary and Romania in 1973 to uncover additional information regarding his life and career in Europe.

What was it like working with the Lugosi family and was there anything that was a no-go area?

Lillian was adamant that the biography reflect both Bela's personal and professional life accurately. She said more than once, "Bob, it has got to be the whole truth and nothing but the truth." She lived up to this statement in every respect, even when it so often came to painful memories and tears. For this reason there were never any "no-go areas" regarding interviews either for her or for the relatives and close friends I interviewed. It even got to the point, where I brought extra Kleenex along for weekend-long interviews, because Lillian recounted extremely painful memories that frequently brought her to tears. At no point did I ever get the impression that those I interviewed skirted unpleasant issues or attempted to avoid uncomfortable questions. While there is a tendency to equate 'family-authorized' biographies with whitewashing the truth, nothing could have been further from the truth in this case.

Bela famously stated that he was a 'lone wolf' – do you think that's the case and if so, do you think that hindered his career? Or was it all for publicity?

Like Karloff, Bela was not enthused about the

Béla Lugosi
THE MAN BEHIND THE CAPE

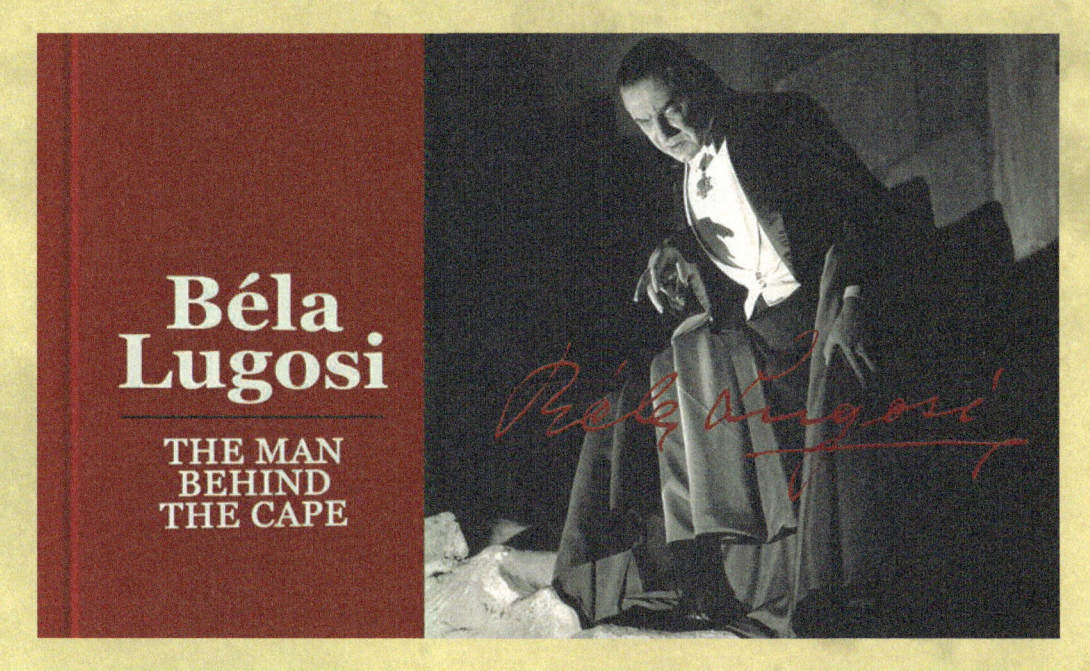

Hollywood High-Life, where the stars talked shop and jockeyed for publicity opportunities. In that sense, he was a genuine lone wolf. He preferred to spend his time with Hungarian friends, some of whom were involved in the film industry, but, even with those friends, he refused to talk shop. His parties were legendary, but few outside of the Hungarian community every experienced them. In this regard he exuded a certain mystique to the Los Angeles press corps.

This secluded lifestyle certainly reinforced his mystique – being a native of Transylvania, possessing a mysterious but unmistakable accent, and having provided his unique portrayal as Count Dracula. However, this aloofness was more the result of the lifestyle he deliberately chose for himself than a publicity gimmick. He was extensively involved in supporting various Hungarian organizations with fundraising activities and personal appearances, and he devoted a great amount of time to his love of soccer, the Magyar Athletic Club team and the Los Angeles Soccer League as Honorary President. In these activities, he was anything but a lone wolf.

You mention interviews with Lillian, Bela's fourth wife. Were you able to interview Hope Lininger before she passed?
No, unfortunately not. She was living on Hawaii at the time and there were issues regarding her participation that remained unresolved.

Out of all the films that Bela made, do you have a favourite?
This is truly a question I cannot answer. The reason goes back to Bela's philosophy of acting and his intrinsic commitment to providing a stage or screen audience with every ounce of ingenuity, creativity and energy he could muster. Regardless of the film, Bela lost himself in his role, and provides what I consider to be an outstanding performance, whether the film be *Dracula* or *The Devil Bat*. Two of my top favorites are *Dracula* and *Son of Frankenstein*, because they epitomize the range Bela was capable of in his interpretations of characters. Even his soliloquy in *Bride of the Monster* ("Home? I have no home!…") affords us a hint at the power of his performances on stage in his prime. I would have to say almost without exception that a performance by Bela is one of my favorites.

Thank you, Bob, for your time and answers.
Mr. Cremer's book comes with a foreword by Bela's son, Béla Lugosi, Jr. plus an afterword by film historian and Lugosi scholar Dr. Gary D. Rhodes, and is accompanied by over 700 photographs from the Lugosi Family Archives, many of which have never been published before.

It provides a detailed account of Lugosi's life and career, from his early years in Hungary as a soldier, actor and union activist through his Hollywood years and fame as Dracula, and his diminishing star in skid-row horror films, to working with director Ed Wood on films like *Glen or Glenda* and *Bride of the Monster*. The book includes numerous interviews with figures like Wood, Lugosi's former wife Lillian Lugosi Donlevy and many others.

You can pre-order 'Bela Lugosi – The Man Behind the Cape' via the Kickstarter webpage shown here, with an expected release date for May 2024:
https://www.kickstarter.com/projects/cloverpress/bela-lugosi-the-man-behind-the-cape-by-robert-cremer

We Belong Dead

STAGING DRACULA

by David M. Nevarrez

As is commonly known among fans, Bram Stoker's novel 'Dracula' was published in 1897, either May or June. What is less known is that Stoker was at the time the business manager of the West End's Lyceum Theatre, and assistant to the owner, the great actor Sir Henry Irving. Being part of the theatre world, it comes as no surprise that Bram himself wrote an adaptation specifically for a staged reading, a marathon at 5 Acts of 47 Scenes, in order to establish his connection to any theatrical production. Sir Henry's performance of Mephistopheles in Goethe's *Faust* was a major model for the Count, along with the peppering throughout the novel of another of Irving's triumphs, Shakespeare's *Macbeth* (not counting the similarity of the three 'brides' to The Three Weird Sisters of the Bard's play), but legend has it that the Maestro himself came in only briefly, then walked out declaring it "Dreadful!" That arrogant, insensitive dismissal does suggest he would have been good in the title role.

Sadly no stage production hit the boards in Stoker's lifetime.

In the early 1920s another actor-manager, albeit provincial, so without the kind of production values seen at the Lyceum, had the idea of staging it after forming his own company. Hamilton Deane was no Henry Irving (though he had been in the latter's touring company, and his family had been neighbors of the Stokers in Dublin, so had connections with Bram), but he was successful in his own right.

Problem was, Deane could not find a dramatist to tackle the unwieldy novel (a problem many have found adapting a number of famous novels). During a severe cold, causing him to be bedridden, Hamilton wrote out his own first draft.

His proposal was welcomed by the widow Florence Stoker, who was currently in litigation against Prana-Film for their unauthorised use of her late husband's work in *Nosferatu* ('22), as an authorised drama could reassert her control of the property (and hopefully make much-needed finance – since being a widow who had never had a job outside the home, who neither came from nor married into wealth, had left many in her time destitute). And so Stoker and Deane struck a contract, which favored the former.

Deane was enthusiastic, and finished writing the play in 4 weeks. In order to make it work on a low budget in a theatre lacking big production facilities, he cut the story down to fit conventional drawing-room melodrama. Gone were both the first part of the novel at Castle Dracula, and the adventurous chase at the end. There was briefly a prologue with Dracula crawling down a wall, and the effect could have been technically done, but it was cost-prohibitive, so cut (but still appeared on the posters – why completely waste a good idea?) He also whittled down the character list (as many film versions wisely did, too, and some unwisely did not) to a manageable cast, also changing Quincey Morris to a woman, so as to have a third female part. At the same time, Lucy Westenra ended up being the subject of conversation, but does not appear.

Another big change was to the Count himself. Gone was the fetid breath coming through visible fangs, plus pointed ears and hairy palms (ironically *Nosferatu*'s Count Orlok was a closer match to the novel's version). He became the suave devil who could be invited into polite society, albeit the makeup was highly stylised for the audiences' benefit (and it has been conjectured that Mrs. Stoker approved of his domestication). Deane initially intended the role for himself, and he had the features for it, but decided to play Van Helsing, for more stage time. In the important title role he cast one Edmund Blake (stage name of Frederick Alkin). Deane's future wife Dora Mary Patrick played the heroine, Mina.

Granted license by the Lord Chamberlain on 15 May, 1924, it preview-premiered at the Grand Theatre in Derby, central England. The censor's only cut was not to show the vampire's death, but to let it be suggested by the actors' movements. Deane got around this with a dummy in a trick coffin that appears to disintegrate into Fuller's earth.

The play was a popular success, and Deane went to work on a properly mounted production in Wimbledon (no, not involving tennis). In order to have smooth negotiations with the difficult widow Stoker, Hamilton went through her agent C.A. Bang (who had been a manager at Heinemann when they published several of Stoker's books). During business discussions Deane met Bang's brother-in-law Raymond Huntley, a tall, sharp-featured, resonant voiced 22-year-old aspiring actor. Deane hired him for his company (perhaps, as Huntley suggested later, to curry favor with Bang). Though young, he could play older character parts. And so he was cast in the title role for the new theatre. He had to provide his own costume, except for the specially wired cape, with the overly high collar, created so the actor, with his back to the house, could drop down unseen through a 'vampire trap' (invented for James Planché's 1820 adaptation of John Polidori's *The Vampyre*), leaving the cape upright till one of the other actors knocks it down.

The play remained so popular throughout the provinces that not only did it take over Deane's repertory, but after initial resistance from him he was tempted to a London production by Jose Levy, owner and operator of the Little Theatre. And so it opened there on 14 February 1927 (on that same date 4 years later Universal's classic film version would open generally, following previews in New York City). The reviews were generally hostile, or humourously dismissive, but it played to full houses. Critics be damned. There was also the added gimmick of a "nurse in attendance", who had smelling salts for any viewer who felt faint. While Mrs. Stoker did see it, she did not introduce herself to the actors, and one can assume this tawdry production was an embarrassment to one used to the glory days at the Lyceum.

Deane was feeling out of place, being a small fish in a big pond, and wanted to return to the provinces, but his backer Harry Warburton was not keen on leaving behind a London success, so he made a deal with Mrs. Stoker behind Deane's back. Deane went to the Society of Authors with a complaint, and G. Herbert Thring, an old hand with experience of this property, urged Mrs. Stoker to mediate, calling her position "rather hard." Over the ensuing year a compromise was reached, extending Deane's touring rights. He lost his lead, Huntley, though, as the actor signed on with Warburton.

Mrs. Stoker, dissatisfied with having to share with Deane, or anyone else, got Bang to hire a playwright to adapt a version she could own outright. He hired Charles Morrell who also used the drawing-room mystery genre, but pulled whole bits from the novel, including chunks of dialogue verbatim, making for what sounds like a bloated vanity project. It played briefly at the Royal Court Theatre, Warrington in September of

We Belong Dead   Page 39

He wisely employed London-based playwright/journalist John L. Balderston to not only doctor the play, but charm the widow during negotiations with Bang. Balderston did well, though he was uncertain about trying to fix this shocker, and a deal was reached. Balderston did accept the assignment, though initially didn't want his name attached. He used only the bare-bones of Deane's original, streamlining, cutting characters Morris and Godalming, changing Mina Harker to Lucy Seward, making Dr. Seward her father, shifting the setting of the Harker residence to Seward's sanatorium, and fixing the stilted dialogue (he eventually did decide to have the byline, to protect his rights). Another change is that Harker (changed from Jonathan to John) is not the Count's real estate agent, but on one of his Continental travels did visit Transylvania, where he heard tales of the Voivode Dracula, connecting him to Vlad Tepes – Van Helsing later identifies him as the same. Gone too was the trick dummy, replaced by an unseen staking with groan offstage.

1927, and was never staged again. The iron widow had to accept that Deane would remain involved regarding stage productions. His version continued to play around London, and was revived under Bang's management the following year, as well as Deane's successful touring companies, at one point having 3 concurrent.

In the cold London Winter of '27, among the audience at the Little Theatre (a converted banking hall with added balcony, boxes and uncomfortable stalls seating) was flashy American publisher and theatrical entrepreneur Horace Liveright. Coming from New York, he was self-educated, a celebrated party host, and a founder of the Modern Library. He saw the play 4 times. Aware of the bad reviews, much of them well deserved, he got "a kick" out of the crude energy and audience response. As a publisher he was aware of the novel's growing sales over the decades. He knew it wouldn't, as is, play in New York, especially with the stilted, amateurish dialogue. But the foundation was there. Was it awareness of the perverse subtext, seemingly censor-proof (he had published Freud in the U.S., after all)?

Meeting with the staid Mrs. Stoker, she took an immediate dislike to this brash, flamboyant Yank.

Not that things went smoothly. Stoker continued to want complete control, and Bang supported her on that; they even decided not to use Balderston's version in London, in order to keep more of the proceeds. Unfortunately for them, the Deane version closed soon after.

Meanwhile Liveright announced a Broadway opening for October '27. He offered both Huntley, and Renfield player Bernard Jukes the opportunity to reprise their roles across the Pond; Jukes happily accepted (he has the record for playing the character), but Huntley demanded more money than Liveright would pay (was this a crafty way of getting out of it?) This latter situation set into motion one of the most iconic castings in theatre (and later film) history.

Broadway in the '20s was not yet the powerhouse it would become, but it was its own world already (Damon Runyon, American short-story writer and journalist, was one of the purveyors of this world, one of his stories becoming the basis for *Guys and Dolls*). One of the popular genres of plays mixed mystery and comedy (such as *The Bat* in 1920, and *The Cat and the*

Canary in '22). While the agents of evil in these plays ended up being human, if thought otherwise, *Dracula* was a different twist. And it took the Great White Way by storm.

In the title role was exiled expat Hungarian stage performer turned American character actor Bela Lugosi. Emigrating to the U.S. from Germany in 1920, he first worked as a laborer, then entered the theater through New York's Hungarian immigrant colony. Soon he moved into English-language productions, at first learning his lines phonetically (he apparently also spoke French fairly fluently, and during the run of *Dracula* took English lessons at Columbia University from director Arthur Lubin). This new role garnered him much female attention, including Hollywood star Clara Bow, with whom he had an affair, which ended his second marriage (for many years a nude painting of her hung in his home).

According to Lugosi biographer Robert Cremer, Bela came to the attention of Liveright through a chance meeting with director Jean D. Williams, who had been in negotiations to mount a different version of *Dracula* in New York (Stoker's commissioned version seems likely), and had wanted Lugosi to star, but plans fell through when Stoker would not sell the film rights along with stage. Williams highly recommended Lugosi as the perfect choice.

Lugosi's style – to focus on lines and blocking during rehearsals, saving the acting for performances – made Liveright and director Ira Hards nervous, so that the producer talked with the actor, who explained his method. And the backers' preview was a great success.

The play had a brief tryout at the Shubert Theatre in New Haven, Connecticut, before opening at the Fulton Theatre (later the Helen Hayes Theatre) on 5 October, where it ran until May 1928. Along with Lugosi and Jukes were Dorothy Peterson (longtime companion of Liveright) as Lucy, Terence Neill as Harker, and two other cast members who would appear in the film version, Edward Van Sloan as Van Helsing and Herbert Bunston as Seward.

Critics were much more taken with this revised, better produced version. Despite the success, Liveright was reluctant to tour. This frustrated Deane, who wrote to Balderston telling him he was working on a completely different vampire play, which he would tour the U.S. with, and John alerted his agent. As the New York box office began to wane Liveright overcame his reluctance, and subcontracted O.D. Woodward to present it on the West Coast, where it opened at the Biltmore Theater in Los Angeles, California on 25 June 1928. Originally booked for a 4-week engagement, it held over till 18 August. Both Lugosi and Jukes reprised their roles.

After that success, and in San Francisco, Liveright mounted a touring company and enticed Huntley to come over to the U.S. to star, beginning in Atlantic City, New Jersey on 17 September, 1928. It would play other countries, such as Australia in 1929-31.

Lugosi himself would return to the stage role several times throughout the 1930s, 40s, and into the 50s. He tried bringing it to the West End in '51, premiering at the Theatre Royal in Brighton on 30 April, touring shortly, ending at the Theatre Royal in Portsmouth where it closed on 13 October. It did not make it to the West End, and it was Lugosi's last performance in the role.

There were also a number of other revivals, including one in 1942 in which the lead had a Hitler-moustache, and in '51 starring John Carradine; other tours; and stock company productions, such as in 1930 with Victor Jory. For the 50th Anniversary of the Broadway opening a new production was mounted, with iconic sets by Edward Gorey (I have the toy theatre version of them) – which had first been used regionally in '73, and starring Frank Langella in the title role (he had played it 10 years earlier in Massachusetts). I saw it when it came to Los Angeles with Jeremy Brett in the lead, who was marvelous.

The 1960s produced a number of parodies, many being musicals. The drawing-room style would be copped by other playwrights starting in the 1970s and beyond. There was even an Off-Off Broadway version, *Dracula: Sabbat* ('70) by Leon Katz, as a black mass, with nudity, and simulated sex. I myself wrote a playlet, *The Dream of Dracula*, in the '80s, later expanded to *Undead, Dreams of Darkness* ('98), incorporating J.S. Le Fanu's *Carmilla* as well. The Count also featured in operas and ballets.

As one tagline from Hammer put it "You just can't keep a good man down."

DAVID J SKAL: UNTANGLING THE WEB OF DRACULA

by Alistair Hughes (interview by Derek M Koch, with kind permission)

The global horror community was shocked in early January with news of the tragic passing of author and scholar David John Skal.

To say that he founded the vocation of 'horror historian' is not an exaggeration. Expert fans had always existed, but none with the industry connections or professional writing and research credentials which Skal had already honed, before revisiting his 'monster kid' passions.

Studying journalism at Ohio University, David J Skal began a career in theatre publicity and communications, promoting companies in Connecticut, San Francisco and New York. He eventually founded his own Manhattan based marketing consultancy for the live arts in 1982, and during this time also authored three well received science fiction novels. An invitation to pitch a reference book idea led to the publication of his definitive work on the first theatre and cinematic adaptations of 'Dracula': 'Hollywood Gothic: The Tangled Web of Dracula from Novel to Stage to Screen', in 1990.

Not only did the wide reaching success of this volume allow him to realise a new career specialising in the classic horror genre, but its popularity even set in motion a full restoration of the 1931 Spanish language screen version of *Dracula*.

He went on to produce many more acclaimed analyses of horror cinema, as well as writing and directing several DVD and Blu-ray documentaries examining Universal studios horror and science fiction.

This interview is an abridged transcription of a 2020 conversation between Mr Skal and Derek M Koch, writer and producer of the excellent 'Monster

Kid Radio' podcast. (The full episode can be found here: http://www.monsterkidradio.net/2020/09/monster-kid-radio-487-david-j-skal.html)

The following is reproduced with Derek's kind permission, and with deep respect and gratitude to the memory of David J Skal.

Derek M Koch: *I've learned more about Bela Lugosi and Bram Stoker from you than anybody else out there with books like 'Hollywood Gothic', 'The Monster Show' and 'Something in the Blood'. You're living the dream, researching and writing about these movies and getting paid for it?*

David J Skal: I do get a lot of mail from people saying they'd really like to be a film historian and have a career exactly like mine; how should they do it? And I reply with 'first of all keep your day job', because there aren't many people who have pulled off what I seem to have. It's a fairly small field; I've kind of created my own brand within the horror brand.

I was interested in monsters from the age of ten, discovering 'Famous Monsters of Filmland' and the old Universal pictures which were just being released to television for the first, or second time around. You couldn't just access movies in those days. There was no streaming or home video, you had to wait until a television station decided to schedule a film or some art house would revive it. But in its place you had the magazines and fan clubs, so you could swap pictures and and have pen pals all over the United States, who were into what you were into. And I was very much part of that generation: I like to call us 'monster kids'. It's an interesting generation; so many of us took media into our own hands because we couldn't see these films as often as we wanted, but we could make our own 8 mm extravaganzas in the basement or the backyard, made up like a cemetery. Some of us became Steven Spielberg, and a lot of us had interesting careers in the media. My big interest was theatre, so I put away monsters for a while, to work in the marketing and promotional end of non-profit theatre for almost thirty years. Actually, Bram Stoker and I have that in common – we worked in the theatre professionally for most of the time we were also writing about horror. I'd been writing science fiction stories and novels for quite a while, right out of college, and I had got good reviews, but didn't make a lot of money at it. So my agent suggested I try a nonfiction book, and were there any subjects I'd ever wanted to tackle? I told her that as a kid, I was really into monster movies and *Dracula* especially just obsessed me, but I>d never read anything about the real backstory and the personalities involved. All the books that were out there just basically said the same things and were not satisfying my curiosity. She said "OK, I'm going to be on vacation for a couple of weeks, put together just a one page description for me of this book you'd like to do." So I called the treatment 'Hollywood Gothic: The Tangled Web of Dracula, from Novel to Stage to Screen' and handed it over. Two weeks later, she got back to me and said "I've got twenty publishers interested."

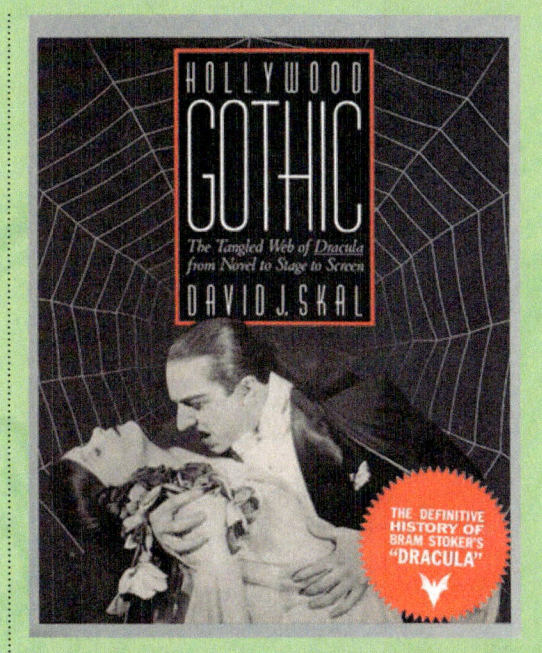

That's amazing, how did that happen?
The good thing about nonfiction is that you can get a contract and an advance based on sample chapters and an outline, unlike a novel where you almost always have to submit the whole thing. So I said, "Well, this sounds like fun."

I thought it was going to be a 'one-shot' and I'd go back to doing my theatre work, but lo and behold, the book was very successful. I had publications like 'Newsweek' calling it 'the ultimate book on *Dracula*' and selecting it as one of the top gift books for the Christmas season in 1990.

'Hollywood Gothic' has never gone out of print, and I realise that's unusual. These kinds of books are usually a flash in the pan and don't go into a second printing, much less stay in print for thirty years. So I get to update it every once in a while.

That book opened up my eyes to so much more about Lugosi, Dracula and what was going on at the time. It enriched these monster movies in such a way that I don't think would have been possible without some of these things you explain and describe.
Well, thank you. I uncovered a lot of untapped material for 'Hollywood Gothic' because I was working in the theatre. One of my clients at the

adopted a kind of approach which has informed all of my books: using novelistic techniques to talk about the people and the personalities. I've always relied on a combination of anecdote and analysis in my books that seems to work for me, and here I am three decades later, still at it. What I did find is that almost everybody associated with *Dracula* was crazed and obsessed, themselves. It's as if anybody who crossed the path of that literary property and wanted to control or exploit it usually drove themselves or everyone around them crazy.

Sadly we're kind of in a place now where a lot of these performers and crew just aren't with us anymore.
When I started out I suddenly realised, my God: I'm talking to some of these Hollywood people for the first time they've ever been asked to go on the record. So much of Hollywood history has just gone forever because nobody ever sat down with a tape recorder to talk to these people about their lives. When I started, in the late 1980s, some were approaching the limit of human memory of those films and times. It was so much fun to meet the actor Raymond Huntley, who originated the part of Dracula in the West End, and on tour and in England in the 1920s. He was a very young man at that time – only about 20 years old. But he was one of those character actors who could project much older, and that's the only reason we could still be in the same room together. Bela Lugosi had died when I was four years old – and this was the man sitting in front of me who gave Lugosi the part of Dracula by refusing when it was offered to him for Broadway. Through 'Dracula', I got to meet so many of the people and became very friendly with David Manners (John Harker), who otherwise really resented people approaching him. He was in his early nineties when I first met him, and he was used to turning people away because, as he told somebody who really irritated him: "you don't care about me, I'm just a surrogate for you for Bela Lugosi!" But I got to know him well enough that we talked about all kinds of things and the transcribed result has a 'you are there' quality which you can't fake. You've got to find the living people, or documents that nobody's ever seen before. So I'm not sure I've got another Hollywood book of the same type in me because I've kind of strip-mined the available resources. I suppose if I could get access to the legal files of the studios, Universal especially, there would be just a whole new cycle of books I could do. The legal and contract battles and all that, but I'm never going to.

I look at the film reference books you did in the nineties, and there wasn't a lot of that happening in those days. Now we've got a number of other people also publishing and a lot more books out there, but maybe not at the

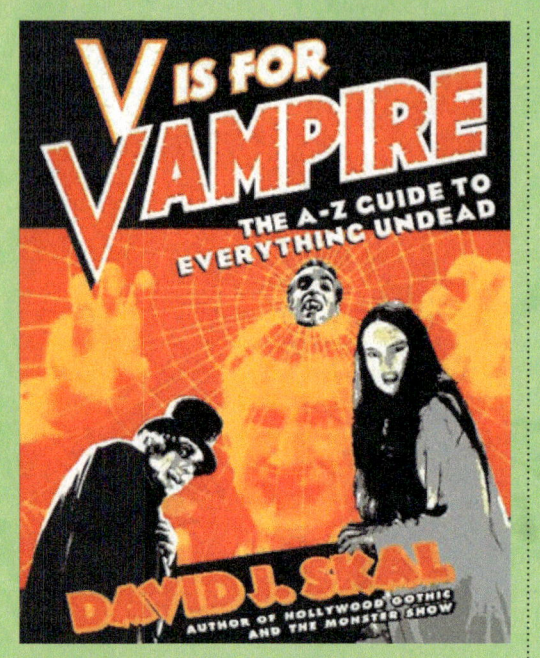

time was a producer on the Frank Langella revival of *Dracula* on Broadway, the Edward Gorey production which was such a hit for so many years. I asked her who represented the estates for Deane, (Hamilton Deane, the first playwright to adapt 'Dracula' for the stage in 1924), Balderston (John L Balderston, who rewrote the play for Broadway in 1927), and Stoker, and wondered if there were any negotiation files from back in the 1930s still available. I was given an introduction and walked into one of the older Times Square skyscrapers, and there, in a battered filing cabinet that hadn't been opened in sixty years, were all of the negotiation correspondence, contracts and everything having to do with both the stage and the film version of 'Dracula'. So I realised it was kind of a gold mine.

I had approached Universal from the outset but they just weren't interested in working with me at all. They said that the film was classic and they were not going to do anything that would cheapen its value for them. It was kind of insulting. So I had to figure out a way to do this book without access to any documents proprietary to them, but I did it. There's not a single Universal internal memo, or anything that is not already out there in the public, that I used.

There's a novelistic approach to some of the material, a journey that you take us on while you're researching. But you never get lost in that, you still give us the facts, and it's presented in such a unique way.
People are always asking me why I write the kind of books I do. And I tell them I write the books that I can't find anywhere to read. That's the simple and true answer. As I'd been a novelist already, I

same level as you are in terms of working with a publishing house in New York.
I'm so glad that since I started publishing there have been so many film historians who have begun doing the same thing, and in a much more comprehensive way. Just by going out and getting these people to give an oral history for the first time. When actors retire from Hollywood, some of them are somewhat embittered or their careers didn't go where they thought they might, and the idea that anyone would want to talk to them comes out of left field, but they're usually very happy to do so. So I think now we're getting much more documentation of the older films, and modern too. There's a whole crop of journalists and magazines like 'Rue Morgue' and 'Fangoria' that do really quite credible journalism. Real interviews, not studio handouts, so that future generations will be able to delve into our pop culture expressions. And, I think, much more easily than some of us did when we started.

I love that phrase 'pop culture expressions'. Speaking of which, do you have a favourite Lugosi/Karloff collaboration?
Oh, it has to be *The Black Cat*. I think it was the best script and the best director they had for any of their collaborations.

David Manners was also in *The Black Cat*, although he didn't think much of Hollywood. He came from a stage background and found all the methods of moviemaking to be completely antithetical to what he knew he could do as an actor. He told me that they just put chalk marks on the floor and shoot out of sequence, the actors aren't in control of anything. But he said *The Black Cat* was the first time that a director had actually sat down with the cast and tried to explain to them what he was trying to accomplish, artistically. He didn't treat the actors like cattle.

Of course, I also like *The Black Cat* because it illustrates one of my great theories that World War One was the driving cultural force behind horror entertainment in the 20th century. And here the story itself is explicitly about that. It's the only film that David Manners did in Hollywood which he could bear to watch, and insisted he had never even seen *Dracula* because he just found it so unpleasant to make. But I'm not sure I believed him…

Karloff and Lugosi would also have done *Dracula's Daughter* together, had James Whale gotten his way. Whale wasn't crazy about doing the film, so he concocted this script with his screenwriter R.C. Sherriff that neither Universal or the censors would ever allow, but it was tailor-made for Karloff and Lugosi. It would have shown Dracula's backstory of how he became a vampire, which had to do with a wizard played by Karloff, who put a curse on him 500 years ago. It would have been a remarkable film. The script still exists, and the dialogue is written with both of those actors very specifically in mind. You can just hear them speaking the words.

People always ask me if I have a favourite *Dracula* movie. I'm not sure I have one; there are many films I really admire. I guess my favourite version of *Dracula* would be a 'mash up' edit, with all of the familiar scenes, but taken from different movies, spliced together. And let the familiar dialogue 'ping pong' across productions. I hope somebody out there runs with that, because I'd love to see it.

That would be amazing to see: a 'master Dracula cut'. David, thank you so much.
Oh sure, this has been a lot of fun.

by Darrell Buxton

CARS OF DRACULA!
ADOLFO CELI MEANS BUSINESS IN ...
HANNO CAMBIATO FACCIA

If asked to name a lurking, chilling presence, one that is most often unseen and ominous, and yet every bit as petrifying on those confrontational occasions where they do happen to loom before you, most of the world's workers would probably cite their boss first and Count Dracula some way down the list.

But what if your boss and Dracula were one and the same?

It's always hard to countenance that there are self-professed fans of horror out there who tune out whenever the genre gets too political, or if social comment begins to supplant physical torment. I often wonder what these folk garner from a viewing of, say, *Invasion of the Body Snatchers*? There's a switcheroo there too, where admirers of Lindsay Anderson's *Britannia Hospital* or Pasolini's *Salo* hold their noses (or even exit the cinema – I've seen it happen!) the second that the genre-style excesses rear up on screen. Both camps would probably baulk at Corrado Farina's 1971 satire ... *Hanno cambiato faccia*, which, translated as the cumbersome and under-representative *They Have Changed Their Face*, has recently debuted on Blu-ray worldwide as a welcome outlier inclusion in Severin Films' Italian box set *'Danza Macabra 2'*. It's one of those releases that usually prompts online postings of the "never heard of it!" variety, people forgetting that they may have read about the movie in the pages of 'The Aurum Encyclopedia: Horror' in the mid 80s or in Jonathan Rigby's 'Euro Gothic' more recently.

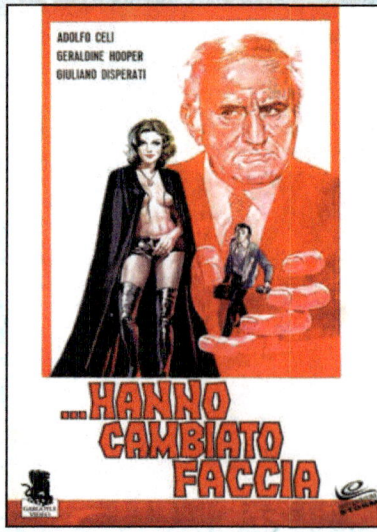

Farina, if known at all by the fan community, is more lauded for directing *Baba Yaga* (1973), but as a major admirer of any filmmaker who uses our favoured genre for satirical purposes, I'm all about ... *Hanno*. The very mag you are currently perusing is, after all, published by Eric McNaughton and edited by me, both of us committed activists and proud supporters of left-wing causes, and while we tolerate views of all hues and extremes, I'd say that many of our contributors share our position. By its very nature, horror generally holds greater appeal for the free thinker – any Venn diagram depicting Tory/Republican voters and avid 'video nasty' collectors is, after all, likely to produced two separate circles! And the traditional 'monster' figure, certainly when shown in sympathetic guise (Frankenstein's creation, the Gill-Man, etc.), can present as an avatar for the working classes, the dispossessed, the downtrodden, the misunderstood. Dracula is of course an exception to the rule – he's scary because he's got an aristocratic title and bearing, he lords it over surrounding villagers who cower in thrall, he's in charge and knows it and abuses his control.

Hammer's *The Satanic Rites of Dracula* pitches the notion of the Count masquerading as a high-powered city businessman, as a front to place himself at the heart of metropolitan London (though only about as successful here as he is in his confined status during Dracula A.D. 1972), and with officials in his pocket and efficient hog-riding henchmen employed on security duties. Since ... Hanno cambiato faccia seems to have not received a UK cinema release, I hesistate to suggest that anyone at Hammer had been influenced by Farina, but maybe it was a zeitgeist thing – after all, Horror Hospital (1973) saw the grounds of Michael Gough's grand-looking health farm patrolled by helmeted bikers and that extraordinary decapitating car (might the lone motorcyclist hurtling through Scottish rural beauty in Jonathan Glazer's 2013 SF mindbender Under the Skin be performing a related function?)

... Hanno cambiato faccia could easily pass as a forerunner of Michael Mann's Ferrari (2023) for any 'face value' viewers out there, as it seems to unfold the tale of a somewhat Lindsay Anderson/Malcolm McDowell-style ambitious innocent's unexpected rise through the ranks of an automobile manufacturing firm. The company has fingers in several other pies too, and at one point late on we witness board members congregating, their throng including Bunuelian stereotypes such as a cleric, a censor, and a young gunslinging filmmaker. The latter-mentioned hip director's duties include the devising of commercials for the company wares, and a Pythonesque sequence offers up his Godard, Fellini, and Marquis de Sade (!) pastiches, with the third of these naturally proving most to the liking of the boss.

Ah, the boss. He's played with a knowing charm by screen legend Adolfo Celi – and, even if you skim over the surface of ... Hanno as opposed to embracing the deeper meanings, you'd have to be asleep to fail to notice character names like 'Harker', 'Helsing' etc. peppered throughout. Celi's character, who to modern eyes seems to anticipate the overbearing and scandalous Silvio Berlusconi, probably believes that the abbreviation 'CEO' stands for 'Count Engorging O-Type' – he's specifically named 'Engineer Giovanni Nosferatu' in the dialogue (is it accident or by design that the 'N' topples from his tombstone nameplate, leaving his initials as 'E.G.O.', at least for English-language viewers?) but all of the trappings around the character suggest that yes, this is Dracula, no less.

Although there's a character called 'Harker', it is one Alberto Valle (Giuliano Disperati) who ventures out into the bleak wilderness, having received the surprise promotion which elevates him to hitherto forbidden access to the company's 19th floor, and then on to the rarefied heights of the 20th, to encounter the office chief and hear of his assignment to attend the remote premises in which owner Nosferatu resides. In place of any "don't go up to the castle" shenanigans, Alberto reluctantly picks up a sexy hitchhiker – Marialaura di Franceschi, billed under psuedonym Francesca Modigliani, as the free-spirited and barely-clothed 'Laura', more than willing to travel and point the way to our ineffectual hero's destination. Her ultimate fate is perhaps the most crushing of all here, an almost 100% transformation from the bubbly wild-child we initially see her as, and a cruel reinforcement of the screenplay's emphasis on corporate dominance. Unusually for a movie covered in the pages of 'We Belong Dead', it's the fact that she survives and walks away at the end that is utterly devastating.

Ok, the ultimate message is no more than "directors of big companies are like vampires" – again, you don't exactly have to be a keen socio-political student to recognise that, especially here in the billionaire's paradise of the 2020s. Yet Farina's use of this basic metaphor is given a fun-but-frightening treatment, the horror clichés are well integrated (Alberto's descent to Nosferatu's tomb, the Fiat-driving guards whose bluish-white vehicles are choreographed to take on the aspect of a pack of protective feral wolves at times, the brief hints at actual vampirism), Werner Herzog could well have repurposed certain elements for his Nosferatu: Phantom der Nacht at the end of the decade, and Amedeo Tommasi's varied score (though lifted from the composer's previous work elsewhere) is a constant joy, in particular a light electric piano piece with choral accompaniment which is an earworm and a half.

... Hanno cambiato faccia was the recipient of the Golden Leopard award at the Locarno International Film Festival in 1971, presented for the year's 'best first feature'. One for the open-minded and politically savvy horror hounds, and a most unusual take on Stoker. More 'satire' than 'satyr', I suppose.

CINEMACABRE

by Steven West

NOT *THAT* FRANCIS

It was among the key conundrums facing a small clique of pupils at Fakenham Junior School in the late 1980s. Yes, one to rival the endless debate over "Who's better – Tiffany or Debbie Gibson?" (obviously, Tiffany, though *Mega Python vs Gatoroid* would make it trickier much later on).

There weren't many evident horror fans in Norfolk back then; it's entirely possible they were shipped off to Wisbech during the "Nasties" panic. Huge thanks, however, to Gavin Chan for taping the best *Friday the 13th* for me (yes, Part 5) from Sky so I could keep it forever on a Memorex blank tape with something raunchy / foreign filling up the rest of the three hours. Still, a select few would engage in the age-old "Best Dracula?" debate. With Debbie and Tiffany sadly never cast in the role due to Hollywood's eternal sexism, it usually came down to just two choices.

Most stupidly thought the Lugosi movie a bit boring and plumped for Lee. I loved both, and still relish every revisit to the two movies that sparked their forever-association with the role. In the decades since, though, things have shifted. As much as I enjoy watching Lee as Dracula, I love watching him in *Howling II* more. Plus, he's really just a guest star in most of the Hammer Dracula movies and my favourite is *Brides of Dracula* anyway. I yearn for a whole film to centre around the transformation of Barbara Shelley's Helen Kent, or to spend more time in the company of charming deviants like Klove and Lord Courtley. Or a story from the perspective of enslaved priest Ewan Hooper of *Dracula Has Risen from the Grave* fame.

These days, I'm most likely to plump for Udo Kier as the personal fave. *Blood for Dracula* is a beautiful, hilarious, tragic thing. He's possibly the most attractive of all screen Draculas; I'd understand taking a horny fancy (not a Mr. Kipling product) to Langella or Oldman or Hamilton or Claes Bang but can't recall meeting anyone with the hots for Lugosi or Lee. I adore the scenes of Kier's ailing Count banging on about furniture and fashion, Italians putting too much oil on everything and their country's poor range of vegetables. I shudder at the vivid physical agony he suffers while in pursuit of desperately scarce "waregins". We've all been there.

But then there's Francis Lederer, Prague-born star of *Pandora's Box*, who got two shots at the role at the beginning and near the end of Lee's cycle. He retired from screen acting after his second stint but lived to be 100. Lederer played a range of Nazis, gigolos, cheats, stalkers and romantic heroes and, although it was typically reduced to a vaguely disparaging footnote in obituaries, he made a marvellously menacing Count Dracula.

I love the two modern, suburban Gothic horrors directed

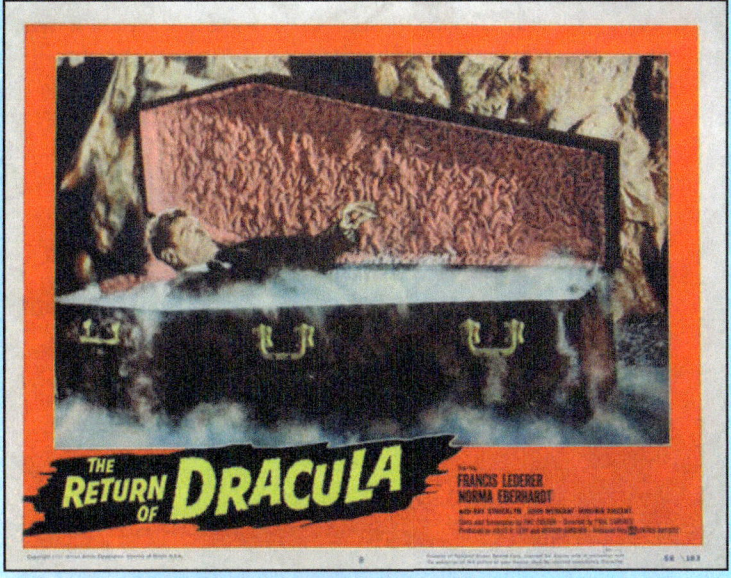

than the majority of screen Draculas) assuming the identity of a murdered European immigrant. Masquerading as a long lost family member of an almost sitcom-like American family, he is welcomed with open arms by Californian "relatives". High school student Norma Eberhardt is quickly seduced by his European hand kiss and effortless exoticism, and the movie has fun contrasting the charisma of a parasitic, ancient monster with her boorish, juvenile boyfriend: "You can tell he's refined just by looking at him!".

There are playful revisions of oft-recited Lugosi-Dracula quotes: Lederer shuns a blueberry pie offer with a knowing "I have already dined". But, clad in a tuxedo and sporting a modern haircut, this Dracula is as much of a convincing physical threat and outspoken misanthrope as Joseph Cotten in *Shadow*. His grim dismissal of the "dull and useless world" is juxtaposed with an attack on blind Virginia Vincent in her bedroom that's as scary as anything in a Dracula movie. Timely parallels to the McCarthy witch hunts add further edge, via an American immigration official who turns out to be a vampire hunter in disguise and is swiftly bumped off by Dracula in wolf form.

By now even older than David Niven's *Old Dracula* (1974), Lederer got to play the Count in a period piece set between Stoker's novel and the events of *The Return of Dracula*. Probably the best of *Night Gallery*'s more gimmicky horror-leaning episodes, 'The Devil is Not Mocked' (1971) offers a charming 14-minute homage to Universal horror, even casting *The Mummy's Curse* participant Martin Kosleck in a minor role. Framed as a yarn told by Grandfather to Grandson, it has an ominous looking castle in Eastern Europe stormed by Nazi forces, believing it to be the HQ for a resistance movement. Lederer, strikingly clad in black suit, white cloak, bowtie and white gloves, provides them with unmistakeable hospitality and offers another verbal variant of Lugosi's classic lines ("I don't sup before midnight") before howling wolves, an off-camera massacre and a Nazi scraping his nails along the floor as he's dragged to his doom, leads to the big, guessable reveal.

Said reveal confirms Lederer's fabulous screen presence in the role. Catch me on a certain, contrary day and I'll say he's my fave screen Dracula.

by Paul Landres for Gramercy in the late 1950s. *The Vampire* (1957) is an intelligent stew of classic horror tropes fastened to a cynical, self-aware, contemporaneous story about modern medicine ("Aspirin never hurt anyone, did it?") and empathetic to John Beal's tragic "monster". Landres' follow-up, *The Return of Dracula* came out the same year as Hammer's first *Dracula* and, despite a title sounding just as generic as *The Vampire,* also feels fresh and modern. It feels slightly subversive from the get-go: a documentary-style narration reminding us Dracula really existed, and a tense opening set piece defying expectations by giving us climactic-style action (a vampire-hunting mob ready to exterminate their nemesis) at the start.

The narrative neatly repurposes Hitchcock's seminal *Shadow of the Doubt* and has Lederer's Dracula (he was almost 60 at the time, older

TREASURED FILMS PROUDLY PRESENTS
A WEEKEND WITH CULT DIRECTOR JEFF LIEBERMAN
SAT 2 - SUN 3 NOVEMBER 2024
KIDDERMINSTER LUME CINEMA
FULL ADMISSION: £30
This was the night of the CRAWLING TERROR!
SQUIRM
Did you ever hear the words
BLUE SUNSHINE
Try to remember... your life may depend on it.
JUST BEFORE DAWN
REMOTE CONTROL
SATAN'S LITTLE HELPER
LIEBERMAN'S FIVE FEATURES + MORE TBA+ LIVE Q&A's
MEET & GREET - TRADER STALLS - LICENSED BAR
TIX AVAILABLE AT TREASUREDFILMS.CO.UK
LUME CINEMA - GREEN ST., KIDDERMINSTER, DY10 1JF

VAMPIRES AT THE VILLAGE HALL!

'We Belong Dead' ed Darrell Buxton reminisces about an eventful evening in the cheap seats…

I've lived in or around Derby for my whole life, growing up in a place called Willington, situated a few miles from the city, and currently resident in Ilkeston, from which such stellar acting talent as Robert Lindsay (*Citizen Smith*; *Bert Rigby, You're a Fool*) and William Roache (Ken Barlow in *Coronation Street*) sprang to major fame. So I've seen my fair share of am dram, from participating myself in school Nativity plays aged six to watching my talented nephew Andrew in comedies, dramas, and even musicals – he's breaking new ground in the 'renaissance man' stakes, currently managing to secure professional lead roles at a regional level (playing Jack Black's 'Dewey Finn' character in *School of Rock* most recently, during a short run at Burton-on-Trent Brewhouse) while combining that with ambitions to enter the diverse worlds of music and wrestling!

Derby itself is reasonably well-served for stage production. Our major local venue, formerly Derby Playhouse but redubbed as the rather prosaic-sounding Derby Theatre, often offers horror/thriller-themed fare, and I really do wish I could get there more often – I have seen *Little Shop of Horrors* there, as well as a rather impressive recreation of Morecambe & Wise's stage act, a live performance by the BBC Radiophonic Workshop (which was the nearest thing we'll ever get to seeing an English Kraftwerk, frankly), and several other shows. They've staged *Dracula*, *Dr Jekyll and Mr Hyde*, and various Agatha Christie adaptations, amongst other presentations during the theatre's busy lifetime. Long may this, and their predictably precarious funding, continue. I hope you all support your own nearest theatres, wherever they may be.

Between 2012 and 2020 I lived in Spondon, a couple of miles from Derby – a typical small suburb, most notable entertainment-wise for being the place where Blur guitarist Graham Coxon grew up after his family moved back from Germany to England; I've seen interviews where Graham still describes the local chippy as being the best in the UK! Just down the road is Locko Park, site of an 18th-century country house set amid expansive grounds and in the past a popular arena for showjumping/horse trials/equestrianism. It has also lent its name to the Spondon theatrical troupe, The Locko Amateur Dramatics Society (or LADS for short); performing since 1990, the LADS' website indicates that their extensive repertoire has ambitiously ranged from stage versions of *Wuthering Heights*, *Dad's Army*, and *The Titfield Thunderbolt*, to the inevitable thrillers/Christies, plus farce (*No Sex Please, We're British!*) and even a stab at one of legendary horror scribe David McGillivray's proto 'play that went wrong' concoctions, *Chase Me Up Farndale Avenue, s'il vous plait!*

And in Spring 2014, the Locko Amateur Dramatics Society presented, within walking distance of my home, *Count Dracula*…

Myself and my partner Carol decided to amble along for what turned out to be an unforgettable night, for all the wrong reasons! I really wish I'd seen this bunch performing the McGillivray now, as I'd love to witness the experience of seeing a 'play that goes wrong' going wrong! As we took our seats for what seemed a popular attraction, though maybe it was the promise of interval tea and cakes that had drawn a crowd, the first thing we spotted was a horizontal wire positioned high at a 45-degree angle directly over the rows of hard-backed individual seating. Hmmm…

Immediately prior to the show, we were informed that sadly, the company's 'Van Helsing' was too ill to perform and had been substituted by an understudy. As the performance began, and we caught our first glimpse of this replacement vampire hunter supreme, we surmised that he must have unfortunately been given extremely short notice about his spot in the limelight – since I have to say that this is the only time I have ever seen Dracula's nemesis reading his lines rather uncertainly from a flapping bunch of script pages, to which he was clinging for dear life! Carol added to the fun by leaning over to me and whispering "that's the man who MOT's my car!"

I have to admit that the Locko players' Dracula was an imposing fellow, though you did sense that he'd probably been cast by virtue of being the youngest and tallest cast member by some considerable distance. Rather good, and in comparison to his co-stars this was like watching Lugosi or Lee (in fact he favoured a romantic Latin lover/Langella-like reading of the role.)

Time came for that prominent/evident wire to come into play. Even those audience members, possibly relatives of the performers, who had hitherto been supportive and appreciative, couldn't resist a guffaw as a pound-shop rubber bat came squeaking over our heads, its emittances more than likely accidental due to someone failing to oil the stage crank gears earlier in the day. I prayed and prayed for a future announcement that they might mount a stage version of *House on Haunted Hill* at a later date, and give 'Emergo' a go, but no dice…

I'll end this brief account of a truly special entertainment by saying that yes, we enjoyed tea and cakes during the interval, took our seats for the second act, and – well, you're way ahead of me – try as the stagehands might, the stage curtains failed to open. Well, of course they did…

Dig the Narration, Kids! Hammer on Record

by Simon J. Ballard
With expert assistance from David Huckvale

Seizing an opportunity, the then Chairman of Hammer Michael Carreras played an excerpt from the *Hammer presents Dracula* LP to Dan Farson on the latter's 1974 documentary *The Dracula Business*. Carreras Jr was somewhat ahead of his time with the creation of the short-lived Hammer City Records, acting as what would nowadays be termed a brand manager. As moviemaking diminished, he sought ways to diversify the Hammer brand, and although nothing came of these plans, most of what he proposed eventually came to pass after his enforced resignation; a TV anthology show, spin-off books, even an immersive theatre production.

That first record was released through EMI's label Studio 2 Stereo. This was ironic given that EMI Films shunned Michael when he enquired about the six-picture picture deal they'd made with Hammer shortly before he bought out his father James at the beginning of 1973. Its head, Bernard Delfont, casually informed Carreras the younger that the deal was with his father, not the company.

A musical reunion brought together Hammer's regular composer James Bernard and Philip Martell, as conductor and musical supervisor rather than his labelled credit as 'arranger' – Bernard in fact performed his own orchestrations. In the event, neither would be paid for their endeavours, with Bernard remaining philosophical, stating, "Well, one is always glad to be able to hear one's own music." Martell did not share this view!

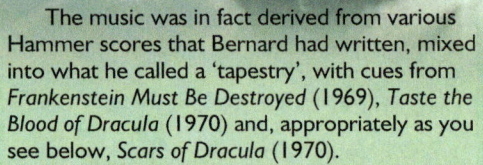

The music was in fact derived from various Hammer scores that Bernard had written, mixed into what he called a 'tapestry', with cues from *Frankenstein Must Be Destroyed* (1969), *Taste the Blood of Dracula* (1970) and, appropriately as you see below, *Scars of Dracula* (1970).

Given his disdain for their treatment of the character, Christopher Lee was coaxed into performing narrative duties, which may have been how he was tempted by the offer – Lee is recalling a story, not playing the character as such, working from a script provided by recent Hammer scribe Don Houghton. This was the man who had mangled the character into an apocalyptic image of the Devil and shoved him into the contemporary-set milieu of *Dracula A.D. 1972* and *The Satanic Rites of Dracula*, as far as Lee was concerned, so I wonder if they told him who had written the LP script?!

After Bernard's familiar bombastic opening score, with his traditional 'Dra-cu-la' refrain, an opening narration from the sonorous tones of Bill Mitchell in a vague Hungarian accent introduces us to this aural House of Hammer, warning, "There is no room for superstition in your mind, is there… is there?" and that "Fear is born of the Devil… it is here, a finger touch away, especially when you are alone!" Mitchell would lend his deep, doom-laden vocal skills to *Doctor Who*'s own spin-off LP adventure *'The Pescatons'* (1976) as the villainous Zor opposite Tom Baker's Doctor and Elisabeth Sladen as Sarah-Jane Smith.

Christopher Lee then assumes the mantle, relating a nightmarish tale that has echoes of *Dracula Prince of Darkness* (1966) and *Scars of Dracula*, seeming for once to relish Houghton's flowery words as he informs us that Dracula's "…breath was sweet with the stench of the grave." As for the arch-vampire's demise (hardly a spoiler!) Lee informs us that, "The monster's mouth stretched wide, and then the body began to age. The skin rotted away, the bones shone yellow in the dull light, and the flesh of Dracula turned to dust."

It's all a load of hoary clichés guaranteed to scare no one, but the sound design is impressive, with the stereo sounds of creaking doors, screams, thunder and the baying of wolves lending great atmosphere to proceedings. It demands to be heard beside a roaring fire, and if you don't have a fireplace, you could always watch one courtesy of Netflix!

Actually, thinking about it, the very fact that it plays safe meant that it would have been an acceptable listen to the children denied the X-rated pleasures of horror on the big screen. Indeed, in that documentary on how Dracula has infested society, Farson interviews a bunch of kids munching fiendishly on their recently purchased Count Dracula's Secret lollies, so the market was there!

The original album release came in a lavish gatefold sleeve that featured the story of the vampire of superstition and popular culture, written by Basil Copper, a writer whose big break came with the short story 'The Spider for 'The Fifth Pan Book of Horror.' The B-side featured suites to four Hammer productions, *Fear in the Night* (1972) from John McCabe, Bernard's *She* (1965), *The Vampire Lovers* (1970) from Harry Robertson (again credited as Robinson) and David Whittaker's *Dr Jekyll and Sister Hyde* (1971).

A few months later, Warner Bros. released the story album of Hammer's Shaw Brothers co-production *The Legend of the 7 Golden Vampires*. It was similar to the Dracula album, with a mix of music and narration – Peter Cushing on fine form, naturally – only this time relating an abridged version of the plot of Don Houghton's third contribution to Hammer rather than an 'original' story.

As with the Dracula album, there is an opening scene setter by actor David de Keyser, who had dubbed John Forbes-Robertson as Dracula in the movie itself. Also featured was Pik-Sen Lim as the voice of Mai Kwei. In another *Doctor Who* connection, she had played the part of Captain Chin Lee in the season eight serial *'The Mind of Evil'* (1971) as written by her husband Don Houghton! Pik-Sen was in fact instrumental in brokering the deal between Hammer and The Shaw Brothers in the first place.

The adventurous, somewhat imperialist nature of *The Legend of the 7 Golden Vampires* has often been likened to a 'Boy's Own' yarn, and with Cushing's pith helmet and air of authority, it is not hard to see why. This translates well to audio, with the actor's refined, clipped enunciation a joy to listen to as he speaks of how, "The Legends of Ancient China have their roots in the midst of time" and describes one vampire's demise at the hands of the poor farmer thus; "Deprived of its mystical life force, the creature twisted in agony and screamed. The body crashed to the ground… until all that remained was a smouldering golden mask." You read that in his voice, didn't you?

The original scores now belong with Blu-ray musical commentator and my co-writer on our book 'Edgelands of Fear' (a fiver, if you keep that bit in, Darrell), David Huckvale. I asked him how he came to own the pair.

"I acquired the scores from Phil himself. They were, when I discovered them, part of a grand symphonic spillage of material that was disgorging itself from his kitchen cupboard and being spilt with milk. The stains remain!"

Hammer City Records had planned a follow-up, naturally *Hammer presents Frankenstein* with a story narrated by Peter Cushing, but according to Michael Carreras the man in charge of album production buggered off with both the master tapes and profits, such as they were!

The two Hammer LPs sat alone for many years, seen by some as something of a folly. But in 1992, Silva Screen re-released *Hammer presents Dracula* on CD as *The Horror of Dracula*, jettisoning the B-side in favour of scores from Hammer's *Dracula* (1958)*, Dracula Prince of Darkness* and *Taste the Blood of Dracula*. It was a huge seller. *The Legend of the 7 Golden Vampires* was released on CD in 2010 by BSX Records, while five years later Dust Bug Records released the solo soundtrack and the LP narrated version together. There have also been a large number of Hammer soundtracks from both Silva Screen and GDI Records, so when all is said and done, Michael Carreras was certainly on brand with his decision to spin Hammer off into the records market, needling none but hitting the groove for many.

We Belong Dead

DRACULA ON THE AIR

by David M. Nevarrez

Orson Welles was a Renaissance man. He was first a child musical prodigy, but when at age 9 his pianist mother, Beatrice, died from hepatitis, he turned his back on music.

After travelling about with his alcoholic father for several years he was sent to a seminary school, where, with encouragement from a teacher, he adapted, directed, and starred in plays.

He was big for his age, and his sonorous voice developed early, so that he was able to talk his way into a professional stage debut (lying about his age, and his experience) in Dublin at age 16, while on a painting tour of Ireland.

After returning to the U.S. he wrote 'Everybody's Shakespeare', a series of educational books, which remained in print for decades.

By 1933 through a series of lucky circumstances he was acting in Katharine Cornell's repertory company. His first radio job came the following year, and he became very in demand, working at different broadcasters, often going from one to another on the same day. (At one point he hired an ambulance to take him through Manhattan traffic, from one studio to another, since there was no law against it.)

That same year while acting on Broadway he met producer/director/writer/actor John Houseman, with whom he would later form The Mercury Theatre. Houseman would also get Welles involved in the Federal Theatre Project, part of the Works Progress Administration that was putting people back to work during the Great Depression through government programs. With this Welles staged an African-American cast *Macbeth* (1936 – often referred to as *'Voodoo Macbeth'*), now conquering Broadway as director (Houseman was co-head, with Rose McClendon, of the FTP's Negro Theater Unit).

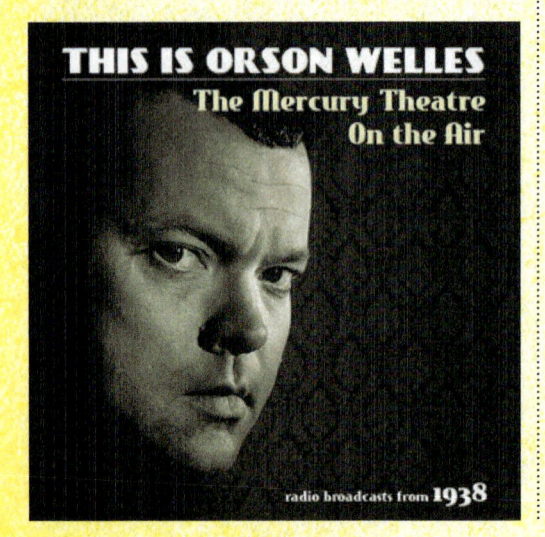

He went back and forth, often literally, between radio and theatre. In 1938 CBS contracted Welles for a weekly series dramatising classic stories, using his Mercury Theatre talent. Initially titled *First Person Singular*, later to be changed to *The Mercury Theatre on the Air*, Orson went into it with the intention of utilising and experimenting with the medium's techniques, rather than just doing straight radio plays. He built the structure around the power and intimacy of the narrator, with himself taking on that role. He and Houseman raised the bar on radio storytelling, creating an immersive experience for audiences.

On 11 July, 1938 the first episode aired, an adaptation by Welles and Houseman of Bram Stoker's novel *Dracula*, in which Welles voiced the narrator, Dr. Arthur Seward, and, with accent and sound effect, the title character.

Welles as himself makes a short intro, then dons the character of Seward, who has gathered together various documents, including his own notes, to tell the unbelievable story of a Transylvanian vampire's journey to England.

First are excerpts from the journal of Jonathan Harker (George Coulouris, *Citizen Kane*), telling of his travels to Castle Dracula, where it does not take long (the story has been truncated to an hour) for him to realise he's a prisoner. The journal entries end after the Count has left Harker alone in the castle.

Seward then reads a newspaper clipping of a foreign schooner being beached after a sudden storm at Whitby. A huge dog was seen leaving the ship, and the only occupant found on board was the dead captain lashed to the wheel. We then hear the events of the voyage of the Russian Demeter, as recorded in the ship's log by the Captain (Ray Collins, *The Magnificent Ambersons*), of the gradual disappearance of the crew, and the discovery by the Mate (Karl Swenson) that drove him mad. The only cargo consists of coffin-shaped wooden crates full of earth.

As we hear different voices narrating portions of the story, we see why radio is really the perfect medium for Stoker's epistolary usage.

Seward telegraphs to his former mentor, Dr. Van Helsing (Martin Gabel), to come to England to examine his fiancée Lucy Westenra (Elizabeth Farrell), who is deathly ill, with Arthur unable to diagnose the cause. His mentor responds, again utilising this medium well. Van Helsing is savvy to the cause upon examination, but keeps his cards close to his chest. He warns Seward she's in grave danger and not to leave her side.

Arthur sits by Lucy's bedside all night, much to the annoyance of a large bat at the window (guess who!). The next day the doctor is urgently called away (surprise, surprise) to his hospital in Purfleet, drawing him away from his vulnerable fiancée (what was he thinking?) And so with no mother to watch over her, the character being cut from this production, she receives her sanguinary visitor that night.

She dies the next day, after trying to give Arthur one of those special kisses (wink-wink, nudge-nudge), but being stopped by Van Helsing. And soon the newspapers are telling of the "beautiful lady" nipping at little nippers. The two men set off for the cemetery in Hampstead; only the elder knows what to expect. A difficult task is carried out.

Next Seward receives a new patient, found on the border of Transylvania, talking wildly of wolves, boxes of earth, and blood, he being Jonathan Harker. His wife Mina (the underrated Agnes Moorehead) brings his journal for Seward and Van Helsing to read. The three of them then have a war council. The men go to Carfax where they find 38 of the 50 boxes, which they sterilise. While they're gone Mina gets an unexpected visit, which she believes is a dream.

The following day the men, joined by Harker, go to an empty house in Piccadilly, also purchased by the Count, where they find 11 boxes. They encounter the dread vampire himself there, who brags that Mina is his, before disappearing. His last box is also missing.

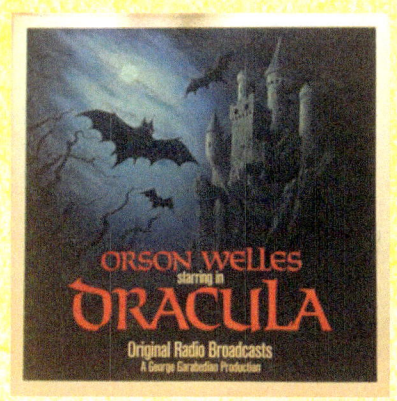

Van Helsing hypnotises Mina knowing of the psychic connection, and they trail Dracula back to his castle. As the former two watch at sunset, the wagon carrying their quarry is chased by Seward and Harker on horseback, and crashes. As Dracula mentally calls out for help, Harker goes to stake him, but Mina, who can 'hear' the vampire's summons, grabs the stake and hammer from her husband's hands... and does the dead herself. Van Helsing describes a final look of peace upon the vampire's face, as he dissolves to dust.

In an epilogue Welles, himself again, assures audiences that this was all fiction, so sleep easy, but then after assuring them a wolf's howl is just a sound effect, he takes on the voice of Count Dracula as he adds "Remember... there are wolves... there are vampires... such things do exist." Then we fade out on Bernard Herrmann's score, as he composed and/or conducted for the entire series. (His first film score would be for Welles' *Citizen Kane*).

Radio was the home entertainment before television came along and stole some of its thunder (having itself made its predecessor, toy theatre obsolete), but despite predictions to the contrary it still goes on, and there are still radio plays performed now and then (including versions of *Dracula*). In the 1930s families would gather to listen to all kinds of programming. Welles' program was a great success. As said before, it set a new bar for radio drama. One aspect the maestro concentrated on was sound effects, particular to getting the right sounds, so that many were newly created for his series. For instance, there were the two staking effects, which challenged the sound team. They first tried driving a sharpened broomstick through a savoy cabbage, but Welles declared it "Much too leafy". He suggested drilling a hole and filling it with water because "We need blood." This did not satisfy him either, and after considering a while, Orson asked for a watermelon. When one was brought, Welles himself hit it with a hammer, and hey presto, chilling sound effect.

Though this episode was certainly creepy, and the next one shifted gears by being adapted from Robert Louis Stevenson's *Treasure Island* (originally to be the first episode), it would be the notorious Halloween special that would truly frighten listeners, an adaptation of H.G. Wells' *War of the Worlds*.

We Belong Dead   Page 55

ANSEL'S ASYLUM FOR THE PSYCHOTRONIC

NO. 13

COME SEE HOW THE VAMPIRES DO IT

My very first monster movie, long before I ever saw any classic Universal Monster film or any episode of *Dark Shadows*, was the 1979 John Badham-Frank Langella *Dracula*. It was also the first R-rated movie I ever saw... I was about 5 and I still don't know what possessed my mom to put her MCA VHS tape (luckily a full color version and not Badham's desaturated version) into our VCR for me to see at such a young age – my only answer is she probably wanted to rewatch it herself. She said "If you get scared, we're taking it out" though luckily I never did get scared (Mina's glowing red eyes did creep me out, but I remember wondering how they did it.)

The Phantom of the Opera and the world of *Dark Shadows* eventually became my real foundational love of the genre and of filmmaking – but *Dracula* 1979 holds a special place for me, it was a prologue to the world of "gods and monsters" I would soon discover, and I think it's a great version of Stoker's tale... adapted from the Hamilton Deane/John Balderston play.
In this installment of 'Asylum for the Psychotronic', I'm going to shout out a few of the various Dracula films I enjoy every Halloween season. You're reading this magazine, so you've probably seen these more than a dozen times, but here are my excitable feelings on some of these classics:

Dracula (1979), the sexy sweeping seventies Universal remake starring Frank Langella and Laurence Olivier, and the stunning Kate Nelligan... with John Williams' operatic score pounding away (seriously one of his best and most unappreciated) and the laser light show a la Pink Floyd which I think is a cool scene regardless of what the haters say; John Badham directed the hell out of this, and thankfully Scream Factory finally released the original Technicolor version to Blu-ray.

Tod Browning's *Dracula*. We all agree the opening Transylvania sequences are the best, and indeed in the original Stoker novel itself, the first third covering Transylvania and Dracula's immediate arrival by ship to England is the best part, so it's no wonder the film reflects as such. It's eerily quiet, with carefully chosen moving camera shots and close-ups. There is attention to detail and precision with the unfolding of the story. Today, we are so used to Dracula as a figure, he exists, he simply 'is' and has been in our lifetime. But we forget, back in 1931, audiences hadn't seen anything like this. Yes there was *Nosferatu*, and a few other German 'fantasies'. But here – American-made, in English, in talking pictures no less, something genuinely supernatural – a real live talking vampire who was not a hoax, as most bogeys of the silent era had proven to be. But Dracula – he's real – and this was unheard of in 1931. And Browning, in his carnival showman way, carefully chooses to present us with evidence in act one and two of a well dressed man with obvious powers of hypnotism. And then act three – the English drawing room, with moving cameras and close ups (still a novelty in talking pictures at the time), and still a quiet graveyard eeriness, he begins presenting us with offscreen stories of fantastical events... of rats, and bloodletting – we haven't seen them, did they truly take place? Are Renfield and Mina just under a hypnotic spell..? Is Dracula truly a vampire..? But he is – and the original conclusion (removed in 1938 by the Hays Office), the curtain epilogue delivered by Edward Van Sloan's Van Helsing speaking directly to a talking picture audience of 1931, reminds us 'just pull yourself together and remember that after all, there are such things as

Page 56

We Belong Dead

vampires!' Browning invites us in to the game, we have to choose to believe. I think Browning knew exactly what he wanted, his vision was to quietly present a truly supernatural series of events, and like any good carnival audience we'd fill in the rest with our imaginations.

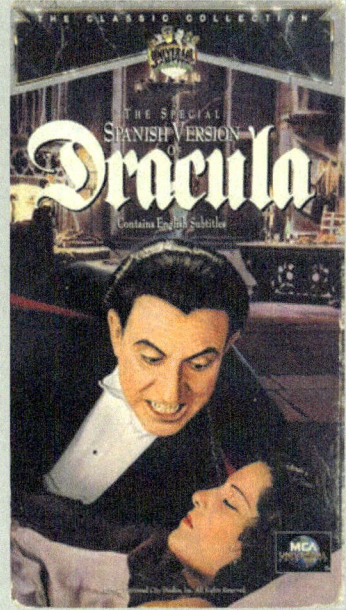

The fascinating Spanish version of *Dracula*, which I really watched this time with a contrasting eye to Tod Browning's directing… there are more camera setups and cutting, which gives it rhythm, but I had an epiphany with how Browning directs Dracula in particular, and while George Melford is being more showy here, there is method to Browning's restricted madness and I like his setups more. But the script is ultimately talky, both here and in Browning's film, and that's the issue I think newcomers have. We are told about too many things and don't get to see them.

Dracula's Daughter remains an elegant classic, with a hypnotic performance by Gloria Holden. The first 19 minutes are atmospheric and exciting, and my favorite part of the film. I always felt like this is happening a street away from the events of *WereWolf of London*.

Nadja, Michael Almereyda's 90s indie remake/remix of *Dracula's Daughter* – and there's quite a bit of it which remains faithful to the 1936 film. I can't remember how I first discovered this movie, but I got the DVD in 2007 and was sucked in by its pixelation camcorder photography, black-and-white style, and rebellious Gothic nature. Elina Löwensohn is the daughter, Peter Fonda is a long-haired hippie Van Helsing, Martin Donovan is his nephew; Suzy Amis and Jared Harris also turn up – and the whole thing was exec-produced by the great David Lynch, who also turns up as a morgue attendant. It's a weird, fascinating movie, and it's kind of fallen through the cracks. Who else remembers it..?

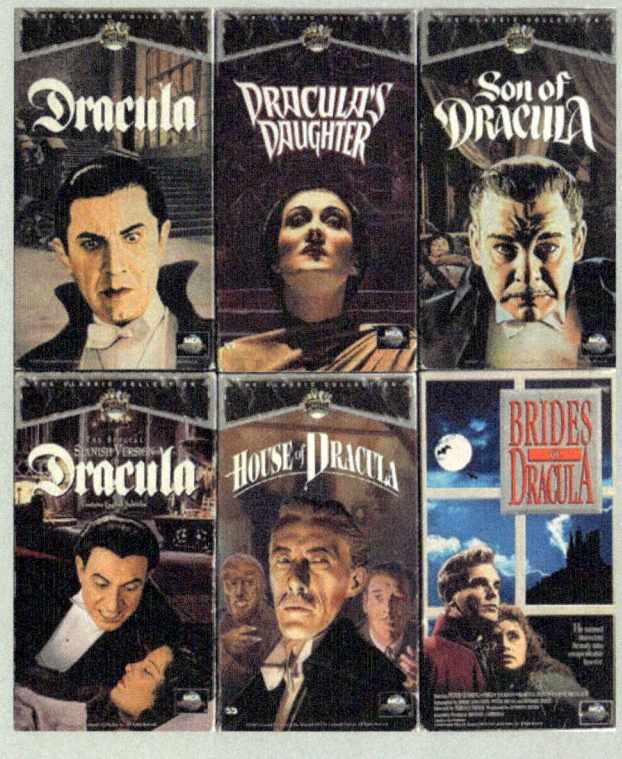

Son of Dracula – Count Alucard appreciation post. I always thought Lon Chaney Jr. did a very admirable job as the physically imposing Count Alucard, he is quiet and commanding when required but when he lashes out with animal ferocity you'd better run (and in the script he truly is the Son… his name is in fact Anthony Alucard according to the shooting script, making him the brother to Gloria Holden's Countess Zaleska, and not Dracula in disguise as some would argue). It's a classy film noir, rich in atmosphere and production value not usually found in B programmers, this is due to the inventive direction of Robert Siodmak… a dark grim love story set in the Voodoo swamps of the south. (The Hasbro posable figure from the early 2000s doesn't quite look like Lon, but it's the only merchandise I ever saw of the character and I really wish they had made a figure of Dracula's Daughter to go with him.) An excellent noir/horror hybrid with Louise Albritton as the vampiric femme fatale, manipulating all the men around her – plotting the murder/sacrifice of her father and playing both Count Alucard and Robert Paige's Frank… and that final devastating close up of Robert Paige, numbly watching as the woman he has always loved is destroyed by the fire he's started – is a gut-punching moment of emotion, beautifully underplayed by Paige.

We Belong Dead

Page 57

Blood for Dracula, aka *Andy Warhol's Dracula*. Wickedly funny and perverse, one of the movies I snuck past my parents when I was 12; all they knew was it was in the Criterion Collection so it must be "artsy". Uh-huh. The blood of these whores is killing me.

I have always enjoyed this one above its companion Frankenstein film, it's funnier and crazier in many ways (which is saying something). That last third is so wonderfully bonkers, and the dialogue is more quotable, though best quoted in the proper company.

Herzog's reimagining of *Nosferatu*… I love Murnau's original and definitely agree it's still a frightening masterpiece. But this version (particularly the German language print *Phantom der Nacht*) is one I revisit frequently… beautiful scenery and a haunting melancholy score by Popol Vuh, Kinski giving a restrained yet nuanced performance that takes the rat king Count Orlok to levels of tragedy, all while Herzog captures it like a hand-held fever dream.

The Brides of Dracula, perhaps the quintessential Hammer Horror. I love this film and the color scheme of red/purple, the score, there's so much goodness on display, and even though the script doesn't make sense we consistently accept everything because it's such a fun colorful ride with Peter Cushing riding in to save the day.

Dracula Prince of Darkness – probably my favorite Hammer Dracula. I love the haunted house feeling of the first half, and the ferocity of Christopher Lee's wordless reptilian performance in the second half, plus Bernard Robinson's wonderfully cozy sets (I'm twisted in the head for these bedrooms, have you noticed?); and wonderful gel photography. Barbara Shelley as we know walks away with the film. I always wish Andrew Keir's Father Shandor had returned in another adventure.

Dracula A.D. 1972, a psychedelic romp a little too late for its time; but still fun never the less, and finally everyone has caught up to how good a time it actually is. Peter Cushing is back as Van Helsing for the first time since *Brides of Dracula*; and there are some truly scary closeups of red-eyed Christopher Lee. I love the design of Johnny Alucard's apartment and the purple hued 'Cavern' coffee bar. At least Hammer was trying something new, slightly misguided, but still atmospheric and well directed by Alan Gibson. Dracula pursuing Van Helsing up the staircase still makes me anxious and I've seen this almost a hundred times. (And 'Alligator Man' is a good song too hahahah.)

The Satanic Rites of Dracula, when they just went full comic book – and ended up with something colorful, violent and fun, kind of frightening at times (even if it's slightly cheap) and another unique Dracula outing, more in spirit with AIPs unique *Scream and Scream Again*. It lacks the camp of its predecessor *A.D. 1972* – and is instead a serious thriller. It's Peter Cushing's Van Helsing vs Christopher Lee's Dracula – so it can't all be that bad, and it doesn't feel as slapdash as *Scars of Dracula* nor as embarrassing as *Legend of the 7 Golden Vampires*.

Bram Stoker's Dracula – Coppola's last great movie, over the top in style and borrowing (stealing) heavily from *Dark Shadows* (probably another reason why I like it) – so much so Dan Curtis filed a lawsuit against him and the film, citing plot points from his own 1974 *Dracula*. I won't apologize for my love of this one. The theatrical sets and old school trick-photography FX work, combined with Eiko Ishioka's Oscar-winning costumes and Wojciech Kilar's memorable score, have always made this a favorite in my book. And Tom Waits as Renfield is seriously underrated.

Van Helsing. It's been a long time since I last saw this movie, and this year this film will turn 20 years old. Just let that sink in a moment. When this came out I was incredibly excited because I was the right PG-13 age and all I could think was "Universal Monsters!!!!". It wasn't the Universal Monster movie I was hoping for (I was also disappointed the Creature did not make a cameo appearance as had been discussed/rumored when the movie was in production – if you scroll through some of my older posts, you'll see I shared some storyboards of the Creature's scene), but now I look at it and it's a wild comic book movie on acid driving at 150mph and everyone is totally committed to their performances, clearly having fun making this movie. There's maybe too much CGI, and it feels a bit long, but in the pre-Marvel world, it's kind of imaginative, and a hell of a lot better than the dumpster fire of Tom Cruise's *Mummy*. I do love the vampire masquerade, and the secret entrance to Dracula's castle is neat. I wish in hindsight there had been a sequel with the Invisible Man, the Creature, and maybe Arnold Vosloo's Imhotep – cross-over *Van Helsing* into the *Mummy* movies… they were both Stephen Sommers films after all. (I also have the cartoon *Van Helsing: The London Assignment* which goes more into the Jekyll & Hyde story.)

Renfield. I have to admit I was very excited for this movie, it was one that I'd been tracking since it was first announced, when Universal wanted Benedict Cumberbatch as Dracula and Dexter Fletcher (*Rocketman*) directing. Then silence. Then the pandemic. Then the pandemic was over. Then they said Nicolas Cage as Dracula, and I was even more excited, because it was fulfilling my prophecy that Nic Cage is going to be my generation's Vincent Price. The first trailer looked fun, he reminded me of Count Yorga more so than Dracula, but whatever – then that TV spot with the 1931 recreations dropped, and I was a happy ecstatic monster kid. The movie is… good. Maybe I was too hyped and it didn't meet those expectations, but I don't fully suspect that's the truth. I wish there was more vampire movie than cops-and-robbers, but I understand how inner studio politics would 'get' that less 'risky' movie aspect instead of diving in full-bore vampire… When Cage and the always excellent Holt interact, these are the best scenes in the movie. I wanted more of that. They are both great and Cage is clearly having a ball. He was sooo good. I hope they do another and really just focus it on the two of them, because they both deserved more time just together doing monster-comedy. Which brings me to the other half, I strongly suspect that there was a great deal more vampire/Universal Monster material shot (and then some) because those closing credits all look like scenes cut from the final narrative, including what looked like a musical number involving Nicholas Hoult. Those closing credits really let Cage go full Lon Chaney *London After Midnight* and again – I wanted more of that… the Blu-ray deleted scenes hopefully will be worthwhile. In short, it's a mindless cartoon that's not taking itself seriously at any point, and that's fine and cool. Was it awful? No. Not at all. Did I love it? …no. But I would rewatch it again, for Cage and Hoult.

The Last Voyage of the Demeter, saw this at the movies – it had been trapped in development hell since 2009 and I honestly never thought it would ever get made, but it did at last – and was a good Gothic slow burn, some great atmosphere, and a bloody R rating. There's one sequence I disagreed with, since Dracula should rightfully be limited to staying on the ship and not 'crossing water' – but other than that minor quibble, it was a nice old school horror outing. This one felt more 'Universal Monstery' than *Renfield*.

Award Winning independent filmmaker Ansel Faraj has been making movies since he was six years old. His most recent film *Todd Tarantula* is a Los Angeles sci-fi mystery streaming on TubiTV and available on Blu-ray. His Folk Horror thriller *Loon Lake* is streaming on Amazon Prime and TubiTV, and is available on Blu-ray & DVD. He is the writer/director of *Doctor Mabuse* (2013), the H.P. Lovecraft-inspired *The Last Case of August T. Harrison* (2015), and the love story *Will & Liz* (2018). His official Internet website is www.hollinsworthproductions.com.

THE DRACULA SAGA
AKA LA SAGA DE LOS DRÁCULA

by David Dent

Film director León Klimovsky (1906-1996) was a former dentist who had thrown over his previous profession for the lure of movie making, entering the Argentinian film industry in the 1940s.

At the time, the country was under the leadership of President Juan Perón, and its state funded film industry was subject to direct intervention. While some filmmakers found this a difficult environment in which to work, Klimovsky thrived; it was only after the fall of Perón in 1955, and the subsequent closure of many film studios, that he took the decision to relocate to Spain, which was then under the rule of General Francisco Franco. Franco, like Perón, exercised control over both domestic moviemaking and imported films, while waging war against the liberal elite; again the director proved adept at navigating this environment.

The final years of the Franco regime saw some relaxation in film censorship and the type of movies that could be produced; Spanish studios responded with a plethora of horror films. Klimovsky, while not particularly interested in the genre *per se* (he continued making movies in a variety of genres throughout the 1970s), was happy to participate.

His first two such films, 1971's *La noche de Walpurgis* (*The Werewolf vs. the Vampire Woman*), and the following year's *Doctor Jekyll y el Hombre Lobo* (*Dr Jekyll vs. the Werewolf*) were both vehicles for Paul Naschy, the Spanish actor who had made a name for himself with the character of troubled werewolf Waldemar Daninsky.

1973 saw Klimovsky again teaming up with Naschy on the truly bizarre *La rebelión de las muertas* (*Vengeance of the Zombies*), followed by two Naschy-less fright flicks. The first was *La orgía nocturna de los vampiros* (*The Vampire's Night Orgy*), the second being the subject of this piece; *La saga de los Drácula* (*The Dracula Saga*).

The movie opens with Count Dracula, played by a splendidly emaciated Narciso Ibáñez Menta, explaining to the audience in voice over that he is the last of the Draculas, and that he had invited his pregnant granddaughter Berta (Tina Sáinz) to stay, with a view to using her for the continuation of the vampiric lineage.

On the way to Dracula's castle, Berta and her husband Hans (Tony Isbert) have an enforced stay in Borgo and then Bistritz (both locations featured in Bram Stoker's 1897 novel 'Dracula', themselves based on actual places in Transylvania). Here they witness the village being slowly infected with vampirism, although the culprits – the Dracula family – remain unobserved.

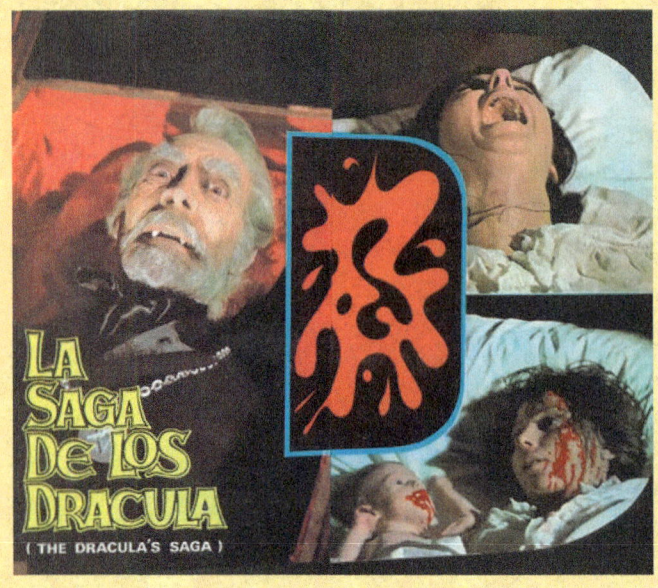

When the young pair are eventually transported to the Dracula home, Berta first wishes to see the tomb of her late grandmother, with whom she was close. She finds the grave together with others for her grandfather, Ivor Vlad Tepes aka Count Dracula, and cousins Irina and Xenia. Although no one seems to be able to explain the existence of the graves to Berta, the audience knows that the family must be dead – or more precisely undead. Later that evening, of course, the pasty faced Draculas and their undead servants are all present and correct in the castle, and Berta is persuaded to forget what she's seen in the cemetery.

Klimovsky's conflation here of the names from Stoker's book and the references to the real Tepes family is clearly an attempt to tie the mythical Draculas into an authentic aristocratic clan; whether for dramatic effect or wider political reasons is not entirely clear. Popular thought was on his side though: In 1972 authors Raymond T. McNally and Radu Florescu published the bestselling 'In Search of Dracula', which attempted to make a direct link between the historic figure of Wallachian warlord Vlad Tepes and Stoker's character. While this theory has since been debunked, at the time it was persuasive.

The reason why Berta has been chosen to further the Dracula name is therefore pretty obvious; the Count is undead, Irina and Xenia are also vampires, and women. There's a further driver for having eyes on Berta; Dracula has a descendent, Valerio (uncredited in the film), hideously deformed because of, as the Count declares, "the excesses and the degeneration of my ancestors." The boy is a webbed handed, one-eyed monster, unable to speak, and was the Count's unsuccessful last ditch effort to keep the line going. He is clearly unable to sire; or even be seen in public.

However, there's a snag; as Berta was already pregnant, the Count needs to ensure that her offspring has the right vampiric credentials. This is achieved, convolutedly, by having the Count's much younger vampire wife Munia (Helga Liné) sleep with and vampirise Hans, who in turn sleeps with his wife and passes on the family trait.

But the transmission of vampirism also carries with it moral and spiritual degeneracy; as her pregnancy enters its final term Berta, far from the demure, upstanding lady we recognised when she arrived, becomes a dishevelled, raw meat consuming thing, on the verge of madness.

At the finale Berta pulls herself together, stabs Hans and locates the bodies of the Dracula family in the crypt, which she dismembers, causing them to disintegrate. But it's too late; the baby, originally thought still born, is alive, lapping up blood which is dripped into his mouth. The bloodline is secured, and the Count, beheaded and lying in his coffin, concludes that the babe is indeed his reincarnation. "The line of the Draculas lives on," he says with a hideous laugh.

It's tempting to read all of this as a critique of the Spanish aristocracy, with which Franco had an uneasy relationship. Indeed some writers have suggested an alignment between Franco's views and those of Klimovsky, accounting for his longevity in the movie business, although this is rather wild speculation. What we do know is that the director produced a little talked-about but very creditable addition to the Dracula canon, a splendid, twisted melodrama which combines soap opera, Hammer horror and grand guignol in pretty much equal amounts.

DRINKA PINTA BLOODA DAY!

Kim Newman Gives You Your Daily Dracula
by Ken Shinn

Since May 2020, up till the present, the prolific and respected author and critic Kim Newman has been proving an erudite and entertaining Renfield. His purpose: to spread the plague of the haemovores. To enable a vast and dread shadow to be cast across the virtual World.

He has come, in short, to give you Your Daily Dracula.

The rules of this Great Game are simple: to present to the observer Dracula in all of his, or sometimes hers, or sometimes its, or sometimes their myriad forms and portrayals. Classics, schlock, cartoons, toys, musicals… all are meat to the Beast. And, with the series showing no signs of succumbing to staking, holy water, garlic, the power of Love or even the passage of Time… I thought that it might be enlightening and entertaining to ask Kim some questions about Your Daily Dracula. And he was gracious enough to oblige.

So: herewith, a short list of questions re Daily Dracula and Dracula in general that I put to Kim – along with a few thoughts of my own in brackets along the way…

KEN: Why Daily Dracula? What inspired you, generally and/or specifically, to Post A Count A Day?
KIM: Obviously, we're now well into the era of social media – I was quite surprised this week that the 'Kim Newman's Anno Dracula books' Facebook group was fifteen years old. It's become a commonplace that writers should have a social media presence – though what with mushrooming controversies about FB/Meta and Twitter/X, that may well have peaked as a notion. Aside from the simple social stuff – being in touch with friends – I realised from the first that I needed to give some sort of value to people who friended, followed or spied on me digitally and ideally it should tie in with my work. I ran movie quotes for a while and posted links to work found online – especially on my own site https://johnnyalucard.com/ - and screen captures/found images.

During lockdown, I realised I had a collection of pictures – frame captures, made by me – from Dracula movies and decided to run them daily (it was called Dracula of the Day first, then I noticed someone else was doing something with that title), presuming it would last a couple of months and I'd move on to something else. I started on May 11, 2020 – and it turned out there were a lot more Draculas than I'd estimated, and furthermore the feature soon ventured into the more unusual efforts beyond just Dracula movies – comedy sketches, adverts, porn, cartoons, TV guest appearances, pop videos, recorded stage productions, ballet, games, etc. It's still going, with no end in sight. I've sourced a ton of things – playthroughs of video games, high school stage productions, obscure movies – I've not yet got round to looking through.

I presumed at the outset that I'd at least seen all the Dracula feature films, but this has turned out to be not even remotely true – so I'm archiving everything at https://johnnyalucard.com/2020/11/10/your-daily-dracula-archive/, which now makes a substantial online resource (and is easier than scrolling back on social media over four years. I post to my page on Facebook (plus several FB groups dedicated to Dracula), X/Twitter, Bluesky, Mastodon and Instagram – annoyingly, the platforms all have slightly different capabilities so it's a fiddle to get them all done first thing in the morning. Usually, there's a link with the images – to a note on my site in the case of films or to the item itself if it's easily online. Instagram is my least favoured SM platform because it doesn't allow links so the images there are often without context. I

Page 62 We Belong Dead

still do all the captures myself – part of the appeal for me in the first place is that this makes the images unique.

(In brief, perhaps, curiosity. That common catalyst to so many great tales of terror. That, and the ensuing joy of revelation of just how vast one's chosen subject can be, and of just what variety it can offer.)

KEN: Why do you think that Dracula – the story and the character – continues to carry such influence even today?
KIM: Because, in several senses, it's adaptable. *(A short but incisive answer. As someone who's written two stories – one where Dracula is very much in the mould of the classic ('Dracula's Tango'), and the other where he doesn't even appear onstage except as an image on an ice lolly wrapper ('Eat One Before Sunset') – on reflection, it's surprising just how flexible and amenable to reinterpretation Dracula is.)*

KEN: Do you have any particular favourite Draculas? Not just the well-known ones, but those that are rather more obscure?
KIM: I'm a Lugosi-Lee traditionalist. I also like Louis Jourdan and Max Schreck a lot.

(I can only say that my tastes and Kim's very much coincide here. Lee is the most iconic Dracula of all in my eyes, Jourdan the most convincing and even compelling. I'd also wave a flag for David Carradine's Count Mardulak (Sundown: The Vampire In Retreat), and – in more jocular vein – Donald Pleasence's Erich, the Count von Plasma from Barry McKenzie Holds His Own.)

KEN: On the other side of the coin, are there any Draculas that you really don't like? Ones that you'd urge Fans of the Fangs to avoid like the plague?
KIM: I had a few qualms about stuff like *Dracula Sucks* – there are a ton of Dracula porn movies – and it's sometimes tricky to find representative images from those which don't violate some sites' policies, and also the process of watching someone else's recorded computer game is fairly mind-numbing… but it was only recently that AI started to take effect, and a few entirely computer-generated efforts passed off as short films have shown up on YouTube. They're horrible, and not in a good way – and I'm iffy on the whole project of using AI to toss off unwatchable cinema (the captured images are misleading too – suggesting qualities the moving versions don't have). My token protest is not linking to the films in those cases. If anyone wants to track them down, they're easily searchable – but I wouldn't recommend it.

(Wise words, and I agree that anyone tracking down those CG efforts in a bid to brandish the title of Ultimate Dracula Completist… well, it's your time, and your life, just please don't try to speak to me at the bar. On a less artificial note, the weedy, wimpy, ginger-bearded Count Downe played by Harry Nilsson (Son Of Dracula) is perhaps my least favourite Dracula of them all – and I also get remarkably bored with Gary Oldman's rendition in Bram Stoker's Dracula.*)*

KEN: And, to complete the trifecta – are there any particularly obscure Draculas, good or bad, that you'd nonetheless urge people to seek out, just for their difference to the usual portrayals?
KIM: I recommend the 'other media' section of the archive - https://johnnyalucard.com/2020/12/16/your-daily-dracula-other-media-theatre-radio-games-comics/ … check out the interestingly diverse range of castings for Dracula in high school or ballet productions. If you need teenage girl Canadian Hebrew Beatlemaniac Dracula, she's there.

(As are vampire ducks and rabbits (both vegetarian), and a whole slew of Dracs of very much any kind that takes your fancy. As Kim suggests, dive in – and marvel.)

KEN: The Count himself has clearly cast a long shadow over your own work. Are any new instalments of the Anno Dracula saga being planned and, if so, can you drop a few tantalising hints as to what we can look forward?
KIM: I'm working on something else at the moment – I've just written a novella ('A Christmas Ghost Story') due out from Titan guess when? And my major work-in-progress is a British superheroine novel called 'Model Actress Whatever', though that does have a tiny Anno Dracula overlap. I'll probably get back to AD in the end, but I've nothing definite planned.

(British superheroines with Anno Dracula connections? I won't lie, I'm very much looking forward to that.)

KEN: Final question. Having given us the Daily Dracula, do you plan to give Facebook any follow-ups? The Weekly Wolfman? The Fortnightly Frankenstein? The Monthly Mummy? Such possibilities!
KIM: Other people can have a bash at that. Dracula isn't likely to run out soon and when it does I doubt any of the other famous monsters are likely to have quite as many entries.

(So there we are – the gauntlet is politely, but firmly, thrown! Please note: I'm having The Periodical Penanggalan. NOBODY is taking that from me. You have been warned.)

I'd very much like to thank Kim for so graciously taking the time to answer these questions for 'We Belong Dead'. REQUIESCAT IN PACE ULTIMA!

We Belong Dead

SHADOW OF THE VAMPIRE

by Sarah Butler

It wasn't until my late teens that I discovered that some people have little more than a passing interest in films as an art form. They may watch them as recreation during a trip to the cinema or on their screens at home but have no real desire to rewatch favourites, make new discoveries or actively seek out more of their preferred genre, actor or director. I have always been torn between wanting to know more about the creators and the process of filming, and finding that it can take away some of the magic of the final product. To me, a truly engaging film is one where I am not thinking about how well-written the dialogue is or how beautiful the photography and music are, but rather to feel completely immersed in the world I am observing. To forget about the craft of it. I don't want to see the workings. As a child, I had no concept that I was watching Mark Hamill, Carrie Fisher and Harrison Ford on the screen or what John Williams had done to enhance George Lucas' vision of an adventure in space, so I was spellbound by a fully realised world. The magic of cinema is its ability to maintain that childlike wonder – to be taken on a journey while watching a moving image and listening to a soundtrack.

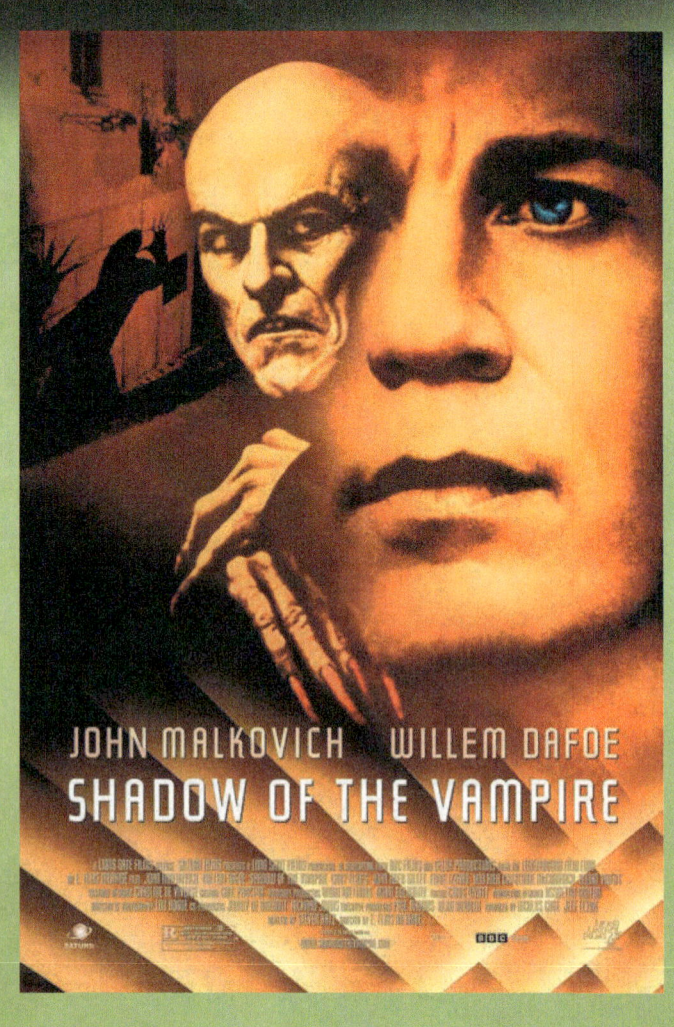

Call it "suspension of disbelief" or "the implicit contract" between audience and cinema, but I would argue it is preferable for a film to quickly make me forget I am watching actors and sets, and not to remind me at any point lest the spell be broken. That is unless the filmmaker intentionally wants to challenge convention in order to make a point. The phenomenon of DVD and latterly Blu-ray extras, which often include behind the scenes footage and sometimes full-length commentaries, added a new dimension to collecting favourite films, allowing us to gain additional insight into the creative process. There have also been a number of very successful productions set in and around filmmaking and movie studios, although not many that are about the shooting of a real film. The premise of *Shadow of the Vampire* is that during the filming of F.W. Murnau's silent classic *Nosferatu*, the actor Max Schreck – playing the vampire, Count Orlok – is either a strict student of the Stanislavski "Method" school of acting or perhaps an actual vampire. This could have been merely a straight recounting of events, but instead we are offered something which adheres more to the conventions of horror than of a biopic, as it is quickly revealed that he is in fact the latter.

In the opening scene, Greta (played by Catherine McCormack), the lead actress in *Nosferatu*, when questioned by Murnau (John Malkovich) as she is complaining about the filming schedule hindering her career on the stage, replies, "A theatrical audience gives me life, while this thing [*gesturing at the film camera*] merely takes it from me." And so we come to the concept of the filmmaker (director in this case) as the vampire and villain of the story. Much as a vampire is driven by bloodlust as his primary inescapable impulse, this director is driven by his desire to capture the most authentic version of the story on celluloid, regardless of the harm it may do to the actors and crew. After completing the opening scenes filmed on a stage set and in anticipation of the crew moving to exterior 'real life' locations, Murnau exclaims, "Thank God! An end to this artifice!" Whilst the characters and events of *Shadow of the Vampire* are based on real people and situations, the writers have taken some artistic liberties – not least in the fact that Murnau was, by all accounts, a kind, sensitive man to work with.

The passage of time (almost 80 years) since *Nosferatu* was filmed means that many viewers will not have any concept of who Murnau was as a man, but will likely be aware of the striking image that Schreck burned into the collective memory when he portrayed Count Orlok in 1922. This allows writer Steven Katz the opportunity to run with the concept of Schreck being an actual vampire, and his director only managing to keep him on side by promising him his lead actress as a blood sacrifice.

Willem Dafoe, as Schreck, does a phenomenal job throughout, lurking in the shadows, watching his prey with strange, alien movements, and ultimately casts a tragic figure having been duped into filming. When asked by the crew if he has read the novel 'Dracula', he confesses that it made him sad that the vampire was so lonely. The orchestral score swells under a scene where he finds a projector which is loaded with shots of a sunny sky and then a sunrise over the sea, something which he will never be able to see. He initially casts a shadow with his long talon-like hand onto the screen, before putting his whole body in front of the lens and projecting the scene directly into his eye. Malkovich, however, seems to pitch his performance just a notch too high, as he regularly does, but his passionate, driven, artist on a mission must be a counterbalance to the predatory power of the vampire – and in the scenes they have together, it requires them both to appear to be on an equal level for the narrative to work. If Murnau didn't hold this power over the production, his cast and crew (including Schreck), then he would almost certainly also become a victim. He reacts to his cameraman being bitten and attacked by Schreck as an inconvenience, as he must replace him in order to continue on schedule.

There are moments in *Shadow of the Vampire* when we transition from watching the filmmakers setting up the shots, to the screen showing the final product as it would have been seen in 1922 – fading from full colour to monochrome.

In fact, on multiple occasions the actual footage from *Nosferatu* is inserted, with set, costume and makeup matching perfectly in the recreated scenes. For those familiar with the original film, these matches are bound to be pleasing, rather like the final scenes of *Rogue One* featuring sets and costumes matching up to those at the start of *Star Wars* or the scenes in the Overlook Hotel in *Doctor Sleep* being careful recreations from *The Shining*.

The opening shot is an extreme close-up of Murnau's eye matched by a second shot of the lens of the camera, and as the film progresses, we come to realise that what we see on screen during filming is the subjective point of view belonging to the director. His vision throughout is what the end product will look like on screen. This difference is most starkly seen when comparing the first shots where we see Murnau directing Greta, and we cut back and forth from the widescreen full colour image of the director and crew to the black and white image framed with the iris in. The demarcation of reality and fiction is firmly drawn but by the final climactic scene of Schreck and Greta; although the fictional camera doesn't physically move from the spot, the viewer sees the pair of them on the bed from two different overhead angles before moving in a much more fluid way, as if we have left the constraints of the static camera. The vampire seems powerless against the director while being captured on film after being told "If it's not in frame, it doesn't exist", but when he is finally able to walk in a continuous tracking shot across the set from black and white back into full colour, escaping the confines of the frame, he become a real threat. At this point the early morning sunlight bursts in and as the vampire vapourises, so the film melts in the camera. The power of the director casting the images to the negative to begin their immortal life finally ends. Schreck's power relies on darkness and Murnau's on there being an image captured on the film in the camera.

Where *Shadow of the Vampire* works best is in its commitment to its metafiction, landing somewhere between a dramatisation of the filming of a seminal horror picture and a darkly comic riff on a 'what if?' scenario. The unnerving moments are derived from the unpredictable nature of having a killer on set and the continued references to him being promised Greta as a reward at the end of filming. This threat grows as we get to the final scene and realise that the director will not stop at endangering her life, having given so little care to previous deaths. The parallels drawn between the immortality of a vampire and to the images caught on screen resonate in relation to a film which is still lauded over a century later.

THE SCARE SOCIETY

Chair of the long-running Dracula Society, Julia Kruk, interviewed by Darrell Buxton

When preparing this special issue of 'We Belong Dead', I decided that it just wouldn't be complete unless we included Julia Kruk. Julia is a familiar presence on the UK fan scene, and only the second person ever to act as chair of the well-established Dracula Society, whose regular gatherings and excursions all help to maintain and further the legend of the Count, while discussing and examining horror literature, cinema, and other media in all its varied forms.

Julia is justifiably proud of the Society's impact, success, and profile. "As I always tell people, we were the first. In 1973 the Society was formed, and last year we celebrated our 50th anniversary." Julia explained how the Dracula Society was "formed by two actors (Bernard Davies and Bruce Wightman) who were obsessed with Dracula and Frankenstein, and, of course, with traveling. Very few people at the time, in the early 70s, had been to Romania, had barely heard of Transylvania – thought it was made up! So they were the pioneers. I joined a few years later, in 1977, so I've been around a long time: it ticked all my boxes. It also fulfils my desire to travel and visit the actual locations and the inspirations for the authors and, of course, the locations for the films. I took over as Chair in 1998. I've been doing it for 26 years now and I'm still just as enthused by what we do, and love it."

The Dracula Society strives not only to celebrate Bram Stoker's immortal character, but to document, preserve, promote, and to educate others in the history and lore of this lynchpin of the genre. Julia mentioned how the novel had developed into something deemed worthy of academic focus: "50 years ago there was very little serious or academic interest in 'Dracula'. It was just regarded as a successful pot boiler. No critical appreciation at all, really. And then in 1970, Bram Stoker's working notes were discovered in the Rosenbach Museum in Philadelphia, and all of a sudden interest exploded." Referencing Radu Florescu and Raymond McNally's initial approaches to the subject, she continued: "They already had a vested interest in associating Dracula with Vlad the Impaler. But it kind of took off from there. Certainly 50 years ago, when I was first studying the Gothic novel, there was very little on 'Dracula'. But now it's taught in universities everywhere, more and more critics and academics are delving into it."

Why is this? "Well, it's such a rich novel. You can look at it on so many different levels. There's the psychoanalytical approach: sexual guilt and repression. There's the medical, physiological side to it, the Victorians' obsession with disease and infection and the scientific advances in blood transfusion and medicine at the time. You can look at that aspect. There's the racial and the political – invasion and Empire, the threat of the East invading the West. That's all there. And that's before you even look at vampires! Vampires are present in all cultures all over the world. So, because humankind has always been preoccupied by death and immortality, and blood is a symbol of life, Stoker took up all these elements and embodied everything in his creation of the Count, in 1897, the epitome of the vampire. I think that's why everyone still wants to have a go and put their own take on it."

I mentioned how difficult the novel is to transfer to visual media, due to its composition via letters, journal entries, and the like. Why have so many creative types looked to 'Dracula', even though there seems to be a barrier in place, as if the book is saying 'don't adapt me, you know you can't film or stage this property'? Julia responded "Yes, that is a tricky one, which is also why there has not yet, even after all this time, been a faithful adaptation of the book. But Wilkie Collins used the same epistolary style in 'The Woman in White', and that has been adapted. So authors and adapters have just gone beyond that, back to the essence of good against evil – the evil rising, taking power, then the gradual buildup of forces of light to fight against evil, and your denouement where the evil is defeated. So that's the basic structure. The middle bit is, of course, where everything seems doomed and people die, but you've got that really powerful dramatic three-act kind of structure, which people can go with."

On her early ventures into discovering fictional frights, Julia surprised me by stating "I probably started reading the 'Pan Books of Horror Stories' before I encountered 'Dracula'. That came along later. So I've always been interested in horror and being scared. I love ghost stories and horror stories. Sadly, I can't remember the first time I read 'Dracula' – sometime in my teens, because I loved all things supernatural and scary. This is what we always tell people when they come across the Society – we're not just about Dracula! So it's Frankenstein, it's Jekyll & Hyde, it's Edgar Allan Poe, it's Lovecraft, M.R. James, and all those wonderful literary sources that began it all. And then, of course, you get the people that adapt it and so that's how you go off into film and stage and TV – and that brings in members as well."

The late David J. Skal had some dealings with the Dracula Society, and naturally Julia was keen to discuss this major scholar and analyst in depth. "David was crucial – he first heard about us back in 1989. He knew that we, the Society, owned the Hamilton Deane archive and then he was planning his book 'Hollywood Gothic'. A seminal work, as we all know, because it celebrated Dracula from page to stage to screen and nobody had ever done that before. David wanted photographs, and of course we happen to have photographs from early stage productions as part of our Deane archive, and he used a couple of them in the first edition of 'Hollywood Gothic' in 1990."

"We didn't actually meet him until much later. This was after he'd published 'V is for Vampire' and other books, on Tod Browning and James Whale and Claude Rains. A really important scholar. But he came over in 2012, which is when we presented him with our Lifetime Achievement Award named after Bernard Davies, one of our founders. And it was wonderful to meet him, because then we just talked about all things Dracula and Gothic, talked a lot about Hamilton Deane – and I think had David lived, maybe he would have been the perfect author to publish a biography of Hamilton Deane."

So, on to screen portrayals of the Count – who were Julia's particular favourites? "Oh, that's impossible! Because I do not have a favourite. One's first Dracula is always important, and Chris

We Belong Dead   Page 69

Lee was the first, for me, when I encountered him in *Dracula Prince of Darkness*. So of course Lee obviously has a very important place in my heart. But of course, since then, when I've seen so many adaptations of the novel, I still say Max Schreck is the scariest. He's probably my favourite scary vampire and I love his presence, his otherness, his foreignness. And then later, I came to appreciate Lugosi: he is wonderful! I also think about the Draculas that never were, those initially earmarked for the role, for instance Conrad Veidt whom I would have loved to have seen play Dracula in the 1930s."

"Much as I admire Gary Oldman, he's certainly not a favourite. I think he could have been a much better Dracula in a different interpretation of the role. He doesn't look as Stoker portrayed him, but he's a powerful presence and an excellent actor. And I do also enjoy the humorous ones! I've got affection for George Hamilton, and for Ferdy Mayne. Ferdy looks and acts the part. He's an excellent actor. I loved his portrayal (as Count von Krolock) in *The Fearless Vampire Killers*. Who else can we look at? Oh, even this past year, I have to admit I did enjoy *Renfield* with Nicolas Cage. It was a lot of fun, he was obviously enjoying himself hugely." An additional recommendation was "Argento's 3D *Dracula*. Whatever you think of the film, I think Thomas Kretschmann did an excellent job," while Julia also praised the star of the recent BBC three-parter: "I'd love to see Claes Bang, who I think looked wonderful, in a serious script. Not wishing to denigrate the BBC's intentions, but I do like my 'Dracula' to be taken seriously. I think Claes is a fine actor, and I'd like to see him in a different interpretation of the role."

As Julia had cited Ferdy Mayne as a favourite, I moved the discussion on to faux Draculas, those examples where we see the Count in all but name. I suggested that this perhaps might have been a topic frequently discussed by members of the Society, but was pleased when Julia remarked "well, now you've provided a subject for a future meeting!" She did reveal that their next planned get-together would feature two guests who have both played Dracula on stage, Jonathan Rigby and James Swanton ("that's going to be really exciting!") I mooted Lugosi's Armand Tesla from *The Return of the Vampire* as a key example of a sort of Dracula avatar, only for Julia to reveal that she had "not seen *Return* for quite some time, so it's not uppermost in my mind. More recently I have re-watched Carlos Villarias, in the Spanish version (of Universal's 1931 movie); when compared, Lugosi has the presence, so he's still top. But going off at a tangent, looking at other faux Draculas and the funny ones, there's *Zinda Laash*, the Pakistani Dracula. That is huge fun. Now that's wonderful. Yes, it's a 'Hammer film', but Pakistani style."

Returning to live theatrical production, and the novel being used specifically as source material for the stage, I wanted to get Julia's informed thoughts on the related potential plusses or possible pitfalls. "Interesting. I've seen so many examples of both disasters and successes. I was counting, I've seen five adaptations of 'Dracula' in the past two years. It just demonstrates how people just want to take it and put their own spin on it. There was a very good one in Lewes a couple of years ago, very faithful to the book, excellent performances. And then another recent adaptation in Milton Keynes with what seemed like a cast of thousands – including a choir! – with two actors playing a young Dracula and an old Dracula. I've also seen the lead character played by a woman. It all depends on what your adapter chooses to highlight, to leave out. For example, one adaptation we saw had a major part of it set on the Demeter. So again, that could be difficult for adapters, but there's so much there that people can pick up on." I mentioned the gothic Edward Gorey sets of the 1970s Broadway version and contrasted those against more sparse, basic live takes, with Julia commenting "When it comes down to it, it's got to be 'does it work?' I really don't have a preference. There was an excellent adaptation I saw a few years back which literally just had a very stripped-down stage, but two enormous screens with action projected via film, very little in the way of physical props, visually just two screens and one or two actors, mostly using stills with very little external location, just going from one point of view to another. It was conveyed really imaginatively. And then again, you can do it with puppets! We've seen adaptations where you have the exterior of Dracula's castle, with shadow puppets climbing up and down. We've seen other adaptations where there's just a carriage and curtains and so that one carriage can be the coach in Transylvania, it could be a coach in London, it could be any kind of vehicle with the actors inhabiting that particular scene, depending on what part of the novel you're adapting at the time. But there seems to be so much scope for imaginative directors."

Now let's get back to the Dracula Society. The Society is well known for its globetrotting; what have been the particularly special places that you've visited?

"My first love has to be Eastern Europe, of course, because you have to go eastward and you have to go to the past, because that's where all the ruined castles are. It's part of our appeal that we describe a cobwebby room in a castle as our spiritual home. There are so many! Romania, of course, the Society visits probably about every six or seven years. But I have to single out Orava castle in Slovakia, because that was used by Murnau when he filmed *Nosferatu* in 1922. We've been there three times! Gosh, has it changed over those three visits! The first time we visited, nobody went there. The custodian had to get a key to let us in and we roamed everywhere. The second time, I think it had changed a little bit more. We couldn't get to that little folly where Hutter writes his letter to Ellen. And most recently, last year, of course, we had to go because of the centenary of *Nosferatu* – hordes of people! Totally changed! All the souvenir stalls you might expect were all there, and there's a grand ticket office, but it's still absolutely beautiful and just as Murnau filmed it, all those wonderful locations. So that was special. Okay, then there's the Blood Countess, Elizabeth Bathory – we've been to Čachtice, which is the ruined castle in Slovakia where she was finally imprisoned. We visited that several times, and we will be going again."

"But one favourite place has to be Geneva and the Villa Diodati, because that's where it all started, that's where Frankenstein and Dracula were born. So to go there was kind of special. We went there in 2016, which was the bicentenary of that 'year without a summer', where it all began. We also had to go to Egypt – just once! – because of mummies. Who doesn't love mummies?"

"As long as there's a peg to justify going there, whether it's a film or a piece of literature, then we will endeavour to go there. This year, for example, at the end of May, we're going to Germany – following in Frankenstein's footsteps. So – Castle Frankenstein, because Mary Shelley undoubtedly had heard of it, and possibly visited it, so we'll go there. We'll go to Ingolstadt, where Victor Frankenstein studied, where he dug up his bodies, so that will be great for the imagination. But also we are going to Laupheim – this really is the birth of Frankenstein, because it's where Carl Laemmle, who started Universal Studios and got the whole thing going, was born."

In conclusion, Julia had this to say about the aristocratic and eternally compelling vampire Count: "Dracula is still the most iconic figure in all the history of monsters. He is the king vampire, the lord of the Undead. So, any excuse, really; go and check out *The Last Voyage of the Demeter*, and we can all look forward to Robert Eggers' new adaptation of *Nosferatu*. It just keeps on adapting and mutating. It's a never-ending story: Dracula lives on."

by Paul PD Donaldson

THE LAST VOYAGE OF THE DEMETER

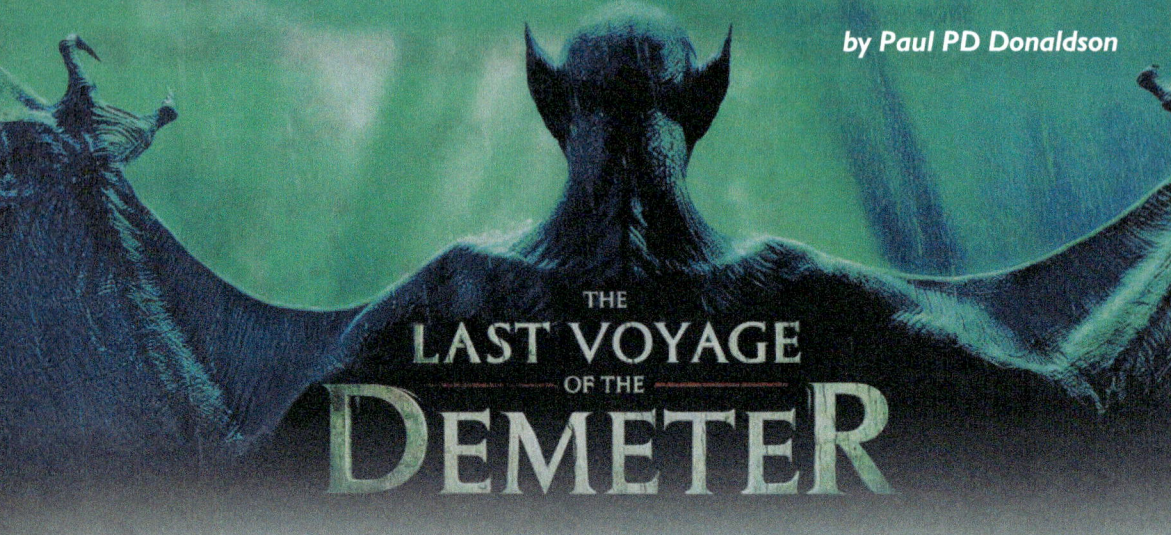

I can first remember hearing about *The Last Voyage of the Demeter* at the time when it was going to be a production by Neil Marshall of *Dog Soldiers* fame, and I started to look forward to it as this episode was always kind of skipped over in any other film releases of the 'Dracula' story – but this time round we get just that, and I for one was looking forward to sitting down and watching this take on the chapter 'The Captain's Log'.

The Last Voyage of the Demeter was ultimately directed by André Øvredal (*Troll Hunter*), and showcases the acting talents of Liam Cunningham, David Dastmalchian, and Corey Hawkins, who deliver cracking performances in their respective roles. Drawing inspiration from Stoker's chapter, 'The Captain's Log' (though see my notes later!), the story unfolds aboard the Russian schooner Demeter. It opens with the police being told about and discovering the wreckage of the Demeter, with them finding the Captain's Log; cut to a wagon train of 24 boxes filled with earth weaving through the land before being loaded onto the Demeter – which is setting sail from Carpathia to London. As the ship begins its voyage, a sense of unease pervades the air. The crew members, unaware of the true nature of their cargo, soon find themselves entangled in a nightmarish ordeal as they are relentlessly pursued by an ominous presence aboard the vessel.

Effectively capturing the atmosphere of impending doom and claustrophobia, the film adeptly uses its setting – the confined space of the ship – to heighten the tension and amplify the sense of isolation. The creaking of the wooden planks, the howling of the wind, and the crashing of the waves create an eerie soundscape that further immerses us on this journey.

The suspense steadily builds as the crew members discover the gruesome fate of their fellow sailors, one by one. Driven to the brink of madness, they desperately try to unravel the mystery behind the malevolent force haunting the ship. The film skilfully employs a combination of CGI & practical effects, plus atmospheric cinematography, to convey the horror that unfolds on board.

I have to give a shout out to some of the cast, starting with the ship's Captain played by Liam Cunningham, who portrays the role with gravitas and intensity. Cunningham effectively conveys the character's growing paranoia and desperation, as he tries to maintain control amidst the mounting chaos and also keep his grandson safe. His commanding presence adds depth and anchors the audience's emotional investment. David Dastmalchian, who is becoming one of my favourite actors (can't wait to see him in *Late Night With The Devil!*), plays Wojchek and delivers a haunting performance as a troubled crew member. His portrayal of the first mate is fantastic, he brings a sense of intensity to the character. Corey Hawkins is great in his role as Clemens – a figure invented for the film. His performance serves as a counterbalance to the mounting terror, offering a glimmer of hope in an otherwise bleak situation.

While *The Last Voyage of the Demeter* holds great potential for a franchise, it unfortunately did not fare well at the box office. Despite this, I thoroughly enjoyed it, largely due to the masterful tension that arises as Dracula picks off the crew one by one.

However, there were a few moments of lacklustre CGI, a common issue in modern big-budget horror films. Though practical effects were present, they were not as prominent as I desired. Personally, I believe that flawed practical effects trump subpar CGI anytime, as they create a more immersive and tangible experience for the audience.

It is worth noting that the inclusion of a wolf's head cane serves as a delightful nod to the original The Wolf Man from 1941. Throughout the film, keen-eyed viewers will spot this reference, which seemed to hint at a potential connection to a new Wolf Man movie – a prospect that unfortunately thus far has not come to fruition. This subtle homage to classic horror adds an extra layer of enjoyment for fans. I also thought that Demeter had a slight Hammer feel to it, particularly with the way it looked. The cinematography and production design deserve special mention for their contribution to the overall atmosphere. The dimly lit corridors of the ship, the weathered and worn wooden interiors, and the ominous shadows cast by flickering lanterns all add to the sense of dread and foreboding. The attention to detail in recreating the setting of a 19th-century sailing vessel is commendable and enhances the authenticity.

It is essential to clarify that although the film's credits claim it is based on the chapter 'The Captain's Log', this statement is not entirely true. More precisely, it draws from Chapter 7 of Stoker's novel titled 'Cutting from 'The Dailygraph,' 8 August (Pasted in Mina Murray's Journal)', which contains the section 'Log of the Demeter'. This distinction ensures a more accurate understanding of the source material and its connection to Stoker's original narrative.

Obviously adapting a single chapter into a full-length movie requires taking some creative liberties, but the essence of Dracula's terrifying and sinister nature remains intact.

'Dracula' is not just a seminal vampire text; it is a cornerstone of horror. It introduces an iconic villain, a heroic protagonist, and sets the stage for the dark and eerie atmosphere that defines vampire lore. While 'Dracula' is celebrated for these elements, Chapter 7 stands out as a standalone piece of chilling fiction, starting with routine entries but soon revealing the presence of Count Dracula himself. As the crew members are preyed upon one by one, the captain struggles to survive. The chapter may be short, but its limited first-person perspective leaves room for expansion.

The Last Voyage of the Demeter finally gives Chapter 7 the attention it deserves, and one I personally always wanted to see. While the movie follows the crew of a cargo ship as they encounter the sinister presence of Count Dracula during their voyage, in order to achieve its nearly two-hour runtime the adaptation adds new elements and characters, such as Clemens, a doctor who joins the crew. These additions provide emotional depth and enhance the storytelling.

Dracula here is a lurking and elusive threat, embodying the essence of terror. He is depicted as a hairless, bony, and feral creature, reminiscent of iconic vampire portrayals from prior films and other media; a kind of cross between Nosferatu, Coppola's Dracula, Salem's Lot and with a touch of 'Doomlord' thrown into the mix. While the physical appearance differs from the book's description, this interpretation succeeds in making Dracula truly frightening.

The climax of both the chapter and the movie sees the Demeter reaching Whitby without any survivors. However, the details leading up to this point diverge. In the film, Clemens and Anna attempt to defeat Dracula, leading to a thrilling escape and a tragic fate for Anna. The movie sets up the potential for a sequel, while the book continues with the main storyline involving the Harkers and Van Helsing.

The film offers a fresh take on a pivotal chapter in 'Dracula'. While it deviates from the source material, it captures the essence of Stoker's work and delivers a scary and exciting vampire tale. Wending its own unique path, it sets the stage for a potential sequel, inviting audiences to continue the hunt for Dracula alongside new characters. We eagerly await the next chapter in this thrilling adaptation.

The novel goes back into its main storyline, involving the Harkers and Van Helsing trying to defeat Dracula, whereas the movie seems to promise a sequel that will follow Clemens on his hunt for the vampire. Given its lack of ties to anything else in the 'Dracula' novel, it seems only fair for it to set up its own path. That being said, Clemens was a sufficiently strong character that you could justify shifting elements of this to craft a new version of the classic 'Dracula' narrative, or to have him hunting vampires and other such monsters. Bring on a sequel to The Last Voyage of the Demeter, we want it! But sadly, because of box office, we likely won't get it.

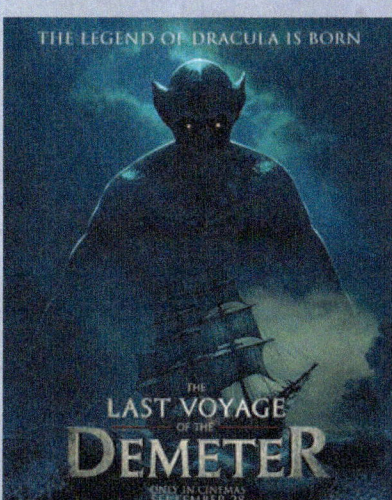

THE UNQUENCHABLE THIRST OF DRACULA

by Parker Stewart

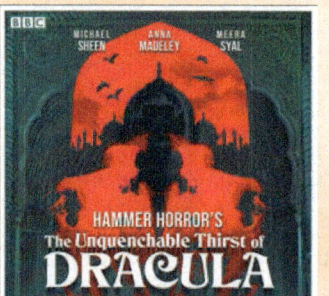

Once lost in the cobwebs and tombs of the 1970s, unable to be resurrected and haunt the screens of cinemas, The Unquenchable Thirst of Dracula emerged alive again via the auspices of the BBC and through the blood-curdling resonance of Michael Sheen's dramatic vocals. Following a 2014 onstage reading at Nottingham's 'Mayhem' film festival run by Chris Cooke and Steven Sheil, with Jonathan Rigby's powerful narration setting the scene while a cast of young actors unveiled this lost treasure, BBC Radio 4 later tasked Mark Gatiss with dramatising this unfilmed Hammer property as a 90-minute audio special just prior to Hallowe'en in 2018.

Featuring an impressive score and incredible acting, the story itself brings a gorgeous view of what could have been another feather in the cap of Hammer's inimitable Dracula classics.

Our story follows Penny, a young London traveler searching for her sister in the uncharted territory of India. Nearly missing her train, she achieves her boarding and settles in, unaware of the events set to take precedence as soon as she arrives.

While aboard, she befriends fellow travelers Prem and Lakshmi, a sitar player and dancer, who are there with their own itineraries in mind. They are set to perform at a palace near some caves – ironically, the same caves Penny's sister was rumored to have disappeared in after meeting an unknown stranger. Their conversations are sweet and gentle, easing all stress Penny once felt at the possibility of missing her train, as the voyage continues to exit the English countryside for the upcoming Indian trip/arrival.

In true Dracula fashion, we learn of an unidentified man aboard who captivates Penny's attention, but only enough to send her mind to a new journey of curiosity. Who is the man and what is so intriguing? Her subconscious cannot refrain from deep thoughts and confusion – however, it is not fully explored.

As the travelers disembark, Prem and Lakshmi are greeted by a Rolls Royce, offer their farewells to their new acquaintance, and wish her well in her voyage. With hopes of finding a hotel in which to lodge, Penny is quickly counselled by Babu, a fellow passenger on the same train. The hotels have all been occupied and filled due to a religious festival occurring at the same time, so she must seek an alternative. Said alternative being a stay with Babu's wife, which Penny accepts. Similar to the infamous Borgo Pass we have seen and heard in the past, Babu offers Penny a ride in his less glamorous "rickety" Morris car.

The greetings of Prem and Lakshmi to the Maharajah and Rani are that of gorgeous Hindu tradition. Connected hands and gentle "*Namaste*" bellow through the palace as the young performers prepare for their exotic routine. Though they are in eloquent trails of thought, their hunger from the trip pauses their display as they plead to the Maharajah for nourishment. The Maharajah grants their wish and allows them to feast. Content and ready to resume, they are interrupted by the introduction of the European guest also in attendance. The guest, proudly announcing himself as Count Dracula, demands a private performance – which the young stars grant.

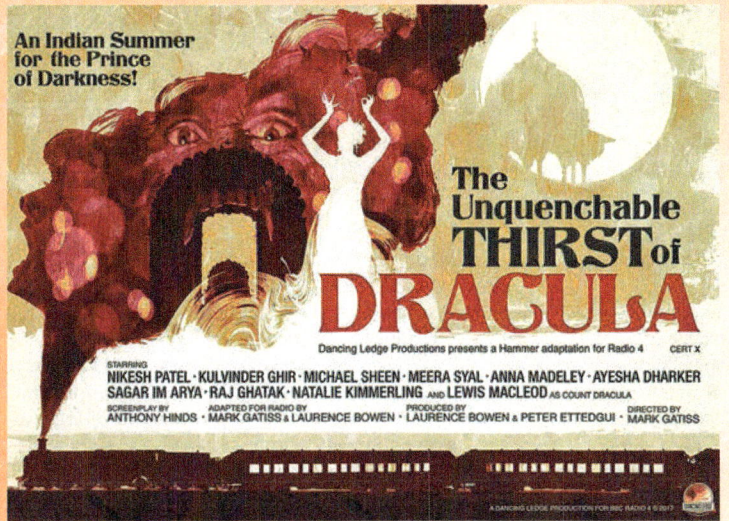

Sitar music and traditional dance bring color to an otherwise gloomy palace. The feelings of pride in their culture are ever-present and enjoyable. But though the glory is felt, the scene shifts into that of downright terror.

Upon the completion of their immaculate dance display, Prem is drugged and removed from the room as Lakshmi becomes Dracula's first official feed of the story. In true Hammer manner, the descriptions are vivid and the sounds can shiver any spine, every bit as effectively as in any of the company's vampire movies. Lakshmi awakens in a room of erotic fantasy and is met by acolytes ready to sacrifice her to the master they have been enslaved to service. With the script possibly paying homage to Vlad the Impaler, she is impaled on a phallic-shaped statue made to resemble the deity of Shiva. Dracula's frustration is immense but his thirst for her is deeper, so he feasts on her completely.

As Prem is released from the drugged state he was in, he is thrown out of the palace where he reconvenes with Penny, unaware of the horror to which his sister had fatally succumbed.

They search through the caves, hoping to find success but instead encountering a king cobra looking to attack. Penny becomes a victim of the vicious cobra but is relieved via the help of Prem's bold thinking.

As they continue to search, they are captured by the infamous Count, looking for another host. He wants Prem since he had previously consumed his sister, but Rani refuses to allow it because her lust for him is stronger than the Count's desire. The scuffle between Dracula and Rani causes his next focus to become Penny, though fortunately, he does not kill her. She begins to turn into a vampire, but one not under the guise of the undead master. She informs him he is not under control, which leads to his frustration. The fury leads Dracula to confront the Rani and Maharajah with the news they are nothing but aristocratic servants, and not leaders or supporters of the religion which they aim to uphold.

Though the story completes spectacularly with the Count assailed by ravenous vultures, the surplus of Indian women who have become this adaptation's version of the 'Brides of Dracula' breaking free of their captivity to stalk the streets of their homeland makes for an unsettling ending, one that proves that the suggested continuation of horror always prevails far deeper than does any resolution-based ending.

Though I have seen countless adaptions of Dracula from Hammer, I must say, this audio take is an immense new favorite. The Indian symbolism, coupled with a perfect symphony of Transylvanian horror, is unique and very well orchestrated. One item I found especially fascinating was seeing how many of my research sources have likened this story to that of *Indiana Jones and the Temple of Doom*, which, in my opinion, is an excellent comparison. Not only is the drama also based on Indian culture, but the sacrificial scenes and torture at the hands of the underground High Priest make for a chilling experience. While the High Priest here doesn't steal hearts and disintegrate the victims as in *Indiana Jones*, you cannot mistake the symbolism and comparison at hand.

It's fascinating and slightly disheartening to believe that *Unquenchable Thirst* could not appear on the big screen, but personally, I believe it's better to have it in an audio fashion. The 'audiobook'-style feeling makes for an even creepier experience because the perceptions and emotions can vary among listeners, yet the vibe is unmistakable. It almost begs my curiosity to know if there were more stories written and conceptualized by Hammer but which were sadly unable to see the light of day and the screens of the cinemas.

As Hammer continues to produce quality horror movies, even to this day, as well as the BBC offering high-quality horror shows such as Claes Bang's Dracula, I wholeheartedly believe – and frankly, I strongly hope – that the possibility for more partnerships with the BBC will be on the horizon.

We Belong Dead   Page 75

Son of Dracula

by Mark Iveson

When my book 'Cursed Horror Stars' got published in 2015, I promoted it through several talks that took place at the Castle Keep in Newcastle city centre, a perfect venue for screening all the classic Universal chillers within the castle's main hall – which is usually freezing, even in the summer.

Prior to giving a talk on Lon Chaney Junior, the organisers asked me to choose the movie that would be screened afterwards. Instead of going for *The Wolf Man* (1941), I opted for a film I always had a soft spot for, *Son of Dracula* (1943).

It may not be best effort from Universal's monster stable, but *Son of Dracula* still holds a special fascination. The script is sluggish, the supporting characters cliched, the rubber bat brings in the required laughs, and the title is a cheat – it's the man himself, or maybe it's his brother, since he goes under the pseudonym of Count Anthony Alucard. The most fatal error in *Son of Dracula* is the miscasting of the main star.

It always puzzled as to me why Bela Lugosi was never considered to repeat the role that made him a star of both stage and screen. Lugosi's Armand Tesla in Columbia's *The Return of the Vampire* (1944) was Dracula in all but name, and the film was intended to be a direct sequel to *Dracula* (1931), but Universal, who had just completed *Son of Dracula* threatened Columbia with a plagiarism lawsuit, forcing the studio to change the vampire's name.

The Return of the Vampire did well at the box office and whether Universal liked it or not, Lugosi is playing Dracula, right down to the cape, and with less of the over-the-top mannerisms. Judging by his performance as Tesla, surely casting him in *Son of Dracula* would have made it a better movie. Lugosi was reported to be furious that he wasn't considered for the role.

With Lugosi firmly entrenched in low budget chillers for Monogram and Boris Karloff treading Broadway in *Arsenic and Old Lace*, Universal had a new horror star to promote in the massive shape of Lon Chaney Junior, the 'Master Character Creator', although there was very little of that on screen. An actor of limited range, who reluctantly took his father's name, Universal previously cast him as the tragic werewolf Lawrence Talbot and had him donning Karloff's legendary makeup in *The Ghost of Frankenstein* (1942), a daunting task for any actor, and while Chaney had the physique, he lacked the facial mobility that made Karloff's performance unforgettable. As he had also played Kharis the Mummy in *The Mummy's Tomb* (1942), the Universal's executives decided to cast Lon as the famous vampire lord, adding another classic monster to his resume. At least the role didn't require heavy makeup.

Son of Dracula is notable for the Count's first visit to America, a place he would go to on and off over the next few years. This trip took him to the Dark Oaks Plantation in Louisiana as guest to the wealthy Caldwell family; like all rich Southern gentlemen, the patriarch (George Irving) happens to be a colonel!

Masquerading as Count Alucard (yes, we all know the drill), the Count has been invited by the colonel's daughter Kay (Louise Allbritton). After meeting the Count on a trip to Europe, Kay has become increasingly reclusive, delving into the black arts and spending her time with toothless old gypsy Queen Zimba (a bizarre performance from Adeline De Walt Reynolds), who quickly succumbs to a fatal heart attack on the sudden arrival of the rubber bat. Dying from laughter might have been the cause of her coronary!

Kay's honoured guest fails to turn up at the party, although his luggage had arrived earlier that day, piquing the interest of family friend Dr Brewster (Frank Craven) who notices the Alucard/Dracula logo under the coat of arms.

The other party guests include Kay's childhood sweetheart Frank Stanley (Robert Paige), who is concerned about his fiancée's melancholic mood. He has good reason to take a dislike to the missing Alucard when Kay suddenly breaks off their engagement without explanation. Another concerned guest is her sister Claire (Evelyn Ankers). While watching the film at the Castle Keep following my talk on Chaney, a friend of mine noticed that the two leading ladies were not wearing underwear under their very tight dresses, quite a risqué move under the staid noses of the Hays Code, and another good reason to watch the movie!

The Colonel dies suddenly, coinciding with the Count turning up after the party ends. In a new twist, the Colonel's had his will changed to leave his house to Kay and everything else to Claire. When Kay marries the Count, they move into the house, to the anger of the jilted Robert, who is determined to find out what exactly is going on, although he's not exactly subtle about it. Confronting Alucard with a pistol isn't going to solve the issue either, and when he opens fire, the bullet passes through Alucard and mortally wounds Kay. Understandably, a confused Robert quickly goes off the rails.

In the meantime, the Alucard/Dracula thing is playing on Dr Brewster's mind, especially after the delirious Robert turns up at his home saying he has killed Kay. Brewster arrives at her house and finds Kay very much alive (albeit undead), and when the comic police turn up the next day, they find her dead in her coffin. What the hell is going on? Now under suspicion of murder, Brewster enlists the help of Hungarian academic Professor Laszlo (J. Edward Bromberg), who knows a thing or two about vampires.

Son of Dracula was originally a story by Curt Siodmak, who was commissioned by Universal in May 1942 to write a script, only for him to be removed from the production when his brother Robert was hired as director. "They only wanted one Siodmak," recalled Curt about their sibling rivalry, further adding that, "This lasted 71 years, until he died. He started on *Son of Dracula*, and they gave him $150 a week. Two years later he was making $2,000 a day at Universal."

Curt Siodmak managed to get the last laugh. Chaney was only required to wear a moustache, but his difficult attitude and violent, drunken outbursts that often got him into trouble at Universal continued during the making of *Son of Dracula*, resulting in the actor smashing a vase over Robert Siodmak's head.

We Belong Dead

Robert Siodmak wasn't too thrilled about his brother's screenplay either. "Universal sent me the script for *Son of Dracula*. It was terrible. It had been knocked together in a few days." With screenwriter Eric Taylor brought onboard, Siodmak started to tinker around with the story. "We did a lot of rewriting, and the result wasn't bad. It wasn't good, but some scenes had a certain quality."

Siodmak managed to make *Son of Dracula* different to the standard Universal programmers. The film works because it has a unique poetry about it. The mist-shrouded Louisiana swamplands couldn't be more ideal for the Count's new home. The most memorable moment sees Dracula's coffin emerging from the marshes and the vapour rising from the coffin to form an all too real vampire. It is an eerie scene that adds to the film's unusual atmosphere, and Siodmak keeps things ticking at a reasonable pace, overcoming the flaws in the haphazard script.

Son of Dracula was unable to correct the one major flaw – Lon Chaney Junior. Not looking remotely like a European aristocrat, the actor is too big and all-American to convincingly pass himself as a vampire nobleman in traditional formal evening attire. Chaney is a bad choice to play Dracula, and it makes one wonder why Universal didn't just hire Lugosi instead.

To his credit, Chaney battles extremely hard against miscasting and manages to achieve a decent performance; his interpretation can be classed as a forerunner to Christopher Lee's Dracula. Chaney may lack Lugosi's aristocratic bearing, but he puts his massive physique to good use by creating a terrifying and formidable vampire presence, and one unafraid of getting into a fight, which happens during the thrilling climax with Frank – cue the *Sherlock Holmes* signature tune as the sun rises to finish off Dracula.

Through no fault of his own, Chaney's Dracula turns out to be a complete sap, since his new bride is only using him to achieve immortality for herself and her former fiancé, who is unaware of all this. It also makes Dracula a sympathetic figure because he has been led astray by a woman with a more sinister agenda. Chaney may not be able to satisfy many Dracula or Lugosi fans, but he deserves ten out of ten for playing the role with complete conviction.

The real villain of the piece is Katherine 'Kay' Caldwell, played with sinister relish by Louise Allbritton, in a vampish (sorry!) role that equals Gloria Holden's memorable turn as *Dracula's Daughter* (1936), but without the redeeming features. Initially withdrawn from her family and friends because of her obsession with the occult, when she materialises in Robert's police cell, she explains her sinister motives that reveal an evil side to her, especially when she intends to kill her caring sister and the affable Dr Brewster for knowing too much. It's an unusual and effective performance, played with quiet menace by Allbritton, who effortlessly alternates from vulnerable heiress to creepy *femme fatale* with only a slight glance. Dracula would have been better off staying a bachelor.

Son of Dracula is interesting for having the romantic leads of Allbritton and Robert Paige as completely flawed individuals; rare for a Universal chiller where the hero and heroine are always sweetness and light. Instead, we see the complete destruction of the couple. While Katherine's obsession with immortality has corrupted her, Paige's Frank is heading towards a downward spiral into madness. Thinking he has killed Katherine and then receiving ghostly visitations from her, he is on the verge of a mental breakdown, especially after his encounter with Dracula and knowing that no one will believe him because of his emotional state.

Frank finally regains his sanity after disposing of Alucard, but it is too late for him. Now a broken man, he pays one more visit to see his undead former fiancée resting in her coffin (what's wrong with a bed?), and, realising she is no longer the woman he loved, he decides against the immortality she has offered him and sets fire to her crypt. Frank has murdered her in the eyes of the law and destroyed himself in the process. This gives *Son of Dracula* one of the most downbeat endings ever to be seen in a horror film.

This is all brilliantly conveyed by Robert Paige's excellent performance. Not the most charismatic of leading men, Paige is a solid character actor, which later became useful when he moved into television in early middle age. The part is sketchy and requires little more than him going off the rails at regular intervals, but Paige adds depth and pathos to the proceedings, playing a man who sees his world falling apart but is unable to comprehend why.

Son of Dracula boasts two Van Helsing figures in the shape of the amateur detective Dr Brewster and vampire expert Professor Laszlo. Frank Craven provides the film's all-important glue with an intelligent performance while J. Edward Bromberg quietly brings out the right kind of Van Helsing intensity when needed, especially when he briefly confronts Alucard. Universal's regular horror scream queen Evelyn Ankers doesn't have much to do except look glamorous and concerned (no screaming here), but she makes the most of her limited screen time.

It is fair to say that *Son of Dracula* is something of a curate's egg. It has its faults, the star performance is hit and miss, and the climax too shocking for those expecting a happy ending, but it has a hypnotic quality throughout, and still retains the power to fascinate with every viewing.

STOKER ON STOKER

Dacre Stoker, interviewed by Ian Talbot Taylor

Ian: I did meet you once before at Whitby when there was the Hammer Glamour event, and I really enjoyed the presentation you did then.

Dacre: Well, they've evolved since then. I'm constantly finding new things and integrating them into 'Stoker on Stoker', with emphasis on different things.

Ian: I've very often spent time on the Northeast coast and any time I've gone to Whitby, for many years, I've always gone to the same fish and chip restaurant which, you said in your presentation, might have been part of the Whitby Library.

Dacre: The Quayside? Absolutely, it was! That was the building that was the library, the museum and the baths. That building was where Bram discovered the name Dracula in a book by William Wilkinson.

Ian: It raised the hairs on the back of my neck because I've been a massive Dracula fan since I was a child and the idea that I was being drawn to somewhere that was...

Dacre: I know! There's something at work there, isn't there? It's bringing this connection because that holiday of Bram's was really his genesis. Although he had other ideas floating around in his head, authors often need, and I think Bram was influenced by, place. Obviously, Whitby was a place that spoke to him in some way because up until that point his notes were kind of discombobulated and he had ideas to set the story – not in Transylvania – but actually in Styria, and he was going to have the Count land in Dover. That one holiday in Whitby, because he finds the Dracula name in the Wilkinson book, and because he falls in love with Whitby, finds the 'Dmitri', turns it to 'Demeter' and everything else, that changes everything. And for you there's almost a talisman for your passion!

Ian: One of the things I love about that area is it doesn't matter what the weather is like, it's always got a great atmosphere. I'm not surprised that it might have inspired him.

Dacre: I'm sure it did. I've probably been there a dozen times now and this last spring when I was there in the end of May, I observed something you've probably seen, but I hadn't seen it before. I'd heard about it, one of these weather/heat inversions, where you have cold water/ hot air, and you have this massive mist that comes in. And Bram described it. He merged all these different weather events for the perfect storm that brought in Dracula, and when I asked the tour guide he looked at me very matter-of-factly and he said "This coastal town, as many do, they have folklore – of the souls of those undead coming to seek rest, and in Whitby we have this interesting history of the suicide graves, and also these graves of bodies that died in Greenland and elsewhere. And these mists are their ghosts that are coming back to seek their resting place". And then I went back to Chapter 7 (of 'Dracula') and thought 'That's what Bram exactly described, the mist coming in, the souls of the dead with their ghostly touch.

I was on top of St. Mary's Church filming with a friend of mine and he caught the whole Abbey being just engulfed in about fifteen minutes with the sea mist that came in. It's so eerie! So, on the most beautiful of days you can get that, and of course at night-time it's just perfect for any kind of horror graphic novel!

Ian: Do you think Bram would have realised just how much 'Dracula' would still be celebrated, loved, studied?

Dacre: It's an emotional question because when you realise Bram's life had involved some highs and lows, some struggles… when you really think about him finding his place in the world, to become a creative, a man of the theatre, it was not easy. He was the only one of the family who was not a scientist or an artist: two sisters – artists, three doctors, one other civil servant. And that was what the Stokers

We Belong Dead Page 79

Courtesy of Greg Lepera

did, elevate themselves in society by education, hard work, determination, and Bram was on that course, but his passion drove him to the theatre and then, as I discovered in the journal that he wrote whilst he was working at Dublin Castle as a clerk, which would have been very boring, he really wanted to write and express himself. So, he went to London and did his writing on the side, which wasn't tremendously successful, but I also think that wasn't driving him at the time. It was a passion to express himself. His passion was to help Henry Irving change the role of theatre in society and to make it respectable and all the rest that goes with that. So, I think he derived tremendous satisfaction by Irving's success, him being knighted and so on.

But it's also human nature that your own endeavour... it's nice to get that recognised. And he did in a certain way, I'm sure he read the reviews and what people get wrong, they say the reviews were not very good about 'Dracula'. There were a few not very good, but most of them were and I'm sure that he's a man that read his reviews like he would have for theatrical reviews. A friend of mine, John Browning, found out that there were many, many reviews worldwide – and had Bram had a chance to read those? Probably not, but the book had good reviews. But certainly, he wouldn't have known the success because it didn't get on the stage until 1924 and he was long gone in 1912.

Would he be surprised? Most likely, but I think he had an idea, when he was well aware of the interest in the occult and spiritualism, and he was a Freemason, that this was something beginning to rise up. This interest. Nowhere near the level it is now, but I think he'd be surprised, he'd be humbled, but also, I think it would give him a wonderful satisfaction. As I say, he was a theatre manager. What a great run that would be, 127 years, even better than 'Les Miserables', you know? To keep going at a high level, never out of print, and it's always being adapted, people are always trying to make a new adaption on stage, on screen, so I think somewhere he's greatly satisfied.

Ian: When you were growing up, how aware of the great family heritage were you?
Dacre: Surprisingly little. When you think about information wasn't available.

When I was in University, I did take an interest, and that's when I read the 'In Search of Dracula' by McNally and Florescu. I think I was the only one in the family that knew about it, so I became the expert. It didn't really change life, not until about 2003/04 when Ian Holt asked me if I wanted to get involved in writing the sequel, 'Dracula the Un-Dead', that I really decided that now it's time to do this properly, go to these conferences, go to the museums, find the notes and really get to know this, rather than just general interest.

Ian: Which came first, the idea to create an official, family-endorsed follow-up novel, or the talks, the tours, the presentations?
Dacre: My wife and I had an interest in our own genealogy. My father was one of three brothers, and he was the first to go, and the others passed away. The oldest one used to send me by fax some of the information about the family and George Stoker, Bram's youngest brother. We flew up to Canada to visit him when he was diagnosed with heart failure. He wanted to show us all the stuff. So that got the ball rolling. It helped me find where 'all the bodies were'. Where the notes were, the books where we could find things, but it wasn't until co-authoring 'Dracula the Un-Dead'... and that was a real nexus point. Now you're going to get serious, you're going to get the book published, you're going to represent the family, Bram Stoker's going to be a character in the book, and you'd better know what the heck you're doing. It took two years to get up to speed, and at that point I was happy to contribute with Ian Holt to write that book. But in the process, I found some very

interesting things that led onto other things. I found Bram's lost journal in his great-grandson's attic in the Isle of Wight. It was during that research that I found those notes, I found where the Rosenbach Museum notes were and got intimately knowledgeable with them. I became aware of where the 'Dracula' typescript was in Seattle, Washington. I went to conferences and discovered the names of biographers and who was good and who was not.

That was the defining two-year period that set me on a course. We're doing the sequel first, we're gonna publish the journal with the help of Dr. Elizabeth Miller, a real expert, but during that time I realised there was a lot more to this story about how the book was written, how it could be fictionalised. Bram's life was so interesting. Different ideas got worked into this and part of that was the discovery by Hans de Roos of the Icelandic edition of 'Dracula' that had a different foreword. It was like building a puzzle and I was in a unique position. I'm grabbing pieces of this puzzle, discoveries that other people had made, putting it together with somebody else's discoveries, and making my own when I slotted in a third piece. That's how I came up with this whole idea of the prequel to 'Dracula', which has been the most popular book, written with J. D. Barker, about what if this story was real, based on letters, the missing 102 pages. All those little pieces finally came together, and to this day I'm still finding more little pieces that work their way into short stories, even the one I'm working on right now, the story of the summer that Bram actually wrote 'Dracula' when he was up north of Whitby in Cruden Bay, Scotland. I found information by going there, meeting a local expert, helping me to open my eyes to things that Bram actually did, people that he'd met, and lo and behold, Emily Gerard, a Scottish writer wrote about Transylvanian folklore. And now I'm leading trips to Transylvania, visiting the city where she lived! So, all these little pieces keep coming together, giving me more fodder to include in the lectures, to include in documentary films, to include in fictional stories that have a sense of reality to them.

Ian: I did enjoy the books very much. It is nice that Bram's there, and in the first one's theatre setting which ties in with his career. It enhances the whole thing.

Dacre: You know very well because you've been to Whitby, Bram made 'Dracula' seem real, and he did it for a specific purpose. Gothic horror had been around, 'Frankenstein' and others, but needed to make his a little bit different… actually based on real things. They had a supernatural element to them, but he made them seem real by basing them

Courtesy of Colin Hamilton

on real places, real people, real events, and that's the tone that comes naturally to me. I'm not just copying him and I'm not sure if its genetic or just because I've researched him so much that I feel it's the right thing to do. That's what I like to do, when I've found places that he has been, where he stayed, people he met. By integrating that into a story you get this ability, this strange way to create this wilful suspension of disbelief. The reader is tricked into believing this is possibly very real.

Courtesy of Bram Stoker Festival

Ian: It's interesting that 'Dracula' becomes the massively well known one, and with so many screen adaptions, and yet he wrote many other books, a handful being of the same genre, but other than the odd film here or there they've not become as incredibly well known. As if magic just struck with 'Dracula'.
Dacre: 'Dracula's Guest' has got a fair amount of attention because of the name. I've now been able to prove that that was once part of the 'Dracula' manuscript because I've actually seen the manuscript and where it's crossed out. But I'm saddened that 'The Mystery of the Sea' hasn't got more attention, a story that he wrote whilst he was at Cruden Bay, similar to 'Dracula' in many ways – there's real-life people in a real-life location much like Whitby and there's supernatural elements that get twisted in. There obviously is a big treasure which is different but there are ghosts and so on. 'The Jewel of Seven Stars' got adapted; and later got turned into a Tom Cruise movie at Universal. So, there's been a little attention.

I've adapted one of his short stories, 'The Squaw' into a graphic novel, with a good friend of mine, Chris McAuley. We've changed the name for politically correct reasons to 'The Virgin's Embrace'. It really opened my eyes to the process of turning short stories into graphic novels, and the expense involved in doing it! But it was well worth it because it's a really good story, it's horrifying. I do have plans to do more of that. That's my way of contributing to the legacy, to get some of his other works out into different mediums.

Ian: You've travelled the world doing presentations. You must be feeling the love and positivity attached to this?
Dacre: I had no idea at the beginning what 'Dracula' meant to many people. Even though it's never been out of print since 1897 there are lot of people that don't read the book, but they know it. Then there's a lot of people who really do read it and read it repeatedly because they *get it*. This story is multi-layered, sort of like an onion. You can read it at one level – it's not an easy read – and you fight your way through some of Bram's garbled dialects, and sometimes unnecessary details, but nonetheless it's a really fascinating story if you just take the time and don't get bogged down on dialects and the details and so on. Every time they read it, people tell me they find different things that pop out to them. You only get that if you do that repeatedly. People will say "I first read it at twelve" and I say, "That's a difficult book to read at twelve." "Yes, but I read it every second year".

So, it is astonishing what a member of my family's impact has been on literature. And then you look at the countless adaptions. A friend of mine did a book on Dracula visual media and found over 700 different movies with a Dracula citation in it, not a movie about Dracula but with Dracula in it. Hundreds of comics and stage adaptations. It's ginormous, when you really think of how it has affected different people and authors who have

Page 82

We Belong Dead

taken from it, screenwriters, playwrights and so on.

At the beginning, many thought that I was just jumping on the coattails of Bram and going to take advantage of the name. After the first books, seeing the research that I've done, really good, decent, hard work, they realise that I'm a contributor to the family's legacy, not a taker. I'll be honest, you don't make a lot of money doing this, but you make a lot of friends, travel to a lot of places, see some very interesting things, have some great adventures. Very satisfying.

Ian: Of the screen adaptions, which do you think is the definitive one?
Dacre: Definitive, to me, would mean the most faithful to the novel. I think many people would agree that is the Louis Jourdan version that the BBC did back in '77. It's dark, it's not glitzy, it's not a lot of special effects, but that's most faithful to the novel. Then there is successful: the 1931 version, very different. That really is an adaptation of the stage play but people don't always get that. When that one was purchased by Universal, they bought the rights to the stage play. Harker was changed to Renfield. They do that often because so many set changes had to be eliminated from the novel to make the stage play to then make a film. But then you fast-forward to '92, the Coppola version. This is one of the things that gets me. The name *Bram Stoker's Dracula* is not really accurate. It's mostly Jim Hart – who I respect and have become friends with – the screenwriter. *'Jim Hart's Dracula Based on Bram Stoker's Dracula'*. He will freely admit he added the love element to it, because in 1992, to have a popular vampire movie, it needed to have a love story. Nothing to do with what Bram did. Still, with an all-star cast, incredible costumes and good effects, it's a very successful movie and it did a lot for the genre. It actually did so much that Ian Holt was so taken by it that that had a big effect on the writing of 'Dracula the Un-Dead'. It even affected us in our writing because we did think about what the fans wanted at the time.

Those to me are big, but I will say that I'm so glad that *The Last Voyage of the Demeter,* which I know has not been easy to see in the UK, has come back to sort of a good old-fashioned horror film. The Dracula is the type of Dracula Bram created. Not a lot of unnecessary sex, good violence, a lot of jump scares and claustrophobia inside the ship. To me, that's a route back to the type of movie that I like to see. Unfortunately, it didn't do great at the box office so maybe that's an indication that people want the super CGI and everything else, like *Dracula Untold* which was a decent movie, but it had nothing to do with Bram's story, it had to do with how Vlad the Impaler possibly became a vampire, which is something else.

Ian: I love the Hammer films myself, but in order to have a clear, concise tale they just whittled it down for *Dracula* (1958).
Dacre: Exactly. There was so much action, so many different perspectives, which was such an interesting part of the book, all in these letters and journals coming out of people's heads. Because it wasn't just pure narrative storytelling it's not easy to adapt. But if you want to you can take the different characters, sometimes they merge the characters, sometimes they take them out, sometimes you change where Carfax Abbey is, move it around. All those things have been done for the sake of movie budgets, simplicity, but that's just what makes it interesting because if it was all the same, a pure-on adaptation of the novel, we'd get kind of bored with it. As it is, a new one comes out: "Ooh, what are they doing now? I hope it's a realistic take on the story."

We're still striving for that. While it's still out there I'm still going to the theatres looking for it.

Ian: And what's next for you, Dacre?
Dacre: I'm trying to do a Bram Stoker biopic. It hasn't been done. I would really love to see it. I've got treatments, I've got contacts in the theatre and film world that are looking at them. I think the story of Bram Stoker, accumulating events in his life, the stories that came into his awareness, the things that he studied in the different books in the London Library and the Whitby Library… nowadays, so much can be edited, taking bits and pieces from locations and plugging them in together, sort of backstories. For instance, I can envisage Bram walking into the Whitby Library, opening up the Wilkinson book and then the viewer seeing all these scenes of Vlad the Impaler being depicted as the Devil and the dragon, and that could be Bram's imagination as he's reading the book by William Wilkinson, and we know how it got into his story and can see him sitting down writing it. That's my next biggest goal, to have that on film. Maybe I need to put that in book form first and that's something I might do.

Now that technology is so advanced, the other one I'd like to have is an electronic version of the book 'Dracula' with *moving* images so that you could actually click onto a page as you're reading the story and get to the end of a chapter, and you could have a menu of things to click on and you could see the notes he took or where he got the information. How did he learn about going to Klausenburg? How did he get Harker into the Borgo Pass? You can actually see the map that he had in the library.

Those are down the road as well as continuing to find new things to put in my Stoker lectures, continue to take my tours, lead people to Whitby, Robin Hood's Bay and Cruden Bay and to Transylvania. I thank you for your continuing interest.

ARGENTO'S DRACULA

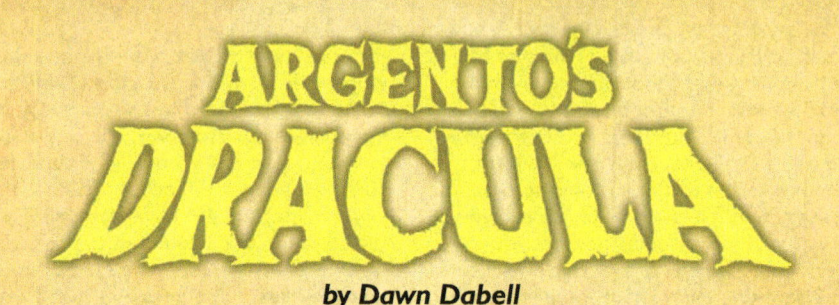

by Dawn Dabell

Widely panned and sometimes cited as the worst Dracula movie ever made, it's hard to argue that *Dracula di Dario Argento* (aka *Dracula 3D*) is anything but unloved. A smattering of hardy souls stick up for it from time to time ("oh yes!" – editor), but the general consensus among horror fans and casual movie-goers is that it sucks (pardon the pun). I'm certainly not here to try to change anybody's mind (my conscience prevents me from heartily recommending this greatly maligned version of Stoker's perennially popular novel), but I will admit it has a few positives which are too often overlooked, and there are effective scenes scattered within the wider mess. While it's true that many of the cast members belong on a spectrum of awfulness somewhere between the amateurish and the downright terrible, at least three of the actors involved rise above the material to give performances which, if not exactly good, are at least intriguing. More about them later.

One of the recurring criticisms levelled at this movie is that it is somewhat unworthy (e.g. far below the once-high standards) of its director Dario Argento. Argento had enjoyed an extraordinary run of classics between 1970 and the mid '80s – helming the likes of *The Bird with the Crystal Plumage* (1970), *Deep Red* (1975), *Suspiria* (1977), *Tenebrae* (1982) and *Opera* (1987) – but sometime after, his Midas touch deserted him and it began to look like he'd lost the ability to make movies that were universally adored by the horror fraternity. You'll still find fans who speak highly of such films as *Trauma* (1993), *The Stendahl Syndrome* (1996) or the TV episode *'Pelts'* (2006), but for every loyal Argento acolyte there seem to be three or four others who grumble bitterly about him being "past it" and feel he never again replicated the brilliance of those early halcyon days. They're not entirely wrong, either. I don't get the sense, for example, that Argento poured his heart and soul into this Dracula adaptation. In fact, if I'm being brutally honest, it feels like he was simply glad to have a job, even if it meant tapping into the popularity of screen vampires (2012 was, after all, the height of the *Twilight* craze) and contemporary audiences' appetite for 3D. Argento's *Dracula* feels like a 'gun-for-hire' assignment rather than a passion project. That said, it does offer a few glimpses of the old magic and occasional bursts of trademark gore.

Argento had resisted making a version of Dracula for decades, claiming he couldn't come up with a fresh angle to justify revisiting such oft-filmed material. The resurgence of 3D prompted him to change his mind and give it a go. The resulting film was shown at Cannes in 2012, opening with an on-screen tag expressing thanks to the Ministry of Cultural Affairs in Italy for its funding contribution, as well as claiming (earnestly if hilariously) that the film "is acknowledged to have national cultural relevance". (Hey, if the opportunity is there to put some important-sounding bullshit at the start of your film, you'd do it, right?) Critics and audiences were unimpressed, and the pic was almost instantly lumbered with a rotten reputation that it hasn't managed to shake – and isn't likely to – more than a decade on.

The opening 15 minutes are tough to endure. On my first viewing, I was strongly tempted to switch off. The theremin score is bad enough, but ghastly digital effects – resembling something from a computer game – are a further hindrance, and the acting in these early scenes is ropey in the extreme. The script seems off-key too, with characters behaving and speaking very unconvincingly. There's some early sex and nudity which feels like it's been shoehorned in to generate softcore thrills rather than natural story progression. The story proper gets underway with the arrival of Jonathan Harker (Unax Ugalde), and at this point things begin to improve. Ugalde himself is pretty underwhelming as Harker, not helped by bland dubbing (or possibly looping), but at least things start moving meaningfully once he arrives.

The locations and sets are actually quite pleasing to the eye. The whole story takes place in a fictional town called Passburg (which sounds more Germanic than Transylvanian). Numerous scenic spots in northern Italy are used for the exteriors, and several evocative interiors are utilised for the indoor scenes. To accommodate the 3D aspects, most of the internal and external scenes were shot in broad natural daylight or on very well-lit sets. This helps to capture the majesty of the beautiful surroundings, but an unwanted side-effect is that it lessens the dark, foreboding atmosphere so desperately required. How can you feel scared or even mildly chilled when everything takes place against such a bright, sunny, gay backdrop? Dracula does not travel to England in this version, remaining instead in his own territory (Harker arrives to catalogue Dracula's extensive library, not to help him buy a property on British soil like in most other versions.) Cue a lot of cheery, sun-drenched location lensing which doesn't complement the horror aspects.

One facetious reviewer remarked: "Cheap CGI, meet Dario Argento. Dario Argento, meet cheap CGI." I agree to a point that the less-than-stellar effects hamper the film. Neither Argento nor his cinematographer, the prolific Luciano Tovoli, seem at ease with the digital shooting style they are using, and the film never quite looks right as a result. Several years ago I bought a new television and had to turn off the motion smoothing setting (nicknamed the 'soap opera effect', because it makes even the most grandly shot movies, like *Lawrence of Arabia*, look like daytime soaps). Argento's *Dracula* has a visual quality comparable to the 'soap opera effect', and it is really rather distracting. The low-grade digitised FX and soap-style photography pull the viewer out of the story, lessening their fear, preventing them from becoming totally engrossed in what is taking place. One particularly laughable scene involves Dracula assuming the guise of a giant praying mantis – it's an admirably original idea on paper but pretty terrible on screen.

The best scene involves Dracula morphing into a swarm of flies before materialising in vampire form in an inn where several men are discussing how to defy him. He savagely kills the conspirators, slicing throats, ripping off heads and impaling them with swords. Argento lets loose in this sequence, serving up inventive deaths and plentiful gore. It's also one of the rare moments when the cinematography rises above its flat visual quality.

I mentioned at the start of this article that three actors stand out from the rest. The first is Marta Gastini as Mina Harker. While her line delivery is occasionally amateurish, she shows more emotion than expected and tries, with varying levels of success, to give the character some dimension. The next is Thomas Kretschmann as Dracula. Although sometimes too quiet and lacking the flamboyance of Lugosi or the animal sensuality of Lee, he creates a melancholic, tormented Dracula capable of flying into occasional violent rages. From certain angles, he resembles Daniel Craig; from others, there's a hint of Liam Neeson about him. His interpretation of the character is very muted, as far removed from the flamboyant style Gary Oldman adopted in *Bram Stoker's Dracula* (1992) as you can get, but it works quite well. Lastly, there's Rutger Hauer as Van Helsing. I was initially underwhelmed by him, sensing a lack of effort and energy, but when rewatching the film I noticed he tries to play the character as an old, frail, wearily courageous type who draws upon years of experience to fight the vampires, rather than sheer brawn.

So, yes, it's lower-tier Argento; yes, the cinematography and digital effects aren't great; yes, there are some iffy performances (Asia Argento in particular comes across like she's just finished a heavy session on the hash pipe, plus her nude scene makes me feel pretty uncomfortable since her dad is the director); and, yes, I can understand why there are many people out there who roundly ridicule this movie. But it boasts a few aspects I like, and I think its reputation as the worst Dracula movie of them all is somewhat unfair. It's not amazing, but it does contain a few things that warrant a look.

ANIMATED DRACULAS

by Jason D. Brawn

As an avid lover of this vampiric character, my earliest introduction to Bram Stoker's seminal creation was not reading the novel, nor seeing the movies, like Christopher Lee or Bela Lugosi's portrayal, or even the comic books like Marvel's 'The Tomb of Dracula' and 'Scream! – The Dracula File'. It was watching *Scooby-Doo, Where Are You!* (1969-1970) that introduced me to Count Dracula, in the episode *'A Gaggle of Galloping Ghosts'*.

Terrified by the vampire lord's demeanor, I was never discouraged by the Count's grim visage. Instead, I became a fanatic, noticing the Count's depiction in many cartoons shows like:

Groovie Goolies (1970-1972)
Spider-Woman: 'Dracula's Revenge' (1979)
Drak Pack (1980)
Spider-Man and His Amazing Friends: 'The Transylvanian Connection' (aka 'The Bride of Dracula!') (1983)

And not to forget *Mad Monster Party?* (1967), which I first saw back in August 1983 on ITV as a nine-year-old, and the first horror-themed animated feature film using stop-motion. This was while I braved to watch the countless Universal and Hammer films and eventually got to read the novel at the tender age of 11.

Growing up in the seventies and eighties, there were not many animated shows or films that featured Count Dracula – and please note that the shows that I already mentioned featured other monsters working alongside Dracula, like Frankenstein and the Wolfman. It is interesting that Dracula was never the sole villain, and some animated shows and films did feature a lead vampire, loosely based on Dracula, like the depiction of Count Magnus Lee in *Vampire Hunter D* (1985) and Baron Meier Link in its superior sequel *Vampire Hunter D: Bloodlust* (2000).

Mickey Mouse cartoon *Mickey's Gala Premier* (1933), a short film featuring a representation of Bela Lugosi, in his Dracula guise, attending an all-star premiere laughing alongside Frankenstein's Monster and Mr. Hyde, could be Count Dracula's animated debut.

Let us return to *Mad Monster Party?* A personal favourite that now has a cult following of rabid horror fans who grew up on a diet of Universal Monsters. Scientist Baron Boris von Frankenstein (Boris Karloff) sends out a group of messenger bats to invite every monster to his Isle of Evil in the Caribbean Sea. The monsters summoned are:

Count Dracula
The Werewolf
The Hunchback of Notre Dame
The Invisible Man
Dr. Jekyll and Mr. Hyde
The Gill-man (*Creature from the Black Lagoon*)
The Mummy

Other monsters included in this film, but already resident within Baron Frankenstein's castle isle are:

Frankenstein's Monster "Fang"
The Monster's Mate

Regardless of the monster meet-up, the Baron has achieved the secret of destruction and plans to retire as head of the "Worldwide Organisation of Monsters". This musical comedy produced by Rankin/Bass Productions for Embassy Pictures – later to bring us *The Fog* (1980), *The Howling* (1981), *Escape from New York* (1981) and *Swamp Thing* (1982) – marked a resurgence in popularity during the sixties, thanks to horror TV sitcoms like *The Addams Family* (1964-1965) and *The Munsters*

Page 86   We Belong Dead

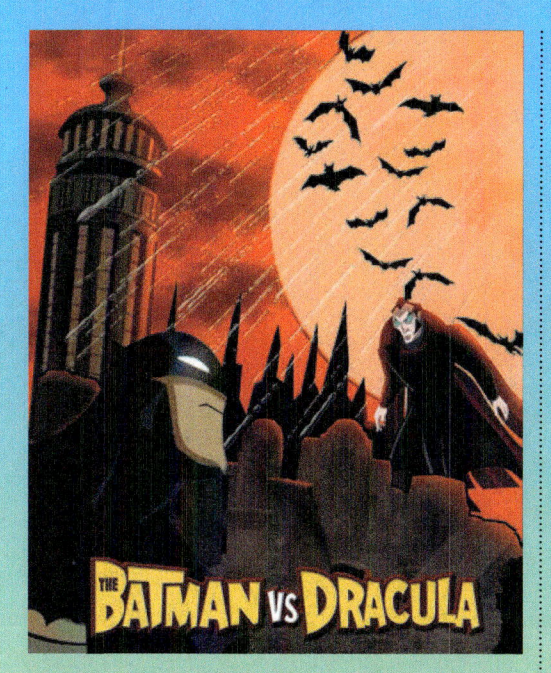

(1964-1965), and did encourage the makers to make a kind of sequel or prequel *Mad, Mad, Mad Monsters* (1972) that aired as a Halloween TV special, using cel animation instead of stop motion.

The seventies had the mighty popular *Super Friends* (1973-1974), a Saturday-morning cartoon lineup, featuring DC superheroes Superman, Batman and Robin, Wonder Woman and Aquaman, and the like; 1978 follow-up series *Challenge of the Superfriends* featured Count Dracula in one episode, 'Attack of the Vampire'.

Drak Pack is about three classic Universal Monsters fighting crime in the vein of *Super Friends* and *Spider-Man and His Amazing Friends*. The series focused on three teenagers: Drak Jr., Frankie and Howler, descendants of Count Dracula, Frankenstein's creation and the Wolf Man, who are determined to atone for the wrongs of their ancestors by becoming superheroes. The cool show also had a S.P.E.C.T.R.E. type evil organisation called O.G.R.E. (The Organisation of Generally Rotten Enterprises or Endeavours), led by Dr. Dred, a blue-skinned master criminal and his cronies Toad, Fly, Mummyman and Vampira. Count Dracula does appear as Drak's great-great-uncle who serves as his counsel, otherwise known as "Big D".

It's interesting how like many superheroes the Drak Pack's alter egos are, in their human appearances before they strike their right hands together and yell "Wacko!" Also, their transportation, like the Batmobile, is an amphibious flying car called 'The Drakster'.

This topic of animation needs to include the anime television movie of Marvel Comics' *The Tomb of Dracula* (1980), directed by Minoru Okazaki, also known as *Dracula Sovereign of the Damned*. Much of the film's story is lifted from the comic book, but it is too condensed, with too many characters, and would have worked better as a series. Regardless, the film is okay and is accessible on YouTube.

Throughout the eighties, except for *Vampires in Havana* (1985), it appeared that the Count did not make many guest appearances in any memorable cartoon shows or films, aside from the character of Count Duckula in ITV's *Danger Mouse* (1981-1992) that spawned a spin-off from the makers of that series that ran from 1988 to 1993. What was quirky about Count Duckula's portrayal were his lack of fangs and his vegetarian diet, predating the vegetarian Cullen family in the *Twilight* franchise.

The 1986 release of *Castlevania*, a Gothic horror action-adventure video game series about Dracula, prompted comic book writer Warren Ellis to produce an adult animated series for Netflix based on the game. The art style carries inspiration from Ayami Kojima's artwork; she also worked on the game. Overall, the series is brilliant in every department, its visuals, characterisation, action scenes and scare tactics.

The nineties and new millennium saw a slew of animated portrayals of Count Dracula in the following:

Mina and the Count (1995-1999) voiced by Mark Hamill as Vlad the Count

Gargoyles, with an episode 'Eye of the Beholder' (1995) featuring a person dressed up as Dracula at a Halloween party in Greenwich Village.

The Batman versus Dracula (2005)
Dear Dracula (2012)
Hotel Transylvania (2012)
Ultimate Spider-Man (2013) – in the episode 'Blade', Dracula the vampire king takes on his modern-day adversary Eric Brooks, otherwise known as Blade the Vampire Hunter, and in the next episode 'The Howling Commandos' the Count takes on Nick Fury's Howling Commandos (Frankenstein's Monster, Werewolf by Night, N'Kantu the Living Mummy and Man-Thing) in his Transylvanian castle.

Avengers Assemble (2013) Dracula became a recurring character in a few episodes.

Hotel Transylvania 2 (2015)
DuckTales (2020) – the character of Nosferatu/Dracula, voiced by James Marsters in the episode 'The Trickening!'

Hotel Transylvania: The Series (2017-2020)
Hotel Transylvania 3: Summer Vacation (2018)
Hotel Transylvania 4: Transformania (2022)

Supposing that these animated features and television shows did introduce me to this topic – in that case, such material will continue to capture younger audiences before they ever get to read the novel or watch the countless movies of the most portrayed literary character in film and TV.

DRACULA HAS RISEN FROM LANCASHIRE

by Ian Talbot Taylor

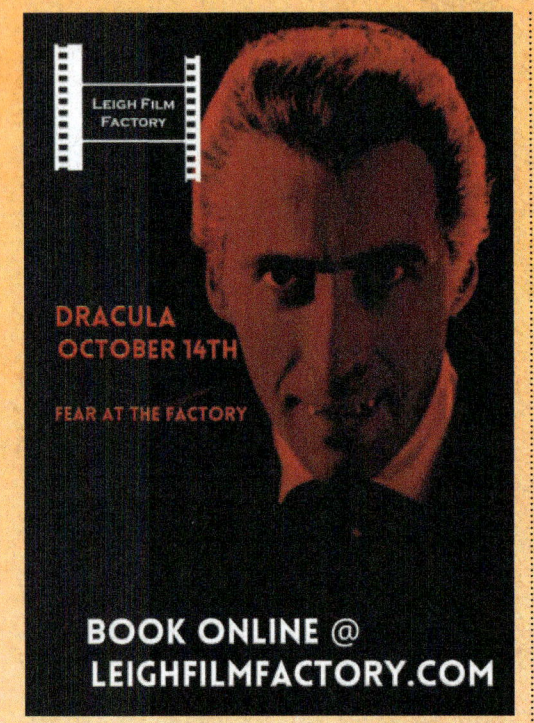

For those of you lamenting the passing of those wonderful trips to the cinema to watch a tasty horror double bill, or perhaps those memorably nostalgic weekends when the BBC might show a couple of vintage Hammer Horror movies back-to-back, I have good news. Last October, Dracula was alive and well and living in Leigh and I was privileged to be invited to introduce both *Dracula* (1958) and *Dracula A.D. 1972* on the big screen at the independent Leigh Film Factory.

Leigh is best known these days for its 2023 Challenge Cup winning Rugby League club Leigh Leopards, or for producing punk legends Buzzcocks' Pete Shelley, but for those of you who need more context, it is a large town, now in the borough of Wigan, that grew as a key coal mining and textile manufacturing area during the industrial revolution. Today, the mills in Leigh and surrounding areas provide homes for independent businesses such as Leigh Film Factory.

For years, Leigh Film Society was a cinematic haven for the town, sharing classics, blockbusters and indie gems, nurturing a love for film across generations. The society's screenings became a part of local culture, and the members were justifiably proud of the togetherness that this fostered. The next step was to set up a proper cinema space, the vision being "to provide an affordable, accessible and welcoming space where everyone can enjoy quality cinema experiences, whether for education, business or pleasure." This they managed to do and now, on the 4th floor of Spinners Mill can be found a fully air-conditioned cinema that is full of the latest technology to give audiences a fantastic film watching experience!

In 2022, Leigh Film Factory launched their 'Fear at the Factory' season of horror movies running throughout the month of October. As a presenter on local community Radio M29 I was aware of this great project, had promoted them and had paid a visit to the premises and marvelled at their work. Whilst there I had chatted with Kevin, one of the team. Some time later I received an email from a mysterious figure calling himself Alan Smithee (you can't fool a film fan with *that* name!) It was actually Kevin letting me know the team were presenting a Hammer Dracula double bill on October 14th, 2023. To quote Kevin directly, "I know you've written about classic horror before, so I was wondering if you'd be interested in doing an introduction to the films? Is this an area you're interested in? Apologies if I've got this all wrong, I am basing this on a conversation we had about a year ago when you came into the cinema."

Yes, I had chatted with Kevin, and might well have mentioned classic horror, including Hammer! He remembered correctly, and it took me less than seconds to accept the kind offer!

The advertising for the 2023 'Fear at the Factory' started as early as August, with the indie cinema promoting via the leading question "Do you like scary movies? It's time to announce the second annual 'Fear at the Factory', and we've got a veritable feast of grisly delights for the discerning horror fan this year. *Saint Maud! Dracula! Dracula A.D. 1972! Enys Men! The Cabinet of Dr Caligari! Hocus Pocus! The Shining!*"

This was clearly going to be an eclectic bunch of horror movies and I was particularly happy to be flying the flag for Dracula at Hammer. Now it was time to start rewatching the movies, making notes and planning what I was going to say to the local movie-watching populace. Would the majority be open to films that were decades old and clearly different in style, tone and execution to many of the other modern movies being shown? The week soon arrived with the announcement by Leigh Film Factory that "This Saturday, 'Fear at the Factory' opens up the Hammer Horror vaults as we bring a double bill of 'Dracula' to our big screen.

We start with the film that introduced Christopher Lee's depiction of the titular Count, along with Peter Cushing as his nemesis Professor Van Helsing – 1958's *Dracula*!

This will be followed by *Dracula A.D. 1972* which sees the veteran actors reprising their roles in a very different environment – London in the 1970s!

The films will be introduced by local writer and Hammer aficionado Ian Taylor."

This was now feeling very real!

I had support in the audience, including 'We Belong Dead's very own Andy Bark and his delightful wife Iryna. I had also noted a Facebook post by the Wigan Cult Film Club: "Anyone going to the *Dracula & Dracula A.D. 1972* double bill tomorrow at Leigh Film Factory?" The group's moderator Dani Foster's question was replied to by 'Group Expert' Anthony Ball. I realised that I would be delivering to knowledgeable folk as well as novices!

Arriving early, I helped myself to a pint of a good ale and chatted to the team. I would be delivering a short intro before each of the two films. I was directed to a central spot between screen and seats and told that I needed to find my mark as I would be being filmed.

Clutching my notes, I now had to decide whether to read them as I spoke or to just go without a safety net! I genuinely didn't know which it would be until I was introduced and took my position to an encouraging round of applause. Of course, I just left the notes in my pocket and flew by the seat of my pants… it's my way!

Talking about Hammer's glorious *Dracula* is easy, of course. Such a cleverly streamlined adaption by Jimmy Sangster, so well directed by Terence Fisher and with those powerful principal performances from Peter Cushing and Christopher Lee. Following a potted history of Hammer, Cushing and Lee up to that point in the late '50s, I dropped in notes such as James Bernard's score marking the name Drac-u-la syllable by syllable and so on. But I also took the opportunity to (kindly and reasonably) burst the bubbles of a few misconceptions such as the 'best friend' status of the two main stars and also addressed the opinions on Michael Gough's performance in (I hope) a fair manner.

After the event, my radio pal Bevan Thompson said he knew I was doing well, because the row of horror film experts in front of him were constantly nodding their heads vigorously in agreement or appreciation!

Following this, I was gratified that the audience watched this great picture earnestly and with full engagement. No ironic 21st Century chuckles. *Dracula* was accepted and enjoyed as intended back in 1958.

Naturally, *Dracula A.D. 1972* was a slightly different affair, something I didn't shy away from admitting to the audience. However, I insisted there was just as much to be enjoyed in the later effort. Again, the audience agreed and whilst there *were* some laughs this time around, they were all in the right places. Two films from both ends of Hammer's work with Bram Stoker's legendary characters – and both entertained to the max.

Afterwards, Leigh Film Factory posted "Thanks to members of Wigan Cult Film Club for joining us at our Dracula double bill last night, and thanks to Ian Taylor for a great introduction." They even suggested that I might be invited back for more of the same.

It was a delightful event, thanks to many people, including two independent groups who are intent on celebrating all kinds of cinema, but also others just happy to catch films on a big screen. As far as Leigh, Lancashire is concerned, Dracula lives!

MYSTERY AND IMAGINATION SPARKED IN BLOOD-RICH ENGLAND:
DRACULA SWOOPS DOWN AT ITV

by Kevin Nickelson

"You can't overdo playing Dracula… the fatal thing is to try to be subtle" – Denholm Elliott

Since the publishing of Bram Stoker's iconic novel 'Dracula' in 1897, the central character has continued to hold a sort of supernatural sway with lovers of horror the world over to rival the fictional creation's own hypnotic prowess. As recently as 2022, the 125th anniversary of the introduction of the so-called Prince of Darkness heralded celebratory events across the globe. The town of Whitby Abbey in North Yorkshire, England looked to make Guinness world record history in the most unusual of categories: most vampires in one location. One might think the mark was shattered by the sheer number of officials in some major government, but that might be a tale for another time. On May 22, 2022, the town sought to attract at least 1,897 folks all dolled up in their best bloodsucker attire to note the occasion of the Count's arrival in the chiller realm. The fervent passion does beg the question, what drives the character's popularity? Is it the idea of breaking from puritan standard toward sexual freedom as Stoker suggested thematically in his book? Is it our curiosity as to what lies beyond our mortal coil? Whatever the impression we get that causes the images of the creepily elegant and caped Bela Lugosi, a skeletal and rat-like Count Orlok assayed by Max Schreck in F.W. Murnau's German classic *Nosferatu*, or Christopher Lee's feral and explosively carnal rendition with Hammer Films of England to parade in our minds, it has kept the name and the character in our collective consciousness without pause for now 127 years. Though the presentation of the lord of the undead has had more alterations than Cher has had Bob Mackie costume changes over time, the central core has remained of an incredibly intelligent, malevolent, passionate being who obsessively seeks power over both men and women in its orbit.

Launched in 1955 in an effort to provide a competition for the British Broadcasting Company and try to prevent a monopoly, ITV was born. A British free-to-air public broadcast network, it has gone on to become the oldest commercial network in the United Kingdom. One such example of the programming offered by ITV was a work directly aimed at fans of the blood-curdler story. *Mystery and Imagination* was a five-series concoction composed of television plays based on the writings of genre stalwarts such as Robert Louis Stevenson, Mary Shelley, M.R. James and the aforementioned Stoker. It ran from 1966-1970 and was produced first by ABC, and then Thames Television.

'Dracula' premiered on November 18, 1968 as the third episode of series four. Denholm Elliott stars as the titular vampiric nobleman, portraying the emotions, temper and motivations with less of an emphasis on dialogue and more on gestures and purposeful movement. As he noted in the quote above (part of an interview with 'TV Times' ahead of the first airing), subtlety will kill the beast faster than the rising sun would. In fact, the entire production features static camera shots as background, behind actors seeming inclined to pose and gesticulate their feelings rather than wrestle with cumbersome words. This is combined with a Harpsichord-infused composition by the magnificently talented Paul Lewis, who served as Assistant Music Adviser for ABC Television prior to becoming a composer full-time. Some changes, courtesy of writer Charles Graham, were made to separate this version from both Stoker's treatment as well as the highly popularized Hamilton Deane 1924 play and 1927 John Balderston revision. Alterations that lean more on functionality of the plot contrivance than on creative ingenuity or expanse of thought, it seems. Gone is the ill-fated R.M. Renfield as Dracula's crazed slave. Insert Jonathan Harker in the lackey role, himself an institutionalized victim who gets to spout "Master!" whenever the big guy is near. Corin Redgrave plays Harker as the decided opposite of both the love-lorn David Manners in the original Lugosi film and John Van Eyssen's flawed vampire hunter in the 1958 Hammer gothic. Like Elliott, Redgrave eschews the stock dialogue for a more visual performance. His is a retreat into the world of extreme facial expressions and an energetic, yet oddly fluid, physicality to his mental patient. His Harker often seems the human puppet for Dracula to use in playing with his foes. Indeed, one scene has the hapless Jonathan being possessed by the creature to speak to the heroic Van Helsing and Seward. Sporting darkened glasses and goatee,

Elliott's Count looks to have stepped out of the Liverpool music scene of 1968 rather than turn-of-the-century London. This aesthetic, along with the unique flashback sequence of Harker meeting the three vampire brides on the stairs in the castle (the medium shot from Harker's perspective, and the combination of grotesquely blackened teeth and pale makeup with the sexualised movements of the actors, is a nod to Hammer and Terry Fisher. That it is one of just a few moments put to celluloid seals that feel), and some superimposition visuals of Dracula's image in a few scenes, helps make the whole affair seem something of an acid hallucination inside a living nightmare.

It is to be lauded that whatever limited budget episode director Patrick Dromgoole had at his disposal is expertly utilised. Plenty of effects, both optical and practical, are on hand for fans to wow over and cringe at. Dromgoole reaches for a simple tool of altering the contrast in the video tape to show the white flashes as sunlight, leading to the bat dude's demise in the final. An image overlay of melting ice on Elliott's face during the biodegrading closeup is an exceptional touch. Cut in a wax model of the Dracula face oozing off the skull, and you achieve an effect that would have Hammer legend Roy Ashton impressed. It's intriguing that the fangs adorned by the actors in this piece were modeled based on the dentition of a bat rather than those of the protracted canine incisors normally used. It draws one back to either the Murnau or Herzog versions of the vampire as vermin-esque monstrosity in *Nosferatu* '22 and '79, respectively.

Of the rest of the cast, the lovely Susan George exudes a barely repressed, raw sexual charisma as Lucy. Once introduced to the Count, she is merely to wait patiently for her otherworldly lover to unleash her from the chains of the physical world. It is a somewhat familiar type for the genre, but George gives it a fresh 'free spirit' approach. Bernard Archard, as Van Helsing, convinces as an authority figure hybrid of old world mysticism and science, even though he is encumbered with a particularly severe beard. Fresh from the BBC's acclaimed 1967 production of *The Forsyte Saga* and her turn as Holly Forsyte, Suzanne Neve steps in as the strong-minded yet doomed Mina Harker, acquitting herself nicely. Nice to see British tv veteran Joan Hickson in a small role as Mrs. Weston, thought it strikes mostly of the part being mainly included to have someone remove the garlic from Mina's room so that Dracula can advance on her one final time. Those dang contrivances again!

Historically, this television project was a first on two fronts. It was the first adaptation of the Stoker tome put to the small screen. Rather odd when one considers all of the stage productions mined for live television in the 1950s. Second, it featured the first black vampire girl ever onscreen. The Trinidad and Tobago-born Nina Baden-Semper took up the protruding teeth long before Vonetta McGee donned them in 1972's *Blacula*, not to mention Pauline Peart in *The Satanic Rites of Dracula* for Hammer, and years before Angela Bassett began vamping in Wes Craven's *Vampire in Brooklyn*. There was a movement in the latter half of the 1960s toward more prominent and meaningful roles for black actors on both the big and small screens. Perhaps ITV saw a trend forming and decided to beat all rivals to the punch.

It is a distinct shame that, of the five series in all, only the six segments from Thames (seasons 4 and 5) and two from ABC ('The Fall of the House of Usher' and 'The Open Door') survive. Network released the remaining eight on a DVD set July 5, 2010. This includes a surviving clip from the third season's 'Casting the Runes'.

As you enjoy your own tribute to the longevity of the supernatural, self-proclaimed ruler of the damned (see his boast under the guise of the Chinese warlord Kah in *Legend of the 7 Golden Vampires*), why not try an entry that is far from the stock bloody fare that has already been fed to you, just like a traveler or village local being handed to the tall guy with weird eyes, fangs and cape who haunts that big, stone house on the hill? *Mystery and Imagination: 'Dracula'* is just that twisted of a ride.

We Belong Dead

LAUGH COUNT
DRACULA VS. SKETCH COMEDY
by Steven West

"You have Booped your last Boop!"

Bela Lugosi, quipping to Betty Boop in 1933, was spoofing his own iconic vampire even before Universal had developed a sequel.

90 years on, we have sitcoms built around vampires, including *Count Abdulla,* and an eclectic range of funnymen have portrayed the erstwhile Vlad: among them, Judd Hirsch, Adam Sandler, Leslie Nielsen, James Daly, Petter Butterworth and, as *Sesame Street*'s Count von Count, Jerry Nelson and Matt Vogel. Depending on your sense of humour, the best Dracula joke of all might be Gerard Butler's Count patrolling the Virgin Megastore in *Dracula 2000* though you'd also be right if you found more laughs in *Bram Stoker's Dracula* (1992) than Mel Brooks' *Dracula: Dead and Loving It* (1995).

It's easy to disappear into a YouTube / TikTok rabbit hole of endless parodies, and your formative years might define personal comedic-Count favourites. Lactose-tolerant New Zealand viewers may fondly recall Russell Smith's Count Homogenised, a milk-loving vampire equipped with dairy-based puns: "Mum's the word or, rather, milk's the word!" Today we can stream a comedy short of Dracula being accused of being racist while taking his first flight or savaging *Twilight* but back in the era of three or four terrestrial channels, Brit monster kids had Dave Allen wonderfully ribbing the Hammer horror idiots who insist on venturing up to Castle Dracula: "Why don't they go at 12 in the afternoon, piss off before the bastard wakes up?"

Allen, who also highlighted the spatial discrepancy between fang placement and the puncture marks on victims' necks, had his observations echoed by *Saturday Night Live* host Sinbad in 1994, while mocking Gary Oldman's "butt head". Eddie Izzard, in *Unrepeatable* that same year, considered garlic bread as a vampire repellent, tracked the doomed journey of typical Dracula movie protagonists (Tabitha, Agatha, Bagatha) and resurrected playground conundrums about the success of crucifix alternatives: "Does fingers work?!"

Coppola's film, itself hovering on the brink of self-parody, proved ripe comedic material: *SNL*'s faux trailer for Coppola's *Bram Stoker's Blacula* – set to Jerry Goldsmith's magnificent *The Final Conflict* theme! – had a kung-fu practising, Afro'd Sinbad in the title role, delivering reheated Wesley Snipes one-liners ("Always bet on black!").

Fox's *In Living Color* (1990-94) aired its lampoon one month after *Dracula*'s U.S. release, with Jim Carrey imitating Oldman's youthful romantic Dracula incarnation: top hat, John Lennon glasses, "I have crossed oceans of time…" His efforts to seduce "Ugly" Wanda Wayne – gamely played in sassy drag by Jamie Foxx and earlier seen in *In Living Color*'s 'Basic Instank' – unravel when he gets a closer look and opts for suicide-by-sunlight rather than intercourse.

Oldman's performance frequently channelled Lugosi, who, of course, had long been the go-to for Dracula comedies on both sides of the Atlantic, with typical examples including Gareth Hale donning the cloak and cod-Eastern European vocals while comic partner Norman Pace gurned and bulged his eyes as simpleton Ygor. The duo, famed for a microwaved kitten, pulled off characteristically crude gags like "She had the sheets… pulled over her face" that only worked in a mock-Bela voice.

The Armstrong and Miller Show brought "Old School Vampires" into the unforgiving 21st century dating scene, with Alex sporting the familiar widows peak and enormous collars and Ben aping Oldman's big hair. They're mocked by younger clubbers, thwarted by archaic chat-up lines and have their centuries-honed glide toward potential prey outshone by young vamps shifting like The Flash. There's something poignant about the line "I ended up with Pat from Barnsley the other night".

Max Schreck's feral interpretation has also been the source of laughs: Paul Whitehouse went full Nosferatu for a memorable *The Fast Show* creature of the night, advancing toward a victim in her boudoir before assaulting her with betting tips in imitation of late DJ / showbiz and football agent Eric Hall, complete with "Monster, Monster" catchphrase. This in turn echoed an early 90s B&Q advert in which a conventional 'Dracula' stirred a sleeping beauty to deliver news of the store's hot deals.

A slew of skits emerged while Hammer Horror appeared to breathe its last. Former Hill's Angel (and occasional Stan Laurel substitute) Sue Upton bridged the gap between W*onder Woman* and *Super Gran* with *The Benny Hill Show*'s super-strong Wondergran. In *Wondergran Meets Dracula* (1979), Benny has a nagging wife with an Elsa Lanchester hairdo, keeps his fangs in a glass of water overnight, bites a mannequin in error and stores attractive young women in Grandfather clocks and glass cases ("For emergency use only"). The plot gets sidetracked by random business including a great police "special branch" visual gag before the resilience of the geriatric ninja defeats the vampire – with help from a Nicholas Parsons picture.

Pre "Eye-gore", Marty Feldman co-wrote and starred in *Every Home Should Have One* (1970), an inventive precursor to *How to Get Ahead in Advertising*. He's an adman struggling to make Scottish porridge "sexy" and distracted by flights of fancy parodying Swedish cinema, soft-porn and Hammer's Dracula. In Thames TV's self-reflexive *Sykes with the Lid Off* (1971), the eponymous star also satirises 70s consumerism (he gets sloshed while promoting beer) and horror films within a wider behind the curtain peek at a calamitous live TV show in the making. The best skit has frustrated director Philip Gilbert's repertory company production of *Dracula* falling apart thanks to Sykes' antics ("Who'd you expect, Prince Philip?") and ill-fitting trousers. In a 1974 episode of *The Tommy Cooper Hour*, the comic quick changes between Dracula, the Frankenstein Monster and his Bride while almost swallowing his fangs and delivering irresistible bad jokes like "Who can afford steaks these days?"

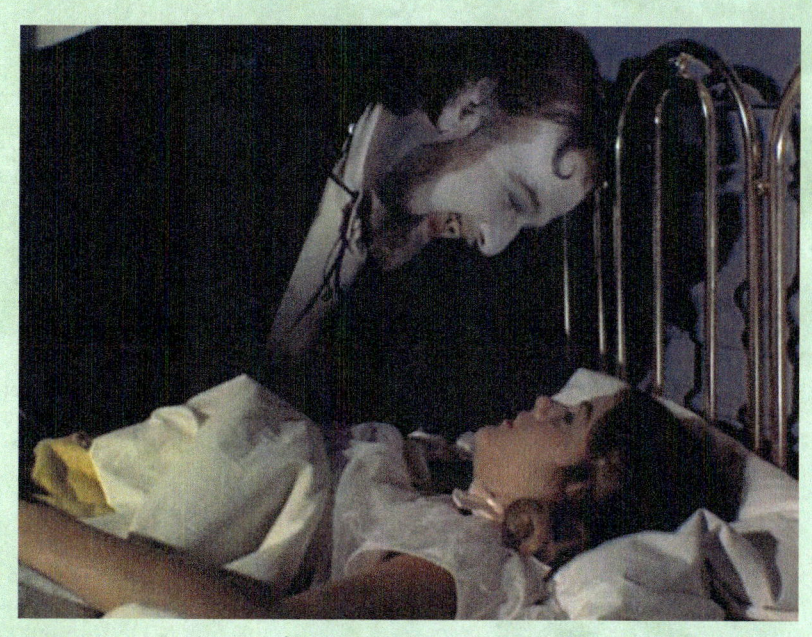

Remember what you watched other than *Ghostwatch* on Halloween night 1992? Perhaps at 8.15, you tuned in to the *Beadle's About* episode featuring the climactic arrival of "Count Beadula"?! The related prank involved a blood bank worker increasingly perturbed by a boss who enthuses about the "bouquet" of a blood vial and has impromptu tasting sessions ("Mmm… white Caucasian") while his work attire evolves into full bow-tie-and-cape majesty. Presumably to avoid complaints from those lame viewers soon to clog the BBC switchboard, the unfolding "hilarity" is punctuated by Beadle assuring the audience that the "blood" is mere blackcurrant juice.

Hipper riffs include *The Young Ones*' classic 'Nasty' (1984), in which the boys' efforts to watch a banned VHS are set against classic horror tropes (Hale & Pace as comedy gravediggers) and Alexei Sayle as a character who might be either Dracula, a familiar Marxist comedian or a driving instructor from Johannesburg. In the ensuing panic, a Pot Noodle is snorted, Mike suggests contacting Peter Cushing (Neil: "I'll get a cushion!") and fears are expressed they'll end up "dead but still alive, like Leonard Cohen".

Further fun japes came from the man who affectionately mocked the Hammer era in *The House That Dripped Blood*'s delicious 'The Cloak' segment (1970). In a 1985 episode of the bonkers *3-2-1* (from the creator of *Would You Kill a Child?*, lest we forget), Caroline Munro was on hostess duties, Kenneth Connor pops up as Merlin and Jon Pertwee plays a spirited Dracula, singing an ode to

We Belong Dead

his homeland: "Condemned to wander the Earth with my children of the night". Before slipping the contestants a suitably baffling clue, he also has an in-character jest with Ted Rogers and creepily slips into a Worzel Gummidge bit.

Across the pond, Lugosi take-offs flourished on TV once the Universal monster cycle had been beamed into households across America and made "monster kids" of many. ABC's Wild West sitcom F Troop (1965-67) was among those hiring a living horror icon for the occasion. Vincent Price's appearance, in 'V is for Vampire', as hearse-driving Transylvanian immigrant Count Sforza mimics Bela in accent and mannerisms, portentously intoning "Good evening" regardless of time of day. Erstwhile Dead End Kid and Lugosi-soundalike Gabriel Dell enlivened The Steve Allen Show with a couple of vampiric guest appearances, notably a classic sketch built around a misunderstanding that could happen to us all: "We use bats, and we have a ball!" / "Umpire?! I thought you asked for a vampire!" Dell voiced both Dracula and the Frankenstein Monster for the 1963 LP Famous Monsters Speak and became debate fodder online about who originated Dracula's "Bleh!" sound onscreen.

Light horror skits became a mainstay of U.S. comedy / variety shows in the 1960s, with CBS' The Carol Burnett Show (1967-78) often straying into genre pastiche. 'The Bat and the Beautiful', appropriately set in Transylvania in 1931, has Burnett as Dracula's unhappy wife bemoaning her "permanent hickey". Harvey Korman mugs as a flappy-tongued, endlessly punning, vowel-stretching Prince of Darkness, rattling out telegraphed jokes like "I have the heart of an 18 year old boy…" Burnett's other horror comedies showcased Lyle Waggoner making heartburn jokes as Dracula while Price, who showed up as Dr. Frankenstein and joined a Mummy spoof, often showed up for similar career-mocking guest spots in popular fare like The Dean Martin Show. Here, amidst gags about the cost of meat and Sinatra's womanising, the genre legend bites the host, lamenting "Don't know what you've got in your veins but it's 100% proof!"

Sporting funky eyebrows and a Ronnie Corbett-shaped hunchback assistant, Price also relished a fabulous showcase in a March 1970 edition of Frost on Sunday, welcoming a wide-eyed, long-fanged Dracula (Ronnie Barker). Similar gags pop up in several TV sketches: Barker delivers the overdrawn-at-the-blood-bank gag found in The Kopykats (1972) and, with slight variation, a short Night Gallery gag featuring Victor Buono's grinning, rotund Dracula ('A Midnight Visit to the Neighbourhood Blood Bank'). Barker loses a fang at a pivotal moment a la Graham Chapman in the "You're no fun anymore" Monty Python sketch and Ernie Kovacs in his self-named show (Kovacs also had a skit in which the Frankenstein Monster thrashes Dracula at pool). The Frost sketch is a real gem, with a marvellous cleavage gag, in-jokes ("Lugosi's Fang Paste"), product placement spoofs ("Fiendus Frozen Birds Eyes") and Price's obligatory gag at the expense of horror 'rivals': "Name your poison!" / "Christopher Lee".

The final episode of The ABC Comedy Hour's impressionist-showcase The Kopykats gave host Tony Curtis an excuse to indulge his Cary Grant impersonation, maintain a running gag about how bad he was in The Son of Ali Baba and feature in a questionable sketch about The Boston Strangler (!). Curtis hams it up as Dracula in 'Gravediggers of 1942', a lively pastiche in which he plots to mate his captured Monster with a "Bride" curated by a bodysnatching Wolfman. Vincent Price impersonations, Invisible Man jokes, jokes about Raquel Welch and a climactic 'There's no Business Like Showbusiness' singalong keep it fun, though there's more invention to be found in some contemporary kids TV equivalents.

Pitched at older children weaned on Count von Count from the same stable, The Children's Television Workshop's The Electric Company (1971-77) provided valuable early exposure for Morgan Freeman, In the ongoing mission to teach kids how to rhyme, spell and enjoy a balanced diet, he swished a mean cape as Vincent the Vegetable Vampire and became the only screen Dracula to employ a turnip in a musical number celebrating the comforts of home: "I love to take a bath in a casket". Freeman's place in Dracula history was secured in a short 1974 "A Night at the Movies" sketch marking the first live-action appearance of Spider-Man. A couple watching "Spidey Super Stories" at the cinema are menaced by Dracula – one of those annoying patrons providing their own commentary during the film ("Isn't she a lovely lady?") – before the teen Avenger captures the Count in his web and the husband moans about Spider-Man taking his seat.

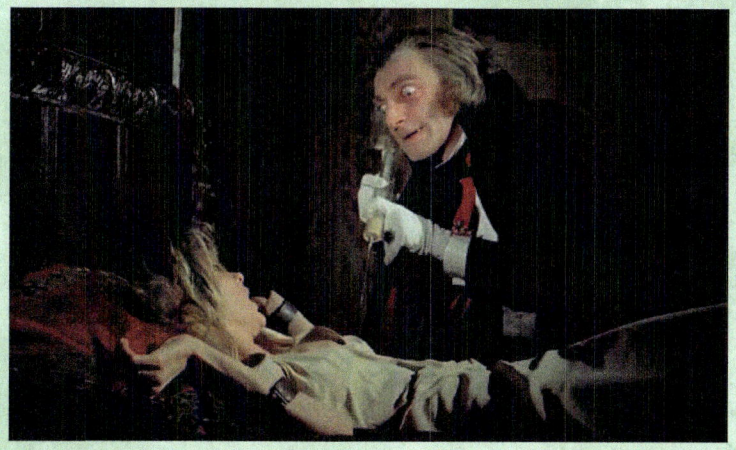

Targeting a different demographic National Lampoon's *Disco Beaver from Outer Space* (HBO, 1979) has Peter Elbling as Gotham's Dragula, "Queen of Darkness", quipping comebacks to homophobic insults and turning macho construction workers gay with a single bite ("I feel pretty!"). He's genuinely funny spicing up lines like "Who are you expecting, cookie, Dick Cavett?"), becoming the only Dracula defeated by an extraterrestrial beaver and a picture of Lloyd Bridges; Lynn Redgrave is also a hoot as Professor Vanessa Van Helsing. Less reliant on beaver gags, Canada's *SCTV* debuted Joe Flaherty's horror host parody Count Floyd in 1977, introducing faux schlock like "Dr. Tongue's 3-D House of Slave Chicks" (with John Candy as Tongue) and howling presumably because of his ignorance to vampire lore. Gimmicks included "Smellorama" (accessible via $19.95 smell cans) and "3-D" achieved by Candy and co thrusting roses and foot longs at the camera.

American chat shows embrace Dracula parodies in times of political turmoil (Al Pacino-soundalike Count Laffula on *Conan* during the Trump era's "Stop the Count" protests) and for Halloween-time gimmickry (Paul Reubens in Pee Wee-as-Dracula guise on *The Tonight Show* with guest host Joan Rivers). *Conan*'s "Halloween Safety Tips" sketch, with special guest Dracula making a string of terrible jokes, endearingly suggests the bad puns found in all these sketches are a speech disorder afflicting vampires and curable via The Lestat Institute. *The Howard Stern Show* memorably paid host to Universal Monsters superfan Gilbert Gottfried as "Dracula Gottfried", sustaining the Lugosi vocals as a Jewish Count with his own rules (no blood drinking on Yom Kippur) and a propensity for filth: claiming to have shagged Christina Appelgate during his *Married with Children* stint, he lecherously and repeatedly intones "Give me your cloogie!" to any nearby female.

Naturally, *Saturday Night Live* has broadcast assorted Gothic spoofs over the decades, with Jason Sudeikis a smarmy, nail-filing Dracula in *'The Curse of Frankenstein'* (2006), in which Bill Hader's Frankenstein Monster dismisses Hugh Laurie's "Fascist" angry mob, deflecting them to his vampiric neighbour. Sudeikis returned to the role, married to Kristen Wiig, in *'The Mirror'* (2008), a clever, elaborate spoof of all those post-*American Werewolf* double-nightmare fake outs. *'Dracula's Not Gay'* (1994) had a huge-collared John Travolta Count, denying rumours of an affair with Renfield ("I'm a man of many secrets but humping a mental defective is not one of them!") en route to a punchline of two male bats shagging.

A standout was *'Dracula Tries to Avoid AIDS'* (1989), in which James Woods' Dracula interrogates potential victims about their recent sexual history, arranging blood tests to quell his paranoia and paying off superbly with the reveal that monogamous housewife Victoria Jackson's only recent partner is (surely no need to panic!?) Keith Richards. Echoing *In Living Color*, the King of Vampires takes so long to find a "clean woman" that he's killed by the rising sun. In a rather different political era, a 2004 *Apprentice* spoof-trailer had Darrell Hammond portraying America's Rapist-in-Chief as an egomaniac dressed as "Donald from Trumpsylvania" / "Count Trumpula", failing miserably to nail the cape swish, evil laugh or Lugosi voice: "I vant to suck your blood but I vont". What's the betting he'd survive a stake through his black heart?

You'll have your own personal favourite comedy business involving his dark majesty, and there's a chance it's been overlooked by this mere breeze through the Count's small screen spoofery. Make your own descent into the YouTube rabbit hole and you'll find much more – and, while you're there, take a moment to relive the glorious Dracula puppet rock opera that never was, yet exists in the dreams of *Forgetting Sarah Marshall*'s lovelorn Jason Segel. His Lugosi impersonation, Count von Count-style mad laugh, musical numbers and cute baby Draculas birthed live on stage are a sheer joy.

We Belong Dead

DRACULA 2000

by David Gelmini

Dracula 2000 (titled Dracula 2001 in the UK) initially opened to a mixed response and underperformed throughout its original theatrical run, although it managed to develop a small but dedicated cult following over the years. The film was directed by Patrick Lussier, also known for helming genre pictures such as *The Prophecy 3: The Ascent*, *White Noise: The Light*, *My Bloody Valentine 3D*, and *Drive Angry*, with Joel Soisson providing the screenplay. And you might also be aware that Wes Craven served as the film's executive producer, as his name was plastered across the poster in letters almost as big as the title, with his involvement clearly being viewed as a major selling point. Despite not being a huge hit with critics or audiences, *Dracula 2000* gained a level of recognition for its unique interpretation of a story which we already know all too well, and it even managed to spawn two sequels. Needless to say, Lussier and Soisson clearly did something right.

The film opens in 1897, the same year that 'Dracula' was originally published, but the remaining similarities between the movie and Bram Stoker's novel are few and far between. Throughout the opening sequence, we are shown daytime shots of the ship known as the Demeter sailing across the sea with Dracula's coffin onboard, superimposed against faded footage of a map displaying the ship's destination. After an abrupt cut to night, the deck of the ship is shown to be littered with mutilated corpses, which was no doubt Dracula's doing. This is then followed by footage of Dracula's footprints on the beach being washed away by the incoming waves after the ship docks, since Dracula clearly lacks the ability to levitate. And the large production budget would certainly have allowed for a recreation of Victorian England, but we were only given two shots of London before cutting to the present day (although we did briefly see more of London during this era in a later flashback scene). Either way, this is still an efficient opening which quickly informs viewers of what will be in store.

Future Oscar-winner Christopher Plummer stars as an antique shop owner called Matthew Van Helsing, with Plummer delivering his dialogue in a surprisingly convincing Dutch accent. Matthew detests the fact that his alleged grandfather, Abraham Van Helsing, served as the inspiration for one of the main characters in Stoker's novel. This makes the gradual revelation that Matthew is actually Abraham Van Helsing all the more gratifying, as we learn that he admirably devoted his incredibly long life to keeping vampires at bay while also shunning any kind of fame or recognition for his efforts. Van Helsing kept himself alive for so long by frequently injecting his arm with a potion which grants him extended longevity, but the strange and angelic visions he experiences upon each dose come as a side effect. One of these visions is presented in the film, and is so bizarre that you really will wonder if it was included simply to baffle viewers.

Jonny Lee Miller also appears as Simon Sheppard, an employee of the antique shop who essentially takes over the responsibilities of vampire hunting after Van Helsing's death. And while he has proven himself to be a gifted actor throughout his other roles, Miller's bland and monotone delivery of most of his lines throughout *Dracula 2000* will certainly begin to grate on most viewers. Even the way in which he loudly demands to know what is going on in one scene comes across as flat and disinterested. To say that Miller was miscast would be an understatement, because no other actor could shout a line such as "Never fuck with an antiques dealer" in such a dispassionate way.

It is gradually revealed that Dracula was captured and bound in a hidden tomb. As you could probably have guessed, he does not stay confined for long, as his coffin is stolen and subsequently opened by a group of thieves, who believe it to contain riches beyond their wildest dreams. Dracula naturally thanks his liberators by tearing them to pieces, before crashing their plane into a bayou. His advanced physiology allows him to survive the crash, and Dracula then celebrates his newfound freedom by seeking out the woman he believes he loves.

Gerard Butler achieved A-list status after *300* was released, but he was still a relative unknown when *Dracula 2000* debuted in cinemas. While he will certainly not be remembered as one of the best Dracula actors, he still brings a certain level of charm and charisma to the role. The way in which Butler broadly smiles while slaughtering his victims will no doubt be burned into your memory, as will the way in which he graciously extends his hand to women before brutally murdering them. Butler's performance relies heavily on non-verbal cues and gestures, and he doesn't utter a single word until over halfway into the film. Not many actors would have been capable of keeping viewers invested without speaking, but Butler's natural charisma allowed him to pull it off. And since this incarnation of Dracula clearly views himself as a charmer, there is even a shot from his point of view as he walks through a record store while being ogled by every attractive woman in the vicinity. His soft and calm manner of speech also seem fitting for a vampire who has lived for centuries, and you almost feel commanded to listen when Dracula speaks. And Dracula is also usually surrounded by plumes of smoke whenever he makes an entrance, because this character is clearly incapable of subtlety.

After the plane crash sequence, the film finally introduces Mary Heller (Justine Waddell), who we learn is Van Helsing's daughter. Heller frequently experiences visions of Dracula after his release from his tomb, leading her to question her sanity. And you will also begin to question your sanity when you hear Waddell gently whispering nearly all her lines, as the actress apparently believed that talking at a regular pitch would have somehow weakened her performance. Waddell seems to be trying to imitate the soft and gentle manner of speaking which Butler employed throughout, and she clearly failed miserably.

Although it would be a stretch to call it an action film, *Dracula 2000* does feature an action scene of sorts, in which Van Helsing and Sheppard used knives and crossbows to eliminate a group of vampires within an abandoned town hall. This sequence seems to have been included to help *Dracula 2000* appeal to action enthusiasts, and it no doubt succeeded. Although it comes across as a little silly to see an elderly man and his apprentice trying to shoot and stab beings who literally leap across great distances and scale walls, in a manner which at times seemed more comical than frightening. But this sequence still proved to be surprisingly fun in its own way.

Most of the kills and gore sequences are also fun and creative. Some memorable examples of the carnage on display include a character being impaled on metal bars after falling into a trap, a leech biting a man's eye, and several heads flying across the screen in slow-motion. The pilot of the plane carrying Dracula's stolen coffin is also impaled on metal blades in the cockpit as the aircraft plummets, which is certainly not something you will be forgetting in a hurry. Best of all, Dracula even uses his claws to slice open a news reporter's neck as soon as she finishes her broadcast. And since this is shown on a camera monitor, and vampires are invisible on lenses and screens, the cuts on the reporter's neck seem to have appeared out of nowhere before she is hastily killed. This was clearly a difficult effect to have pulled off, and it will probably leave viewers feeling unsettled for quite some time.

It's also refreshing to see a film which remembers that vampires are supposed to possess superhuman durability. In addition to surviving the aforementioned plane crash, we also see Dracula laughing while being shot repeatedly in the chest, before pulling out the bullets and examining them with morbid curiosity, clearly unfamiliar with modern weaponry. And, with this being an early 2000s movie, there is an obligatory shot of an arrow flying towards the camera as Sheppard fired upon Dracula in his wolf form. *The Matrix* was at the height of its popularity at the time, so this hardly comes as a surprise.

One of the most striking aspects of *Dracula 2000* is its bold and unique take on Dracula's origin. The film reveals that Dracula is none other than Judas Iscariot, and that he was transformed into an immortal vampire before subsequently being cursed to wander the Earth for eternity as a form of punishment for betraying Jesus. This could be viewed as a daring reinterpretation of Dracula's origin, or just an awkward method of shoehorning an extra dose of religion into a story which already featured Christian undertones. But regardless of your personal thoughts on the matter, you still have to admire the way in which the script thoroughly reimagined Dracula's backstory in such a creative way. There's even a flashback sequence depicting the crucifixion of Jesus, and Judas subsequently hanging himself, making *Dracula 2000* one of the few R-rated films to have depicted these sequences from the Bible before Mel Gibson plastered his dogmatic Christian views across cinema screens a few years later.

It certainly will not be remembered as one of the greatest vampire movies of all time, but *Dracula 2000* still managed to offer viewers a bold and unique take on Bram Stoker's original creation in a way which felt completely fresh. The script could have used some polish, and some of the actors were certainly miscast, but the strong performance from Butler, memorable kills, and unique reinterpretation of Dracula's original all helped to make this into a film which vampire fans will never forget. If you are looking for a movie which ambitiously brings Dracula into a modern setting while retaining all the key ingredients of classic vampire stories, *Dracula 2000* is not a film you can afford to miss.

CROSSING RUNNING WATER
DRACULA OVERSEAS

by Karen Joan Kohoutek

For a supernatural entity who was introduced as unable to "cross the running water of his own volition", Dracula has managed to leave his mark all over the world. Many adaptations took some time to be unearthed, but luckily for the adventurous, the Dracula movies of Turkey, Pakistan, and India have never been easier for western audiences to see.

As far as I can tell, the first post-war film with 'Dracula' in the title is the Turkish *Drakula Istanbul'da (Dracula in Istanbul)* (1953), directed by Mehmet Muhtar and starring Atif Kaptan as Dracula. Most Internet sources agree that this was the first movie Dracula with fangs, predating the Hammer version by five years, and also the first to show Dracula offering a baby to his vampire brides.

The credits mention Bram Stoker's novel, but it's more based on the novel 'Kazıklı Voyvoda' ('Impaler Voivode'), a loose translation of 'Dracula' by Ali Rıza Seyfioğlu, published originally in 1928, with an English translation by Neon Harbor in 2017. Despite that, and changes like making Güzin, the Mina character, a professional dancer, it sticks surprisingly close to the familiar story, adding echoes of Tod Browning's classic adaptation.

Movies like 'Turkish Spider-Man' (*3 Dev Adam*) and 'Turkish Star Wars' (*Dünyayı Kurtaran Adam*) have a camp reputation, but this is a completely straight-faced adaptation, in atmospheric black and white and available on YouTube, with intermittent subtitles. Transplanting the story from a Victorian (or at least quasi-Victorian) time period to the (then) present day, it shows a modern man trapped in a medieval nightmare. The Transylvania section, with its superstitious peasants, bleak and bare-treed Borgo Pass, and hot vampire women, feels very archetypal: so much that it seems like I saw it as a child and picked up my ideas about vampires from it, even though that's obviously not true. There's even a portrait with moving eyes, like every TV haunted house from the '60s and '70s.

The vampire exposition takes place when Azmi, the Harker character (played by Bülent Oran) reads about "the ghost Dracula" in a book, who's "medically dead." It's lucky that Dracula left it lying around, although the pages about how "to kill a ghost" have been torn out. Wherever the YouTube subtitles came from, they're often entertaining: when Azmi is in the hospital, it's said he's raving about "blood suckers, ghosts and women beasts." They also diagnose him with the vivid translation "brain shivering."

Once back in the city, we get a lot of upbeat music and a montage of night scenes of Istanbul, immediately coded as a more modern world. There's even an early version of a horror movie shower scene, with Güzin in the bubble bath. Later she can't wear her protective necklace at the theater, because "she cannot dance with garlics." That gives Dracula an opening backstage, and attacking, he tells her, "You are a delicious creature. I'm gonna drink you drop by drop. Tonight you'll dance only for me." This is clearly not about drinking blood for sustenance, nor does it have anything to do with love. His desire to control her, to possess her beauty and her talent, is foregrounded – the same kind of predator, like her lecherous boss, that she's had to fend off in her showbiz career.

Transplanting a familiar story to a new locale can help view it from a new perspective. It makes sense that Dracula would move to Istanbul. If he wanted to escape his decaying castle and bled-dry village, there were closer cities than London! The distance from Transylvania to Istanbul is 912.6 kilometers, versus 2420.9 kilometers to London, so it seems a lot more doable. Even Paris would be closer! Plus Transylvania was once under Turkish rule, and the historic Vlad the Impaler, so long associated with the vampire, killed plenty of Turks in warfare. It seems fitting for Dracula to haunt the imaginations of Turkish audiences.

Pakistan's *Zinda Laash* (1967), usually translated as *The Living Corpse*, was unusually accessible for

We Belong Dead

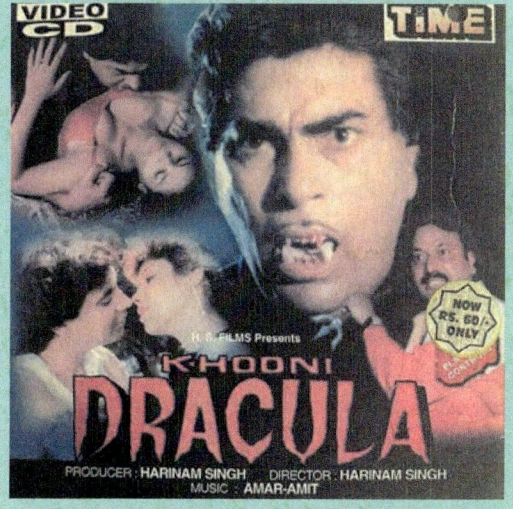

a while, released on DVD by Mondo Macabro in 2003, but it's sadly out of print again. Directed by Khwaja (K.H.) Sarfaraz and starring Rehan as the vampire, the film is often subtitled as 'Dracula in Pakistan', but Rehan's character is Dr. Tabani, "a famous professor, who with the best of intentions, tried to conquer death through scientific experiments." Like *Drakula Istanbul'da*, there is nothing camp about it whatsoever, and Rehan is an excellent lead. The producer and director had agreed that "Rehan was the only actor in Pakistan who could play the part of Dracula." His slicked-back hair, pale skin, and slightly sharp features evoke Bela Lugosi, and once he's transformed, he smiles with his fangs, sinister and gleeful.

This movie came after a whole series of Hammer films, and borrows its plotline heavily from the first Christopher Lee *Dracula* (1958), with a few interesting variations. It's an early example of a vampire being created the modern way, in the lab, and has no Transylvanian elements. Like the Turkish movie, it contains some great musical numbers, and fun driving-around scenes, in this case showing us 1967 Pakistan.

Another notable change is that the death of Shabnam, a Lucy/Mina fusion borrowed from Hammer, is much more in-the-moment than usual. She isn't staked in her coffin, but in the midst of an attack, when her family needs to save each other and the little girl she's targeted. This makes her killing seem less cold-blooded, and more of a devastating family tragedy, which seems fitting; the movie industry that was split into Indian and Pakistani branches in 1948 tended to emphasize relationships and familial bonds.

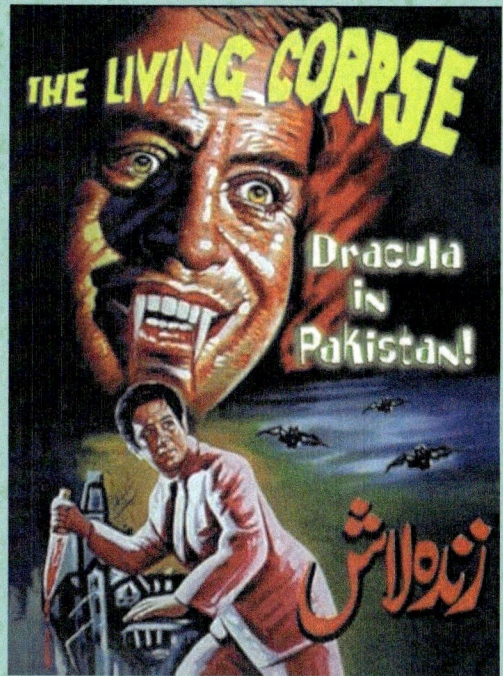

On the Mondo Macabro disc, Pakistani expert Mohammad Yousuf talks about how the movie was "the first of its kind in Pakistan," and Sarfaraz admits he "didn't think it would work" there. Producer Habib (who also played the Van Helsing-esque character) says that "the censor was totally shocked just by the subject matter," making it Pakistan's first 'Adults Only' movie, however tame it seems today.

The featurettes also show an amazing poster with the (all-caps) text "Terrifying suspense! It will shock you out of your seats! Tense, torturous and terrifying ... Strictly for adults only ... The unforgettable human vampire comes to the screen to give you a breath-taking chill horror." And on the same poster, "People Who Have an Irrational, Persistent Fear Or Dread of Demons, Ghosts Or the Supernatural May Not be Permitted to View This Motion Picture Because of its Unusually Shocking Scenes!" (sic) It's somehow reassuring that roadshow ballyhoo happened all over the world.

India has the biggest film industry of these three countries, but despite its habit of borrowing plot elements from Hollywood movies, the Dracula mythos hasn't caught on there. There are movies with 'Dracula' in the title, but they're notably low-budget affairs. That's even compared to the "B"-movie level of the Ramsay Brothers, who more or less created India's horror movie industry. They never did any direct adaptations of the public domain horror icons, but created their own monsters; the home-grown demon Saamri (from *Purana Mandir* and *Saamri 3D*), an ancient demonic being who returns to plague the living, is closer to a Dracula figure than seen in any of India's *Dracula* movies.

I'm always pushing back at the idea that Indian films, with their colorful musical numbers and low budgets by our standards, appeal to western audiences on the level of camp, but unfortunately, their Dracula adaptations hover around the level of *Birdemic*. Not only were there no name directors or actors involved, but none of the movies I've found have a decent transfer, or even subtitles, so I'm unable to comment too much on the plots.

In general, they feature limited scenes of the supernatural, instead filming long conversations, and often some generic police elements. A lot of the scenes in these movies have no establishing shots, and the conversations were seemingly filmed with the actors in separate rooms, plain backgrounds behind them. In *Khooni Dracula* (1992), at least its song sequences, an important element in the genre, were more professionally performed and filmed than in most of the Indian *Dracula* variants. For example, in *Son of Dracula* (1999), a dancing girl is only shown from the shoulders up!

But at least that features some enjoyably cheap monster masks. *Dracula 2012* (a Malayalam film dubbed into different Indian languages as *Aur Ek Dracula* and *Kahani Dracula Ki*) has more competent staging than those sub-low budget releases, but has special effects, like bats flying through an archway, with the quality of a screensaver. When a young man performs a ceremony to set Dracula's spirit free, it possesses his body in an orgy of terrible CGI.

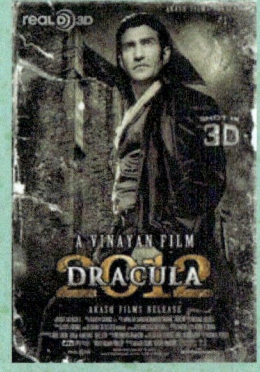

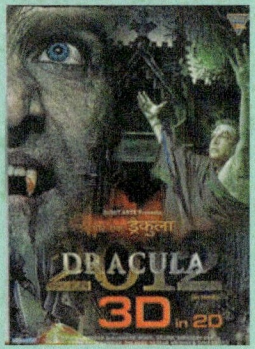

As this issue of 'We Belong Dead' shows, there are countless ways, probably hundreds, in which to depict Dracula. There is just no need for him to be a pulsating, fully animated man-bat, much less one that's onscreen for a long time. Even the Dracula of *Shaitani Dracula* (2006), who's dressed like a park ranger, is an improvement!

Not that *Shaitani Dracula* is a good movie. I have just enough Hindi to know that most of Dracula's dialogue is just him bellowing "I am Dracula!" at the camera. But by embracing its own absurdity, it's the one immensely low-budget, un-subtitled Indian Dracula that can truly be held aloft with *Troll 2* and *The Apple* in the pantheon of indefensibly bad but somehow very entertaining movies. Starting incongruously with the James Bond theme, *Shaitani Dracula* is more a piece of messed-up performance art than a movie, like Ed Wood's *Orgy of the Dead* if everyone had to keep their clothes on. I recommend you check out its reviews by the late Todd Stadtman at the blog 'Die, Danger, Die, Die, Kill', and Keith Allison's at 'Diabolique' magazine, essays that have their own cult status for fans of the more out-there Hindi films.

It's too bad there's been no proper Indian *Dracula*. The late Irrfan Khan appeared as an aspiring actor in *Sunday* (2008), a fluffy action comedy, and spent part of the movie in a Dracula cape for an audition. With the brooding intensity he was known for, it's a shame he never got to play the character for real.

FILL THE GAPS IN YOUR COLLECTION

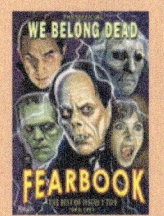

WBD FEARBOOK	 WBD ISSUE 9	 WBD ISSUE 10
 WBD ISSUE 11	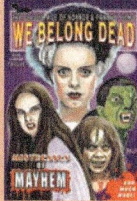 WBD ISSUE 12	 WBD ISSUE 13
 WBD ISSUE 14	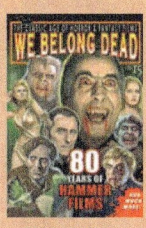 WBD ISSUE 15	 WBD ISSUE 16
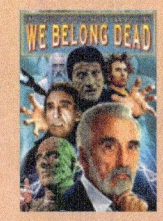 WBD ISSUE 17	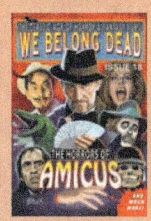 WBD ISSUE 18	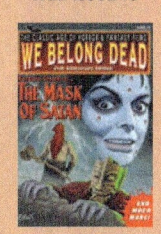 WBD ISSUE 19
 WBD ISSUE 20	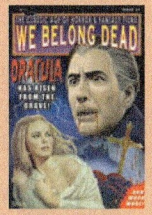 WBD ISSUE 21	 WBD ISSUE 22
 WBD ISSUE 23	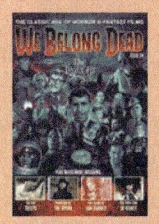 WBD ISSUE 24	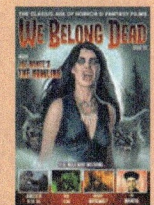 WBD ISSUE 25
 WBD ISSUE 26	 WBD ISSUE 27	 WBD ISSUE 28
 WBD ISSUE 29	 WBD ISSUE 30	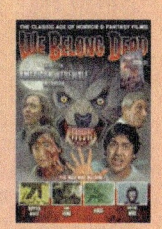 WBD ISSUE 31
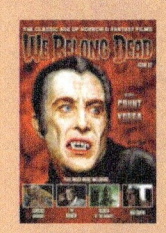 WBD ISSUE 32	 WBD ISSUE 33	 WBD ISSUE 34
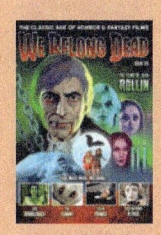 WBD ISSUE 35	 WBD ISSUE 36	 WBD ISSUE 37
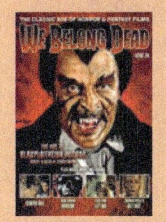 WBD ISSUE 38	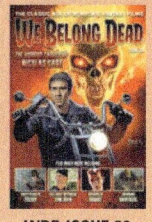 WBD ISSUE 39	 30TH ANNIVERSARY

BACK ISSUES

available via AMAZON

simply search WE BELONG DEAD

or visit www.webelongdead.co.uk for links

We Belong Dead

WE BELONG DEAD

CHECK OUT OUR RANGE OF BOOKS

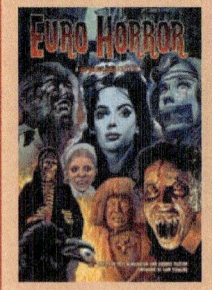

- EURO HORROR
- 70s MONSTER MEMORIES 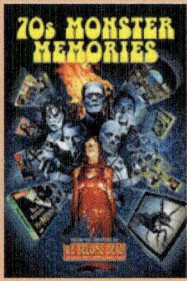
- CHOPPED MEAT 
- SPOTLIGHT ON SCIENCE FICTION 
- PICTORIAL HISTORY OF HAMMER HORROR 
- FILMS OF JENNY AGUTTER 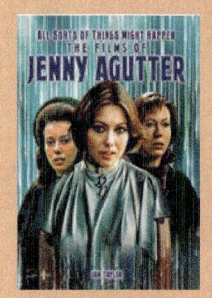
- GIANT MONSTERS OF FILMLAND 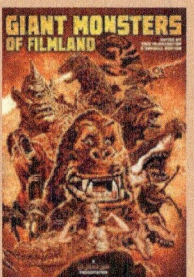
- UNSUNG HORRORS 
- SON OF UNSUNG HORRORS 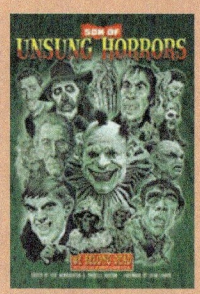
- A CELEBRATION OF PETER CUSHING 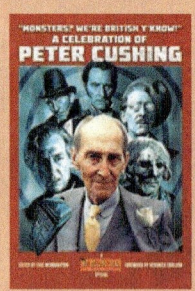
- A CENTURY OF HORROR 
- A CELEBRATION OF VINCENT PRICE 
- SPOTLIGHT ON HORROR 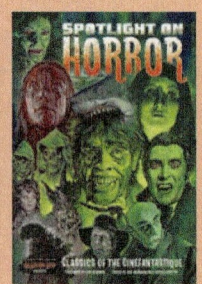

FOR FULL DETAILS VISIT

WWW.WEBELONGDEAD.CO.UK

Printed in Great Britain
by Amazon